by

J. Basil Phillips

Old Bakehouse Publications

Abertillery

First published in November 2002

ISBN 1 874538 69 7

Published in the U.K. by
Old Bakehouse Publications
Church Street,
Abertillery, Gwent NP13 1EA
Telephone: 01495 212600 Fax: 01495 216222
http: /www.mediamaster.co.uk/oldbakebooks

Made and printed in the UK
by J.R. Davies (Printers) Ltd.

Foreword

This is the story of the pioneering generation of Senghenydd which suffered the *'full clutch of circumstances'* during the period when it was being transformed from a rural hamlet into a seething ebullient mining village.

Such was the year-to-year development that I have chosen to relate it more in the style of a chronicle, in preference to a broad-based narrative.

It has been written primarily for the present and future descendants of a generation of men and women whose lives were characterised by sustained endeavour, outrageous tragedy and indomitable spirit.

Dedication and Acknowledgements

This book is dedicated to its author, Basil, whose years of work in writing it came to a sad and premature end with his death before completion.

Its finalisation has been undertaken by his widow, Glenys, and son, Huw, who gratefully acknowledge the assistance of the following:

Mr. David Parry - for advice and photographs

Mr. Gary Plumley - for ideas relating to the cover design.

The Senghenydd Memorial Award Trust - for their encouragement towards finalising the book.

Mr. Gwilym Davies and Mr. Malcolm Thomas of Old Bakehouse Publications - for their expert advice and assistance in the preparation of this book.

Senghenydd 1890 - 1914

A Chronicle

. . . .

'Invictus'

'In the fell clutch of circumstance
I have not winced or cried aloud,
Under the bludgeoning of chance
My head is bloody but unbow'd.'

William Ernest Hanley

MAY 1894.

To Station

Universal Hotel

Gwernymilwr Farm

Proposed new road to station.

Plan in the press advertising land for sale for building.

1898

Two interesting town plans of 1894 and 1898.

CHAPTER 1

In 1890 Queen Victoria reigned supreme, Lord Salisbury was Prime Minister of a Tory Government, David Lloyd George was returned as Liberal Member of Parliament for the Caernarvon Boroughs and the East Glamorgan constituency was represented by Mr. Alfred Thomas, a Liberal, President of the Welsh Baptist Union and a prominent leader of Welsh dissent.

Among the topics of debate exercising Parliament and the press were the Welsh Land Bill, the Welsh Intermediate Education Act and the Disestablishment of the Anglican Church in Wales. All reflected the forging of *'a new Wales'*. Its demographic pattern was changing rapidly because whereas the rural counties were depressed and declining, the dynamic progress of industrialisation attracted ever-increasing populations to the mining villages and urban centres of Glamorgan and Monmouthshire. At the same time, in a society dominated by Liberalism and Nonconformity, a spirit of radicalism and nationalism was abroad in Wales, critical of the existing political, economic and social structure and accompanied by a growing awareness of national identity with a renaissance of pride in the Welsh language and culture.

Whether this *'awakening'* occupied the thoughts of the few adults who lived in a very small rural hamlet in the geographical cul-de-sac of the Aber Valley is not known. Comparatively secluded, linked only to the neighbouring valley of Abertridwr by a bush-lined parish road and to Nelson by a rough cart track, a sylvan retreat surrounded by woods harbouring conies, squirrels and a host of birds, its crystal-clear brooks teeming with trout and harbouring the occasional salmon, the hamlet was so insignificant that it did not warrant a specific name. Sometimes referred to as *'Cwmparc'*, a name derived from that of a brook which meandered through the hamlet, it was invariably included in the general term of *'Aber'* by officialdom and the press. For administrative purposes it was included in the Park Hamlet in the Parish of Eglwysilan in the County of Glamorgan with the provision of its main services the responsibility of the Pontypridd Union which it exercised through various ratepayer elected Boards.

The population numbered less than a hundred and the habitation was composed of fourteen farm houses - Ty Draw, Blaengwawr, Ty'r Mynydd, Caermoel, Craigyrhufan, Glawnant, Maesdiofal, Park, Gwernymilwr, Cefn Llwyd, Foelddu, Parc Newydd, Caerllwyn and Gellifanadlog. All but two were occupied by tenant farmers, their families, farm servants and domestic servants who derived a livelihood from rearing sheep and cattle.

With all but one farm less than 200 acres in extent their *'brinker'* rights over common land were fully utilised. Major occasions in the annual calendar were sheep-dipping, sheep shearing, the hay harvest and the brinkers' meeting on Eglwysilan Mountain for the *'Collection of Strangers'* when *'stranger sheep'* were identified and restored to their owners. Pleasurable relief from the daily toil was afforded by visits to the markets at Caerphilly and Nelson, the fairs at Caerphilly and Gelligaer, and by the occasional Ploughing, Hedging and Mowing Matches, hunting the hare and riding to hounds with the Hunt.

It was a close-knit community basically Welsh in speech and culture, hard-working and thrifty, strong in religious commitment, a sabbatarian society practising a strict code of private and social conduct. Communicants of the Church of England attended Eglwysilan Church in Abertridwr where the Rector, the Rev. Rice Jones, was a very conscientious incumbent. But the vast majority of villagers followed the hamlet's centuries-old tradition of Nonconformity, worshipping at Groeswen Welsh Congregational Chapel and its *'daughter'* chapel of *'Adulam'* in Abertridwr. Both were ministered by Rev. Tawelfryn Thomas, known simply as *'Tawelfryn'*, a powerful evangelical preacher, a passionate Welshman renowned as a gifted poet and prolific eisteddfodic winner. Major occasions at Groeswen were the annual Cyrddau Mawr (Big Meetings), the Cymanfa Ganu (Singing Festival) and the chapel-promoted eisteddfod. Anticipated in both chapel and church were the Harvest Festival and Sunday School treats.

It is tempting to conjure up a nostalgic, idyllic scene of rural contentment, but in reality there were less enviable aspects to the mode of life. The children had to trek to Abermill School in Abertridwr. There was no place of worship, no shop, no Post Office, no inn. The water supply was drawn from wells and the sanitary arrangements were primitive. More significantly, the deserted farmhouses and labourers' cottages of Goldref Fawr, Goldref Fach, Gelli Ddu, Ty'n y Parc, Blaen y Fforch, Coedcae Rosser, Buarth y Parc, Beudy'r Hwch, Pandy Bach and Ty'r Waenwen bore eloquent testimony to the long-depressed state of agriculture.

The farmers were hard-pressed to make a living and with no demand for farmworkers or rural craftsmen the agriculturally-based economy struggled to maintain even this small community. At the same time as its traditional way of life was waning so coal-mining speculation was proceeding apace in the surrounding area. That this secluded hamlet would also be engulfed by *'King Coal'* seemed inevitable.

So it proved.

In 1889 Sir William Thomas Lewis had begun to explore the possibility of developing the steam coal deposits south of Llanbradach. To this end he focused his attention on *'Cwmparc'* and in May he formed the Universal Steam Coal Company, a Limited Liability Company which acquired the mineral rights over an area of about 2,800 acres, mainly owned by the Marquis of Bute, which was one of the most extensive in the country. His fellow Directors were his brother-in-law W.T. Rees of Maesyffynon, Aberdare, as Managing Director, his son Herbert Lewis, Sir Thomas Morel, E.P. Martin, M.W. Martin and Valentine Trayes.

Sir William Thomas Lewis who formed the Universal Steam Coal Co. in 1889.

Born in Merthyr in 1837 of ancient Welsh lineage, formerly Mineral Agent to the Bute Estate before entering the lucrative field of colliery speculation, Sir. W.T. Lewis had created a mighty industrial empire which included much of Cardiff Docks, a host of collieries in the Rhondda, Cynon and Rhymney Valleys and large-scale ownership of miners' terraced houses. He was knighted in 1885 as a reward for his outstanding service as a member of the Royal Commission reporting on safety in mines and also for his charitable works. Living in almost baronial splendour in Aberdare, displaying a feudal attitude towards the coal industry, an upholder of the *'master and workmen'* attitude, implacably hostile to Trade Unions and autocratic leader of the South Wales and Monmouthshire Coal-owners' Association, he has been described as *'a Welsh robber baron on the Texan scale'* and *'the best hated man in the Principality'*.

The Universal Colliery, Senghenydd.

By 1890 the preliminary borings had proved successful, the plans set in motion to sink the Universal Colliery, and in the words of a *'Cardiff Times'* reporter, *'This picturesque little valley is likely to be converted before long from its present peaceable and tranquil condition to be the source of great wealth.'*

Priority was the construction of a railway line to the site of the intended colliery from the Aber Junction in order to convey the heavy equipment necessary for the sinking. In June the Rhymney Railway Bill, *'the object of which is to make a new branch line in the Aber Valley'*, was grouped to come before a Select Committee of the House of Commons and it was sanctioned in July. The Rhymney Railway company engaged Mr. T.W. Davies, head of a Cardiff engineering firm, as Technical Director of the construction and the first sod was cut at the Aber Junction end on January 23rd, 1891. A small number of craftsmen was employed, supported by a few hundred navvies paid 4½d to 5d an hour. The works engine was appropriately named *'Aber'* and was driven by Alfred Dawes of Abertridwr.

The 'Aber' railway engine used in construction of the railway line to Senghenydd 1890.

The Census of this year showed that there was no increase in the number of habitations from the previous year and that the population was ninety one. Enumerated were:

Ty Draw: (180 acres)
James Edwards (43), farmer, born Llanwonno.
Wife Annie (35), born Llanwonno.
Children Annie (10), Margaret (8), John (6), Edward (4), Thomas (1).
An agricultural labourer and a domestic servant, both single.

Caermoel: (45 acres)	Thomas Bussell (65), farmer, born Machen. Wife Martha (64), born Llanwonno. Children Thomas (35), Margaret (21), Evan (1). An agricultural labourer, single.
Glaw Nant: (180 acres)	Thomas Evans (67), farmer, born Eglwysilan. Wife Hannah (60), born Eglwysilan. Children Ann (30), John (28), Mary (25), Edward (22). Margaret (20), Assistant Teacher.
Craigyrhufan: (92 acres)	Howell Phillips (49), farmer, born Wenvoe. Wife Ann (39), born Merthyr Tydfil. Children Watkin (10), Gwen (5), Margaret (1 month). Two agricultural labourers, a domestic servant, all single.
Maesdiofal: (185 acres)	Noah Evans (68), farmer, born Eglwysilan. Wife Jane (64), born Llanfabon. Children Thomas (37), Elisabeth (30).
Parc: (100 acres)	George Packer (44), farmer, born Llantrisant. Wife Margaret (36), born Eglwysilan. Children Jane (12), Hannah (10), John (8), Henry (6), Mary (4), Lizzie (1).
Gwernymilwr: (40 acres)	Daniel Lewis (32), farm labourer, born Eglwysilan. Wife Mary (29), born Eglwysilan. Child Evan (6 months).
Cefn Llwyd: (160 acres)	John Richards (36), farmer, born Eglwysilan. Wife Margaret (37), born Ystradfodwg. Children David (8), Gwen (6), Maria (3), Evan (1), Thomas (9 months). Lewis Richards (71), uncle to John, born Eglwysilan. An agricultural labourer, a domestic servant, both single.
Foelddu: (35 acres)	Jane Jenkins (67), widow, born Llanwonno. Children Christopher (28), farmer, Margaret (27).
Parc Newydd: (100 acres)	John John (69), farmer, born Llanwonno. Wife Ann (55), born Ystradgynlais. Children Thomas (23) coal miner, Lotwick (21) farmer.
Gelli: (350 acres)	Henry Thomas (66), farmer, born Llantwit Major. Wife Jane (64), born Pendoylan. Children William (34), Elizabeth (32), Thomas (24), Leyshon (22).
Caerllwyn: (120 acres)	John Richards (29), farmer, born Eglwysilan. Wife Maria (28), born Eglwysilan. Children Rees (8), Albert (6), Ivor (1 month). Henry Richards (27), brother to John, farmer, born Eglwysilan. Wife Jemima (20), born Eglwysilan. Edward Richards (56), uncle to John. Ann Mary Richards (2), niece. An agricultural labourer, a domestic servant, both single.

Blaengwawr: Joseph Gwynn (37), coal miner, born Breckonshire.
Wife Ann (34), born Breckonshire.
Children Mary (16), Sarah (12), Emily (9), John (3).
A lodger, single, coal miner.

Ty'r Mynydd: James Pingree (29), bricklayer, born Worcester.
Wife Sarah Ann (26), born Montgomeryshire.
Children Sarah (5), George (4), Margaret (2 months).

These statistics show that there were only fourteen married couples in the hamlet among whom were the long-established families of Thomas Evans (Glawnant/Glan Nant), John Richards (Cefn Llwyd), John and Henry Richards (Caerllwyn) and Noah Evans (Maesdiofal), and that there were only fourteen *'scholars'*.

The Census also included a survey of the spoken language, and excluding babies, it revealed that 28 adults and 4 children were monoglot Welsh-speaking, 23 adults and 13 children were bilingual, 8 adults and 6 children were monoglot English-speaking. Those adults who were monoglot Welsh-speaking were the older inhabitants.

Throughout 1891 and 1892 there was no change in the habitation there being no demand for additional accommodation because the work force engaged on the railway line was billetted in Abertridwr in adapted old buildings bearing the names of *'Yorkshire Hall'*, *'Somerset House'* and *'Dudley Cottage'*. Consequently no *'foreigners'* disturbed the comparative tranquility of the hamlet. Not recorded is the response of the very few male voters to the Eglwysilan School Board and County Council elections in 1892 or to the General Election when Alfred Thomas was re-elected to the constituency by defeating Herbert Lewis (Conservative Unionist). Far more interest would have been aroused in the community by the appointment of Mr. Edmund Evans as Head Teacher of Abermill School and the induction of Rev. Henry Morgan, B.A., as Rector of Eglwysilan Church. Highly esteemed in their respective callings, both were also passionate Welshmen, fervent proponents of the language and culture, active in eisteddfodic circles. Henry Morgan (*'Ilan Wledig'*) was an essayist of repute and a successful competitor. Edmund Evans (*'Elfryn'*) was noted not only as a poet and essayist of distinction in both Welsh and English with very many eisteddfodic successes to his credit but also as a gifted musician. Together with the renowned *'Tawelfryn'* they were to exercise a profound influence on the moral, cultural and social development of the hamlet in the years to come.

As the construction of the railway line became ever nearer completion towards the latter part of 1892 so the land around the site of the proposed colliery was cleared and engine sheds, a goods shed, a railway station and some craft buildings were being erected. No doubt this aroused some regret that the quiescent rural way of life was about to be superseded by rampant industrialisation but the farming-based community would have been more than mollified by the prospect of a more secure economic future derived from the sale of produce to an increased population and from that of hay for the pit horses to the Colliery Company.

Nor was the prospect of financial gain confined to the community. In an era when coal was described as *'black diamonds'* there were speculators eager to invest in property and commercial ventures. In the vanguard was Thomas Williams of Cardiff who submitted applications in 1890, 1891 and 1892 at the Caerphilly Licensing Sessions for a provisional licence for an hotel to be built on Gwernymilwr land based on the need that would arise from an increased population and that the nearest public house was 1½ miles away in Abertridwr, all rejected on the grounds that they were premature.

Entering 1893 little had changed since 1890. Still too small to warrant a specific name, lacking in basic utilities and amenities, the hamlet was ill-prepared for the imminent onslaught from *'King Coal'*.

CHAPTER 2

With the completion of the railway line in April 1893 the scenario began to change rapidly. Almost immediately the sinking of the Downcast shaft on the West side was started under the expert management of David Thomas, M.E. from the Cynon Valley, a man of vast experience who had sunk the Abergwynfi and Penrhiwceiber pits. His experienced team of sinkers, mainly from Penrhiwceiber and Mountain Ash, were housed by the Universal Company in the first additional *'habitations'* in the hamlet. These comprised a row of one-storey, two-roomed buildings, roofed and walled with corrugated iron and painted with tar. Enjoying the postal address of the *'Universal Cottages'*, then the *'Universal Huts'*, followed by *'The Huts'*, they were subsequently modified from time to time and occupied until 1928.

The Universal Cottages - The Huts.

By the end of May the *'Glamorgan Free Press'* reported, *'The hamlet of Aber is destined to become a prosperous and thriving neighbourhood. Our representative had occasion to visit it last week and was surprised to see the wonderful development. Just now about one hundred hands are being employed in sinking a colliery and on the railway. The Rhymney Railway Company have erected a large station and goods shed, the engine sheds are put up and there are two engines working. Sinking operations began about two months ago and at the present time they have got down to forty feet. The manager of the new pit is Mr. Thomas, late of the Cape, and this is to be one of our largest. Although the population is not large there is every prospect of it being so as builders are erecting new houses. There is little doubt that a rich seam of coal is to be obtained and it now only means time. The future looks bright.'*

Senghenydd in about 1894 with the Universal Colliery nearing completion but the village itself is still just half built.

Such was the optimistic forecast as to the viability of the colliery that now there was a desperate need to provide accommodation not only for the existing small work force, some of whom lodged in the Huts or travelled from neighbouring villages, but to house the anticipated expansion of the number of workers, family men seeking homes, single men seeking lodgings. To this end the Universal Company was granted permission in August by the newly-created Caerphilly District Board to build 65 cottages and another 4 Huts *'subject to their erecting a system of cesspools and that no drains be discharged into the brook'*. Approved also were Josiah Morgan's plans to build 20 houses, a workshop and a slaughterhouse. So began a spate of building, the stone supplied from local quarries.

In September the sinking of the Upcast shaft on the East side was started. By the end of November the Downcast shaft had reached a depth of a hundred yards and the press was able to report that *'the sinking operations under the management of Mr. David Thomas, a genial and upright gentleman, is making rapid progress, the prospects are very good and before long this place will be very prosperous and business will be on the move.'* Under construction was the Universal Hotel, the Crosswell Brewery granted a provisional licence after a successful submission that hundreds of people came up the valley and had no hotel to go to, the nearest being the Panteg Hotel one and a half miles away. Plans for more houses were approved and it is said that among the first shops to be built were Nos.30 and 40 Parc Road, the former a grocery and china store kept by David Jones who also sold stamps, the latter a butchery served by William Burnett.

The sinkers making good progress 1893.

Inevitably, the incoming villagers were confronted with appalling conditions during this initial stage of development - a water supply dependent on wells, primitive sanitary conditions and overflowing cesspools, unlit roads so rutted by the conveyance of building stone that *'it was dangerous to walk out when it was dark'*, mail having to be posted and collected in Abertridwr, no medical provision in the village, the children having to trek to Abermill School. As one reporter commented, *'This little spot at present is in a dreadful state. We hope the Local Board, or whom it may concern, will see to the improvements which are greatly needed.'*

Yet these pioneering immigrants, small in number, strove to forge a way of life which would satisfy their religious, cultural and social aspirations in the traditional national mould.

Of deep religious conviction, steeped in sabbatarianism, the desire to worship was paramount. Those of the Anglican persuasion attended Eglwysilan Church, the Welsh Congregationalists (Independents) denomination attended Groeswen and Adulam chapels. But the other Nonconformist denominations had no place of worship in the district and yearned to hold services in the village as did the Welsh Congregationalists. So it was that irrespective of denominational beliefs, groups of Nonconformists began to meet for prayer meetings and the occasional service at the farmhouses of Maesdiofal, Park and Caerllwyn, the home of Manager David Thomas, *'Siop Saer'* (carpenter shop) owned by Josiah Morgan and in the open air.

Then as denominational loyalties became more apparent, so side by side with the collective meetings there emerged the will to found separate Causes and to build vestries where the very small congregations could worship in their own tradition. Doubtless influenced by the fact that Manager David Thomas was of this persuasion the first to establish a Cause were the Welsh Congregationalists. They met at his home, at Siop Saer and other venues for prayer meetings and services conducted by *'Tawelfryn'*, and in December of 1893 they secured a plot of land at an annual rental of £2-17-9 to build a vestry.

Next to satisfying their religious needs the villagers had other priorities. Preponderantly Welsh in speech and culture, what was more natural than to seek expression for their passion for choral music? Happily this was satisfied when Edmund Evans of the Abermill School formed a Mixed Aber Valley Choir in December. Assuaged also was the national male passion for rugby football when devotees joined the Aber Valley Stars Club which played its matches on a field adjoining the Rose and Crown Inn on Eglwysilan Mountain. In the team which included full-back Arthur Morgan, three-quarter backs E. Bell, L. James, T. Rowlands, F. Meyrick, half-backs D. Evans and Bob Jenkins, forwards E. Evans, W. Hamer, G. Jones, T. Llewellyn, M. Meyrick, H. Richards and J. Williams, a few came from the village but which ones is unclear.

As the year drew to a close the village was populated by about 300 newcomers, was still without a distinguishing name and largely dependent on its links with Abertridwr. Living conditions bordered on the chaotic and sordid with little if any improvement in the provision of public utilities. Yet some of the basic concepts for a distinctive community had been tentatively forged.

The opening month of 1894 was marred by the first fatality arising from the sinking operations when William Davies was killed and both chargeman Thomas Evans and sinker Henry Lewis were seriously burned as a result of, a shot-firing accident.

February 1st was a joyous occasion, the day when the railway station was opened for passenger and goods traffic. The Rhymney Railway Company instituted four journeys a day to Caerphilly with connections to Cardiff, the single fare to Abertridwr 1d, the return fare 1½d, return fare to Caerphilly 3d and the return fare to Cardiff 9d. The honour of driving the first train was accorded to Fred Butt. Acting as Station Master that day was Mr. Snell of Caerphilly Station but shortly afterwards Thomas Nicholas was appointed to the post with responsibility also for Penyrheol Station. The engine sheds accommodated 11 engines and employed 55 men.

But what marked this occasion as of historic importance was that at last the village acquired a distinguishing name as opposed to being included in the general term of *'Aber'*.

It was originally suggested that the station be named *'Cwmparc'* but this was rejected because it would be confused with that of the Rhondda village so-named and instead it was designated *'Senghenith'*. The *'Glamorgan Free Press'* commented, *'The new place has rather a peculiar name. By what we can see at the railway station it is to be called Senghenith. We have had many enquiries as to the meaning of the word and also as to the coiner of it. Perhaps some readers will explain it. We believe it was Sir. W.T. Lewis, Aberdare.'* The most elementary research would have informed the reporter that the name was derived from the medieval Lordship of Senghenydd which included the Aber Valley. He was correct in ascribing the *'coiner'* to the colliery owner not only because he exercised the dominant influence in the village but also by the fact that he boasted descendancy from Ifor Bach, a famous Welsh chieftain of the Lordship. This is confirmed by Rev. Henry Morgan who recorded, *'It was so-called to meet the wishes of Sir William Thomas Lewis. He wrote to me to say that he wished to call the place by that name and to have it referred to at meetings and in the talk of the place.... The name is appropriate and its use recalls the Cell of St. Cenydd.'* It is interesting to note that Lewis later assumed the title of *'Lord Merthyr of Senghenydd'*.

Although there appeared to be no initial opposition in principle to the anglicised spelling of the name, still perpetuated today on the Conservative Club building, it aroused vehement objection from the proudly Welsh villagers for many years until *'Senghenydd'* was officially adopted.

It has been suggested that the correct spelling of the name is *'Senghennydd'*. Suffice to say that this has no historic basis. Although there were many varied spellings of the ancient Lordship in official documents there is no record of it being spelt with a double *'n'* so far as I can ascertain. It is also the fact that both the English and Welsh names bestowed upon the village were spelt with a single *'n'*.

From March onwards progress in the sinking operations was seriously retarded by the flow of water from an underground stream into the Downcast shaft and at one time it reached a rate of 2,100 gallons an hour. This caused not only considerable operational difficulties but made it necessary to lay as many as 5,000 bricks in some places to wall back the flow. It was not until August that the problem was overcome.The work force then numbered about 150, the engine sheds employed about 60 and the population was about 600.

Despite the setback more ancillary buildings were erected and the Manager and Company offices were housed in Gelli Villas. House-building also proceeded apace, more commercial premises were opened and in May the first streets were allocated the names of Parc Road, Stanley Road, Eleanor Road and Stuart Road. Plans submitted by the Colliery Company for 40 houses on the Parc Newydd Estate were approved as were those submitted by Josiah Morgan and others for 13 in Eleanor Road. The Universal Hotel was completed and granted a full licence and in the process of construction were three huge hotels, the Gwernymilwr for Josiah Morgan, one at Pandybach for Messrs. W. & E. Miles of Pontypridd, the other for Mr. Hurman of Cardiff, although all had been refused a provisional licence. Parc and Grove Terraces were being built.

Monitoring the development in September a press reporter commented, *'We have all heard of the mushroom growth of American cities and the money made in land, but comparatively few people are aware that the same thing is going on only a few miles from Pontypridd. Across the mountain there has grown up within the last few months a district that in all probability will equal if not eclipse the Rhondda Valley as a coal-producing area. So far no coal has been realised but sinking operations are going ahead at full pace and it is estimated that in about eighteen months time coal will be mined.*

Twelve months ago there were only a few huts but today there are 130 houses erected, 90 of which are occupied. There is a boom in land and all sites likely to be used as business premises have been taken. Land that was formerly 2d a yard has gone up to 6d. The roads are being made up by the different estates and the plots marked out. The principal street is Parc Road and the greatest part has been taken by Mr. Josiah Morgan of Porth and houses and shops erected. One large hotel has been finished and granted a licence and three others are being constructed. All round the prospects of the valley are bright. The shops are being occupied as soon as they are finished and capital is being drawn to the place.'

For the growing number of residents it was another year of continual hardship with very little palpable improvement in the provision of basic utilities despite plans being drawn up by the Caerphilly District Board. There was no main sewerage system and the few subsidiary sewers continued to discharge the effluent into Cwmparc brook. The primitive reservoirs provided by the various building companies were little more than large holes in the ground so that the water supply was inadequate and often polluted resulting in frequent use of the wells. The situation was aggravated by the demand for houses exceeding the supply so that overcrowding was becoming common and houses occupied without proper sanitary provision. Builder/owner Henry Williams was served with *'Notices for the Abatement of Nuisances'* with the threat of court action unless he provided privies in houses he was constructing, followed in September by similar Notices for causing five houses in Stanley Street to be occupied without prior Board sanction in that they were unfit for human habitation, and yet again in November when he caused to be occupied a house in Parc Road which was without covered drains.

A fatal case of the dreaded typhoid fever in the Huts served to emphasise the hazards inherent in a situation where it was impossible to maintain adequate health standards. The District Board had appointed a Medical Officer of Health and an Inspector of Nuisances but the absence of a resident doctor was a serious cause of concern.

The lack of educational facilities in the village continued to arouse vehement criticism. This was trenchantly expressed in August by a press reporter who wrote, *'The residents complain bitterly that there is no Infant School, the little ones finding it impossible to go to the school in Aber in all weathers and their children have not the educational opportunities which are the rights of every child. So far the Eglwysilan School Board has not moved in the matter but it is hoped that their lethargy will be short-lived and give the district its needs.'* But despite the election of Evan Sherrah to the Board it remained unresponsive to the public clamour and no progress was made by the end of the year.

The side roads remained as muddy, rutted cart tracks and the main road was little better. None were supplied with lighting.

In respect of the provision of postal facilities there was a limited improvement when the Postmaster General agreed to make them available to the colliery management and the farms. But they were still denied to the general public and the District Board continued to urge the need for a Post Office with a Telegraph Office, obtaining a measure of success in November when a sub-Post Office was sanctioned. The question of a Telegraphic Office was deferred pending the Board's agreement to provide a guarantee against financial loss.

With an increasing population subjected to sub-standard depressing living conditions and lacking public amenities there now emerged the social problem of drunkenness. Prevalent throughout Britain, the problem most acute in industrial areas, a feature in Wales was *'shebeening'*, the illegal sale of beer in homes, the practice most common on Sunday when the public houses were closed in accordance with the Sunday Closing Act of 1881. One reporter wrote that in Senghenydd *'shebeens abound and secret drinking is taking place in almost every house'* and although this was typical journalese exaggeration the situation was one of deep concern.

One villager who was prosecuted was sinker John Mapps whose home in the Huts was raided on a Sunday morning by the police who discovered nineteen men drinking beer. Among them was Ambrose, a barber who went there every Sunday morning to shave the lodgers. Another defendant, when charged, declared, *'It is too bad. It's bad enough for a fellow to have to pay for his beer without having to go to Caerphilly to pay for it again.'* In his defence Mapp pleaded, *'Many are my lodgers. I can give them a drop of beer if I like. I have not sold any'*, but it was of no avail and he was fined £10. It transpired that there were seven lodgers in the two-roomed Hut!

Marshalled not only against shebeening but also the legal sale of the *'demon drink'* was the local Temperance Society led by Rev. Tawelfryn Thomas who was strongly supported by all the Nonconformist denominations. It was mainly due to its opposition that in September the applications for provisional licences on behalf of the Gwernymilwr, Leigh and Parc Hotels, nearing completion, were again rejected. This despite the plea on their behalf that they would provide much-needed accommodation for travellers, a submission typified by the statement in support of Mrs. Miles for the Leigh Hotel that its object was *'to provide good accommodation for commercial gentlemen with 11 bedrooms, increasing to 22, a large commercial room, a large club room, a billiard room and good stabling.'*

The Temperance Society was but one indication of the growing strength of the various religious denominations both in organisation and participation in social affairs. Memorable was the opening of the first vestry in the village. This was *'Noddfa'* built for the Welsh congregationalists in Stanley Road to accommodate a congregation of 350 at a cost of £200, the fund-raising having benefited by substantial loans from Leonard Thomas of Parc Terrace and Mrs. E. Jenkins of Foelddu. The first service was conducted

Commercial Street in the early 1900s with early telegraphic poles and gas-lighting in evidence. On the right-hand side of the street, midway is the Leigh Hotel noted for its high standard of service and accommodation.

by *'Tawelfryn'* on Sunday, July 22nd. Then on Monday the Cause was incorporated with a membership of thirty two when sermons were delivered by Revs. J.T. Davies of Cardiff and V. Stephens of America. This was followed on Tuesday by the official opening when among the visiting preachers were Revs. W. Rees of Glandwr, T. Evans of Pembrokeshire, W.C. Davies of Llantrisant and T. Hughes of Cathays, and the occasion was marked by the presentation of the communion vessels from Josiah Morgan. In the following month Manager David Thomas, Evan Sherrah (son-in-law of the Manager), David James and Daniel Jones were elected as the first deacons and Aaron Jones as the Secretary. By the end of the year *'Noddfa'* was well established under the inspirational leadership of *'Tawelfryn'* as the caring minister, a position he was to exercise until 1901.

Meanwhile, the Welsh Wesleyan Methodists had established a cause in February at a service in Siop Saer conducted by Rev. John Evans (Evans, Eglwysbach) of the Pontypridd Wesleyan Mission, one of the great preachers of his day. After delivering *'an eloquent and impressive sermon to a great attendance'* it is recorded that because the service had continued long after the last train had departed *'the reverend gentleman and about a dozen friends walked over the mountain with him. Before starting, the whole company sang* "Crugybar" *and at the top of the mountain the midnight air echoed with another glorious hymn.'* Subsequent meetings were held at Siop Saer and the Manager's home where the services were conducted by visiting ministers such as Revs. D.K. Jones of Treforest, T.P. Thomas of Hafod and M. Morgan of Pontypridd. Then in December the decision was made to form a church and build a vestry, the congregation in the meantime meeting in a shed loaned by builder William Samuel.

It was also at Siop Saer that the Welsh Baptists held their first service when Rev. Joseph Evans of Maerdy preached to a congregation of four. This was followed by services at the home of Mrs. Margaret Jenkins of 13 Parc Road. A later special service at Noddfa vestry conducted by Rev. Dan Davies of Forth attracted a congregation of sixteen and as the number of adherents continued to grow so a Cause was established and in September a Building Committee was formed under the direction of Rev. J. Davies of Caerphilly. On November 23rd the first established service was held at the Gwernymilwr Hotel by courtesy of Josiah Morgan and two days later Rev. Dan Davies baptised three members in the open air.

Communicants of the Church of England continued to attend Eglwysilan Church where the services were conducted by Rector Henry Morgan.

Still too early in its development to be self-supporting in the organisation of leisure pursuits and functions the village remained dependent on the close liaison with Abertridwr. The parents of children attending Abermill School took a keen interest in all its activities, there was a large following from the village for the Aber Grand Eisteddfod held under the presidency of Manager David Thomas, the choristers played an increasingly important role in the Aber Valley United Choir's concert performances and enjoyed its outing to Penarth. The increased strength of the village contingent which trekked to Eglwysilan each Saturday to play for the Aber Stars rugby team was demonstrated by the election of David Price as Captain and the press report that the team's improving performance was due *'to several good players having taken up abode in Senghenydd'*. The team for the 1894/5 season included full-back Tom Gould, three-quarter backs E. Bell, L. James, Joe Mathews, Fred Meyrick, T. Rowlands, H. Webber and A.J. Williams, half-backs David Evans, George Gould and Bob Jenkins, forwards David Price, James Burnett, W. Hamer, G. Jones, T. Llewellyn, S. Mathews, Ted Meyrick, Joe Meyrick, Arthur Morgan, Windsor Morgan, Idris Williams and William Williams of which about half came from the village. Some, such as Idris Williams, also joined the Eglwysilan Baseball Club, formed in March, which played their games on the rugby pitch or the Rectory ground.

The year saw the first visit of Alfred Thomas, M.P., when he addressed a meeting at Noddfa vestry during the General Election campaign when he received massive support which contributed to his being re-elected. Of great significance in the administration of local government was the passage late in the year of the District and Parish Councils Act whereby the District Board was constituted into the Caerphilly Urban District Council with responsibility for public health, the water supply, the maintenance of minor roads, the provision of street lighting and other minor functions. It comprised four Wards - Caerphilly Town, Taffswell, Ystrad Mynach and Nelson, each represented by three elected Councillors. The Aber Valley was included in the Caerphilly Town Ward, an arrangement which did not please the inhabitants, particularly in the fact that the male voters had to journey to Caerphilly to register their votes. In the ensuing election Edward Thomas of Aberfawr farm in Abertridwr was returned as one of the three Councillors, but the Council had yet to meet by the end of the year.

At this time the sinking operations were making steady progress, the colliery work force was about 160, about 60 were employed at the railway sheds and the population had increased two-fold to about 700.

Over the year little progress had been made in the provision of basic utilities in respect of sewerage and water supply, living conditions were sub-standard and often over-crowded, infant mortality was high, there was no resident doctor, there was no school in the village and drunkenness was becoming a serious problem. However, on the positive side the village had acquired a singular name, the railway station had opened for passenger and goods traffic, a Post Office had been promised, more houses had been built, more shops opened, the first streets allocated names, the first vestry opened. Causes established by many Nonconformist denominations, villagers playing an increasingly important role in the Abertridwr-based choir and rugby Club, all of which reflected a resilient optimistic faith in the future with a firm resolve to improve communal facilities and to bring pressure to bear on the newly-created District Council to provide the essential basic utilities.

The sinking of the Downcast shaft on the West side, named the Lancaster pit, and the Upcast shaft on the East side, named the York pit, proceeded with increased urgency during the first eight months of 1895 as did the construction of workshops and ancillary buildings. By the end of August the Lancaster shaft had reached a depth of 650 yards, locating not only the 2ft 9ins and the 4ft 6ins seams but also the 6ft seam. This break-through prompted the press report that *'the inhabitants of Senghenith are highly elated in the winning of the 6ft seam of coal at their new pits which is of excellent quality. The owners are to be congratulated on their success. We are informed that when the other measures are reached the pits will afford a very large output of coal and consequently find employment for over 2,000 men and boys.'* This optimistic forecast was reflected by a press advertisement in September which announced *'Land to Let. Senghenith, Aber Valley. Valuable Plots of Land for Building at Very Low Ground Rent. In a few weeks a large number of houses will be expected to be required. For plans and particulars apply to E.H. Bruton, Architect, Caerphilly.'* But the prospected report that *'coal could be brought up in a few months'* proved over-optimistic when production was delayed by the disturbed nature of the ground and encountering many *'faults'* so that no coal was mined this year.

Nevertheless, with production only a matter of time and a prosperous economic future assured *'the district was forming into a busy town.'* Already plans had been approved for 77 more houses including 30 in Stanley Road for builder J.E. Lloyd, 20 in Parc Road, and for 12 more shops, and during the subsequent period plans were approved for an additional 98 houses per Charles Taylor, 3 shops, stables and coach houses. Building proceeded on a large scale. More shops were opened and more commercial enterprises were started. More streets were allocated names and now they comprised Parc Road, Windsor Road as an extension to Parc Road, Eleanor Road, Stanley Road, Station Terrace, Parc Terrace, Grove Terrace, Kingsley Place and the Universal Cottages/The Huts. The Gwernymilwr was completed, the Leigh Hotel was almost completed, the Parc Hotel was incomplete.

Commensurate with the development of the colliery and to the great satisfaction of the village came the appointment by the Universal Company of Dr. Philip James, M.R.C.S. Resident at the *'top end'* of Parc Road he became a familiar figure standing at the colliery surface to collect his dues and carrying a hurricane lamp as he made his nightly visits. So began a very long period of dedicated service to the community.

Also very welcome was the first resident police constable in the person of John Hopkins who lived in Grove Terrace.

So was the successful conclusion to the agitation for a Post Office when the District Council and the Universal Company guaranteed to cover any loss incurred by the cost of a horse-drawn mail van. A sub-Post Office was established, Miss Jane E. Samuel was appointed as sub-postmistress, the letters arrived from Cardiff at 9.45.a.m. and despatched at 5.00p.m. But the Postmaster General refused to sanction a Telegraph Office without a guarantee against a loss of £37 per annum for a period of seven years and the question remained in abeyance for the rest of the year while the District Council negotiated with the Universal Company to be responsible for half the indemnity.

The first meeting of the Caerphilly Urban District Council had been held in January when Edward Thomas took his seat. But the occasion was greeted with scant enthusiasm in Senghenydd and Abertridwr, a storm of protest having been aroused by their inclusion in the Caerphilly Ward. As month followed month with no change, the residents submitted a petition to the County Council in August seeking the formation of a Polling District so that the voters would not have to go to Caerphilly. In turn it referred the question back to the District Council for its observation and it responded by requesting not only a Polling District but the creation of an Aber Ward to be represented by three members. But there was no response from the County Council, the position was unchanged and the community continued to fulminate against an *'alien'* Council indifferent to its needs.

On the credit side tenders were invited for the construction of more sewers and a scavenger for the Aber Valley was appointed at an annual salary of £43 plus £1 for each cesspool. Also, the Surveyor/Inspector of Nuisances maintained a close scrutiny to ensure that the builders, land-owners and house owners conformed to the health regulations. Summoned were builders/owners Henry Williams and J.E. Lloyd for breaching the by-law by allowing houses to be occupied without a certificate as to their fitness for habitation. Notices for the Abatement of Nuisances were served on E.H. Bruton as the lessee for the Lord Windsor Estate to complete the sewerage and drainage systems on houses being built, on the Universal Company to connect the drains from the Parc and Grove Terraces to the main sewer and on Josiah Morgan in respect of deficient drains in his houses.

But the sewer system was incomplete and uncoordinated so requiring more cesspools to be constructed. The water supply remained inadequate and often polluted so that some households had to resort to wells although such water was declared unfit for drinking purposes. Infant mortality remained high, there was a case of typhoid fever, some cases of smallpox and diphtheria, all of which were attributable to a large degree to the difficulty in maintaining adequate standards of public health. Plans were approved for a new road to the station and widening the road to Abertridwr together with a proposal to build a road to Pontypridd, but the existing roads were unlit and little done to improve the surfaces other than covering the main one with loose limestone chippings.

Heartening however, was the Eglwysilan School Board being goaded into action when, at the suggestion of local member Evan Sherrah, it secured an agreement with the Noddfa trustees for the use of the vestry to house an Infants' School as a temporary measure at a charge of £1 every four weeks. In the words of a press report, *'Hitherto the poor little children have been obliged to toddle in all weathers to Abermill School, two miles distant, and at some seasons the elements were too boisterous to admit of the children being allowed out of doors so leading to irregular attendance. The Board has been fortunate enough to secure the services of a pain-staking and efficient Mistress.'* This Mistress was Miss E.A. England, a Certificated Teacher from Bedlinog, appointed at an annual salary of £45 plus half the Ministry grant determined on the result of the annual

Young scholars at Senghenydd Infants School which was opened on 12th September 1895.

Inspector's report in regard to the number of passes in the 3Rs and the attendance percentage. She lived in Stanley Road and was a member of Noddfa.

The official opening was recorded briefly in the Log Book as: *'This (Senghenydd) Infant School was opened today, 12th day of September 1895. There were present Mr. Sherrah (member of the Board) and Mr. Thomas Thomas (Clerk). I.E.A. England, commenced duties on the day of the opening.'* Fifty five children were admitted that day, mainly transferred from Abermill School, the distinction of being No.1 on the register accorded to Martha Sands (28.2.89.) of 30 Parc Terrace. In the ensuing week a further thirty-three children were enrolled and Miss Miriam Rowland commenced duties as a Monitress. The staff was completed on October 1st when Miss Margaret Evans, ex-Pupil Teacher, of Glawnant farm, was appointed as an Uncertificated Teacher. At the end of the term there were 98 pupils on roll - 43 transferred from Abermill School, 42 new intake from the village and 13 who came to live there from other areas in South Wales.

A formidable task faced Miss England. In the first few weeks there was a shortage of desks, the vestry was unheated until mid-November when a coke-fired stove was installed, the pupils she found *'in a very backward state'* and with three classes accommodated in the one room she complained bitterly throughout the term about overcrowding.

Nor were the prospects made easier in that both teachers were young and inexperienced, a typical situation in an age when the recruitment and training of teachers was governed by the *'Monitorial'* system. The initial stage was the selection of a *'Candidate'* from the most able 13-year-old boys and girls about to leave school. If approved by the Ministry he or she assumed the title of *'Monitor'/'Monitress'* and taught the youngest pupils for a year, followed by a three-year course as a *'Pupil Teacher'* teaching successively older pupils under the instruction of the Head Teacher and subject to Ministry approval. If successful, it was then possible to try a scholarship examination for entry to a Training College to qualify as a *'Trained Certificated'* teacher. But very few proceeded to College, remaining as *'Uncertificated'* until being recognised in time as *'Certificated'*. This system prevailed until 1914 and long afterwards as did the practice of restricting the appointment of women to those who were single or widows and paid less than men.

There still remained the problem of the older pupils having to attend Abermill School and with the temporary arrangement for the infants proving grossly inadequate, there was no relaxation in the pressure on the Board, and following a series of public meetings it responded in December by purchasing a plot of land on the Gwernymilwr Estate as the site for an Infants' School and a Mixed School.

It was a year when the religious denominations intensified their commitment. At the well-established Noddfa vestry a choir was formed with John Evans as Arweinydd y Gan (Precentor) with services and meetings held on week nights. The Welsh Baptists started to build a vestry. The Welsh Calvinistic Methodists and the Welsh Wesleyan Methodists each purchased a plot of land to site a vestry, and in the meantime the congregations met separately in the Assembly Room of the Leigh Hotel by kind permission of Mrs. Miles.

It was also in a downstairs room of the Leigh Hotel that a Mission was started by Rector Henry Morgan on Sunday, November 10th, when he conducted bilingual services in the morning and evening. Sixty chairs were provided, the lectern was made by Fred Williams, the reading desk was made by Thomas Bailey, the lesson was read by Wilfred Gurney and hymns were sung. The room was overcrowded. Subsequently, bilingual services were held there in the week, Sunday School held in addition to the normal services, Fred Williams and train driver F. Butt were appointed as Rector's Wardens and Thomas Bailey appointed as people's Warden. Then on December 8th, Holy Communion was celebrated for the first time in the Assembly Room, the congregation seated on 120 chairs purchased by the parishioners. Later, with the acquisition of a small harmonium from the parish Church, a choir was formed with George Gould as choirmaster and Miss Powell as organist. Among other early communicants were R.I. Surridge and Miss Miriam Rowland, both of whom played the harmonium occasionally, Messrs. J. Bailey, D.C. Jones, G. Smith, J. Thomas, W. Williams and Mesdames E.M. Ball, W. Edwards, G. Morgan and E.M. Weekes.

That the services were conducted in both Welsh and English was indicative of an increasing number of monoglot English-speaking newcomers although still very much in the minority.

Those who were Nonconformists were faced with a particular difficulty in that the services of all denominations were conducted solely in Welsh. It was natural therefore that they began to seek to establish separate services. The first to do so were the Congregationalists who met as a group at Noddfa vestry on December 1st. At a subsequent service on December 23rd, conducted by Rev. M. Evans of Porth, it was proposed by Mrs. E. Williams and seconded by Miss Jones of Stafford House *'that English services be held with the object of forming an English Congregational Church at Senghenydd and that a start be made as soon as possible.'* The motion was carried with enthusiasm and in pursuance of this objective the first such service was held at Siop Saer on December 29th.

The Temperance Society, led by *'Tawelfryn'* and with particularly strong support from the ladies, continued to campaign against the sale of the *'demon drink'* as the prevalence of drunkenness, shebeening, fights, brawls and assaults was increasing. Once again it played a major role in the refusal of the magistrates to grant ale licences to Mr. Leigh (Leigh Hotel), Josiah Morgan (Gwernymilwr Hotel) and Mary Lawrence (Parc Hotel), a decision which was greeted with loud applause from the body of the Court. In its campaign the Society had now found an ally in the Independent Order of Rechabites, established in April and meeting in Noddfa vestry, a Friendly Society with the primary object of assisting members who suffered adversity but whose members also took a vow of abstinence.

Friendly Societies had long been a common feature in communities throughout the land in an era when there was no statutory provision for financial support in the event of the bread-winner being unable to work as a result of illness or an accident. For those in distress there was recourse to the Poor Law system which was administered in Eglwysilan parish by the Pontypridd Board of Guardians to which Manager David Thomas had been appointed as an Overseer of the poor, but such a prospect was not only demeaning but repellent with the dreaded fear of committal to the workhouse. So to avoid *'going on the parish'* during adverse times other means had to be undertaken to ensure financial support. So most of the Universal miners were members of the Senghenydd Sick and Accident Society which was affiliated to the Monmouthshire and South Wales Provident Society funded by contributions from both the coal owners and employees. But the benefits from this Trust were meagre and hence the need for Friendly Societies, the Order of Rechabites followed in November by the Loyal Order of Ancient Shepherds and the proposal to establish a Lodge of the Ivorites. In addition to dealing with the formal business the meetings included instruction and entertainment.

More choristers joined the Aber Valley United Choir and the preponderant strength was reflected in the election of Idris Perkins as Secretary and Dr. James as Treasurer. Apart from featuring in concerts at Abermill School it competed in a few eisteddfods such as one in Taffswell but without success. Nor was choral interest confined to adults when Edmund Evans formed the Aber Valley Juvenile Choir. It competed in eisteddfods, including the prestigious Caerphilly Castle Eisteddfod, albeit unsuccessfully until in July, augmented by older choristers, it was awarded the prize at Machen eisteddfod. However, as the sole competitor it was a somewhat hollow victory and the pleasure was diminished further when the adjudicator reduced the prize from £3 to 30/- with the remark that the children had done very well but the tenors and basses had not come up to expectation. Furthermore, by expressing the wish that the money be divided between the children he created much ill-will within the ranks of the choir.

Simultaneously and significantly, groups of choristers were now being formed in the village. One such group, under the baton of Charles Jones, won 2nd prize in the Chief Choral Competition at the United Bands of Hope Eisteddfod in Caerphilly. Individual talent was also emerging with bass Idris Perkins, juvenile soloist Mary Elizabeth Price and poet and essayist David Gould (*'Dewi Aur'*) successful in local eisteddfods and together with violinist George Gould were much in demand for concerts which invariably followed tea-meetings and other fund-raising functions.

The year also saw the formation of a Mutual Improvement Society with railway guard W.H. Godwin as Chairman and grocer William Williams as Secretary it proved very popular with a programme which included a Mock parliamentary Election and a lecture entitled *'Self Control'*, the former indicative of the interest aroused by the General Election in which Alfred Thomas was again re-elected as the member for East Glamorgan. It is said also that a small library was set up in one of the Huts.

Then in December a Senghenydd and Aber Chamber of Trade was formed under the presidency of ironmonger Jacob Jones supported by Edmund Evans of Abertridwr as Chairman and stationer David Harris as Secretary. This was a highly significant event in the lack of an Aber Ward because there was now an organisation which would bring pressure to bear on the District Council to accelerate the measures necessary to ameliorate the living conditions.

Senghenydd players dominated both the Aber Stars Rugby Club and the Eglwysilan Baseball Club. Joe Mathews was elected Captain of the rugby team which enjoyed a successful start to the 1895/6 season with victories over Llanhilleth United, Llanbradach Rangers, Great Western 2nds and Treforest Wanderers, losing only to Caerphilly 2nds.

No coal was mined this year but an air of optimism prevailed, the work force had increased, more houses built, the population approached 1,000 and the statement that *'the rosy prospects are fast becoming realised'* was reflected in Kelly's Directory of business people. Listed were: quarry owner and builder Henry Williams & Sons; builders Josiah Morgan and J.E. Lloyd; general dealer David Rowlands; shopkeepers John Bussell, David Davies (Universal Stores), D.C. Jones, Joseph Owens, grocers David Edmunds, David Jones, William Samuel, William Williams butcher and greengrocer John Gould; butchers Rees Thomas, Lewis Walters; greengrocer Andrew Harper; confectioners William Price (Coffee Tavern), David Thomas; tailors William Jones, Thomas Taylor; draper Evan Perkins; bootmaker Herbert Williams; earthenware and glass dealer Edward Jones; earthenware dealer

Daniel Jones; smallware dealer Jacob Jones; newsagent Mrs. Kate Williams; stationer David Harris; hairdresser/tobacconist George Theophilus; hairdresser Peter Stephens; joiner Joseph Williams. Not included was pawnbroker L. Price of 12 Parc Road.

Also listed were Manager David Thomas, surgeon Philip James, station master Thomas Nicholas, sub-postmistress Miss Jane Samuel, Robert Loughor of the Universal Public House and farmers Thomas Bussell (Maesdiofal), Thomas Evans (Glawnant), Mrs. Jane Jenkins (Foelddu), John John (Parc Newydd), Howell Phillips (Craigyrhufan), John Richards (Caerllwyn), John Richards (Cefn Llwyd) and William Thomas (Gelli).

Very many major problems remained to be addressed to improve the barely tolerable living conditions. But the opening of a temporary Infants' School and a sub-post Office, the increase in commercial enterprises, the commitment by more denominations to build places of worship, the promotion of Friendly Societies and a Chamber of Trade, together with a greater involvement in choral, sporting and cultural interests were all indications that the village had reached a further stage in its progress towards forging a virile confident community.

By June of 1896 not only had the Lancaster and York shafts been completed but headings had been driven into the coal face on the West side to exploit the three coal seams including the six-foot, and as the faces were opened up progressively so coal was mined in good quantity. Of very high quality, it found a ready market with the Admiralty and by the end of the year the work force approached 300.

The method of operations adopted by the Manager under the direction of Agent W.T. Rees was that of the *'Longwall'* system whereby the colliers moved forward simultaneously to work the entire coal face. This demanded a high degree of skill, and under dry, dusty and gassy conditions the work was harsh and unrelenting. *'Mabon's Day'*, the nonworking day on the first Monday of each month, came as a welcome relief.

Wages were paid fortnightly. The scales for both *'piece work'* and *'day wage'* operatives were determined throughout the South Wales coalfield by a Joint Committee representing both the coalowners and the miners. Chairman was Sir W.T. Lewis, created a baronet this year, the autocratic and intransigent opponent of any form of Trade Unionism. Representing the miners as Vice-Chairman was William Abraham (*'Mabon'*), Liberal Member of Parliament for the Rhondda, Secretary of the Cambrian Miners' Association, Methodist lay preacher and eisteddfodwr. A charismatic and revered figure, he was the apostle of industrial peace, believing implicitly that the interests of employers and workers were identical, that differences could be adjusted by agreement and that strikes were unnecessary. The best-paid miners were the *'piece workers'* of which the highest rate was earned by the colliers based on the tonnage of coal cut, followed on a lesser scale by such as rippers, roofers and timbermen who were paid by the yardage. Less well-paid was the vast majority of workers, the *'day-wage'* men and boys who were on a prescribed standard rate. Added to the wage rate of all categories was a percentage calculated in accord with a Sliding Scale based on the selling price of coal and adjusted every six months.

The Sliding Scale system provoked widespread discontent among the South Wales miners who saw it as a device to maintain the profit margins of the coal owners and had resulted in wild fluctuations in wages with frequent reductions. But because the system was supported by the supremely influential *'Mabon'* and the fact that the seven small Miners' Associations were disunited and not affiliated to the Miners' Federation of Great Britain the protests were unavailing. So, although the work force at the Universal Colliery shared the general misgivings the year passed without any major confrontations with the management, and in the words of a reporter, *'Senghenydd will not be denied in its rapid progress towards being the Queen of the Mountains.'*

With a population approaching 1,500 by the end of the year the housing programme continued to expand. Approved were plans for 80 cottages submitted by Senghenydd Building Club syndicated by outfitter Mr. Edwards of Dowlais, butcher Mr. Thomas of Porth and Mr. G. Evans of Mountain Ash, together with those for 31 houses and cottages on behalf of residents and speculators such as Josiah Morgan, fruiterer Mr. Brooks, cashier Mr. Edwards, all of Porth. By September over 260 houses houses were occupied or in the course of construction, a sale of ten in Eleanor Road realising a total of £1,475 in one instance. Also built were nine more shops, bakehouses for H. Evans and J. Gibbon, a smithy and stables for Josiah Morgan, another three stables and a coach house. All three hotels were completed. Among the new shops opened were those of draper D. Watkins, outfitter W. Isaac and shoe factor Towyn Jones.

The accelerated building programme served only to accentuate the acute inadequacy of the basic utilities and frequent were the deputations from the Chamber of Trade and the Senghenydd Ratepayers urging the Council *'to take under early consideration'* an improvement in such matters.

In respect of the sewerage system a tender for the extension of the secondary main sewer was approved and some houses were connected, but the situation was aggravated by the reluctance of landowners and builders to lay and maintain connecting pipes until compelled to do so by Notices for the Abatement of Nuisances. Nor was there any improvement in the disposal of sewage by June when the Sanitary Inspector reported that its foul contents were being discharged into the brook so that the pollution was worse than ever. Constant criticism of the scavenging arrangements did meet with a response when the Council appointed a scavenger at an annual salary of £45 plus £1 for each cesspool.

The Sanitary Inspector was equally critical of the water supply in that it could be easily polluted before it reached the reservoirs and also of its inadequacy by stating that 26 houses in Parc Newydd Estate were dependant on one spout and 16 on the Windsor Field were dependant on an unprotected surface well.

The rate of infant mortality remained very high and a virulent epidemic of scarlet fever claimed a number of deaths.

Apart from supplying the usual covering of loose limestone chippings there was no improvement in the state of the roads. As to the vexed question of lighting, an irate resident expressed the general feeling when he wrote to the press, *'Light! Light! We constantly hear the question* "When are our streets to be lighted?" *but the reply is given in silence because no one seems to know'.* The silence was broken in October when the Council accepted a tender of £36 for the purchase of 15 lamp pillars for the Aber Valley, followed early in November by accepting a tender to haul and fix oil lamps at 2/6d a lamp. But with no movement thereafter the Chamber urged the Council of the need for 10 lamps *'to light the by-roads which are in a dangerous condition'.* To no avail, the press reported, *'Winter, with its darkness has come, and still the Senghenyddites are without street lights.'*

An improvement in the postal facilities, the need for a Telegraph Office, better police protection and the *'want of a cemetery'* were other demands made by the Chamber of Trade with the support of Councillor Edward Thomas. Another topic high on the agenda was opposition to the continued use by the postal and railway authorities of the spelling *'Senghenith'.* When draper David Watkins asserted at a meeting that *'as Welshmen we should have a Welsh name'* there was unanimous support for a resolution urging these authorities to adopt *'Senghenydd'* as the official designation.

Bitter that the Aber Valley still had no separate representation on the District Council the Chamber made repeated demands for an Aber Ward and in July it carried a resolution regretting that the Council was failing to give the district the attention it deserves, especially as to forming a new ward, but the rebuke fell on deaf ears.

There was no change in the provision for education, the older children attending Abermill School. The number of infants at Noddfa vestry increased to over 100 and such was the degree of overcrowding that for a period some pupils were transferred to Abermill. Added to the staff were Miss Margaret Jane Gould (Monitress) and Miss Miriam Rowland (Pupil Teacher). Despite the inadequate accommodation and facilities such was the dedication of the Mistress and her inexperienced teachers that the Ministry Inspector was able to report that *'The school has been conducted with care and diligence. The children show every satisfactory proficiency considering the difficulties connected with the premises and it is hoped that the erection of new promises will be commenced as soon as possible.'* When the Chairman of the Board declared that *'Miss England has done wonders'* she promptly requested an increase in salary. This was duly granted and the pupils were rewarded by a treat in the form of a visit to Taffs Well. Then in May the School Board, no doubt influenced by the Inspector's remarks concerning new premises, invited tenders for the construction of two schools and work began later in the year.

There was a marked advance in the efforts by the religious denominations to raise funds for building projects by means of concerts, competitive meetings which took the form of mini-eisteddfods, tea meetings, sales of work and other functions.

The Welsh Calvinistic Methodists opened *'Tabernacl'* vestry. On March 1st the Welsh Baptists opened *'Salem'* Vestry at a cost of £600, the foundations

Tabernacle Chapel.

having been laid by volunteers and the stone provided free by Josiah Morgan. On April 4th and 5th the English Wesleyan Methodists opened their vestry with services conducted by Revs. H.P. Morgan and E. Joliffe of the South Wales Mission and Rev. J. Evans, Eglwysbach.

On February 28th the English Congregationalists, meeting at Noddfa, formed a *'church'* with eleven members comprising Mrs. E. Williams, Mr. & Mrs. D. Harris, Mr. & Mrs. W.G. Llewellyn, Misses J. & P. Jones, Mr. F. George, Miss George, Mr. T. Cross and Mr. L. Rees. Rev. Tawelfryn Thomas agreed to serve as officiating minister David Harris was elected as lay preacher, W.G. Llewellyn as Secretary and Mrs. E. Williams as Treasurer. Thereafter they held services successively at Siop Saer, the Leigh Hotel, Siop Saer, an upper room in a house nearby and then at 98 Parc Road. The Cause prospered and a Building Fund was launched by various efforts including the promotion of the first eisteddfod in the village. So successful was the fund-raising that on November 7th and 8th a galvanised iron building to seat 200 at a cost of £187-18-6 was opened in Windsor Road when the services were conducted by Revs. W. Spurgeon of Cardiff, J. Williams of Carmarthen College, W. Owen (late of China), J. Gwilym Jones of Penarth, J.G. James of Merthyr, W.G. Jenkins of Pontypridd and *'Tawelfryn'*.

Rector Henry Morgan, assisted by Mr. Wilfred Gurney of St. Michael's College, continued to hold Sunday services, Sunday School and a midweek service at the Leigh Hotel while they sought a permanent place of worship. One suggestion for a site was on Craigyrhufan land where once stood an ancient Celtic Church called *'Capel Cenydd'*, but it was rejected. It was on a site donated by Lord Windsor that the foundation of St. Peter's Mission Hall was laid on August 6th by Mr. Leigh Thomas of Brynllefrith, a young student at Rugby, who was presented with a silver hammer and trowel to mark the occasion. The service was conducted by the Rector, supported by the choirs of the parish Church and Senghenydd, with addresses given by Revs. Daniel Lewis the Rector of Caerphilly, T.W. James of Taffswell, W.E. Jones and D.E. Jacob of Llanfabon, D. Davies of Aberdare and G. Jones of Treharris. Underneath the foundation stone a bottle was placed in which were recorded the names of Mr. Thomas, the Rector, the officers and some members. After the ceremony more than a hundred people adjourned to the Leigh Hotel for tea *'where they partook of the good things provided'*. During the construction of the Hall which continued throughout the year the communicants continued to meet at the Hotel.

It was also at the Hotel that the Welsh Wesleyan Methodists held their services.

The English Baptists first met in the open air before moving to the front room of a house in Parc Road, then to a shop in the same street where a Cause was established in June and subsequently to Aberdare Hall.

'Noddfa' elected Messrs. D. Aaron Jones, D. Bowen, D. James (Llansamlet) and David Gould to the diaconate and held the first Cyrddau Mawr (Big Meetings) which extended over two days.

Anniversary and Thanksgiving Services were major occasions which invariably required the closure of the schools. But of particular significance this year was the day in August when the United Sunday Schools departed on their first outing, the village almost deserted. A special train took the Noddfa contingent to Penarth *'where it enjoyed plentiful amusement and fun, especially when several members of the Chamber of Trade rode astride Solomon's donkeys'*. The other denominations, several hundred in number, journeyed by another special train to Caerphilly *'where they partook of two picnic meals and various games in the castle grounds before returning in a train which needed two puffers and was the largest seen in Senghenydd'*.

Once again the three hotels applied for licences at the Caerphilly Brewsters Session with the owners each engaging prominent Counsel in a bitter rivalry. On behalf of Josiah Morgan it was stated that the Gwernymilwr had cost £4,200 to build, that there were eleven bedrooms and *'outside Cardiff it would be difficult to find a larger hotel'*. On behalf of Mrs. Miles of the New Inn, Pontypridd, it was stated that the Leigh Hotel had cost £4,600 to build and was *'an admirable house of three storeys with excellent accommodation, ten bedrooms, a separate sitting room and coffee room for travellers'*. The Parc Hotel, built by Mr. Hurman of Cardiff, was described as an admirable building. Once again the applications were opposed by the police, the Temperance League and the management of the Universal Hotel which asserted that the bedrooms of the hotels were barely used. By the casting vote of the Chairman of the Bench a provisional licence was granted to the Leigh Hotel but it aroused such a volume of criticism that it was subsequently withdrawn in that the Chairman had no legal power to make the decision. So all three hotels and the neighbouring Windsor Hotel remained as Temperance Hotels, restricted to the sale of tea, coffee and soft drinks.

This decision was welcomed by the community in general as the increasing incidence of drunkenness posed a social blight. Particularly turbulent were the week-ends with physical assaults common, the press duly reporting all charges at the Caerphilly Magistrates Court with such headlines as *'Miners Fined for Drunkenness'*, *'Police Assaulted'*, *'Miners in Trouble'*, *'Affray in Senghenydd'*. Offensive was the continuing practice of shebeening centred mainly in the Huts, one police raid on the home of a widow on a Sunday morning surprising a large group of men imbibing from a nine-gallon cask of ale on tap.

The overwhelming mass of villagers sought their pleasures other than frequenting the Universal Hotel and a shebeen.

In June the Chamber of Trade, led by president Robert Loughor and accompanied by about a hundred people from the Valley, sallied forth on an excursion to Weston-super-Mare by rail and boat at a cost of 2/6d a head.

More organisations were established. The Lodge of the Ivorites was formally incorporated as the Gwyngyll Lodge, so-named after the Chairman Gwyngyll Hughes of Pontypridd, with John Evans as President, J. Jones as Vice-President, David Gould as Secretary and Robert Loughor as Treasurer, the meetings being held at the Universal Hotel. A St. John

Ambulance Class was conducted at Aberdare Hall by Dr. James as Chairman, supported by D. Harris as Secretary and W. Isaac as Treasurer. There was also a Mining Class.

The Mutual Improvement Society was replaced by a Debating Society with W.H. Godwin as Chairman and grocer William Williams as Secretary. The session opened in February with a social evening in which *'the tea and edibles'* was followed by a debate on the motion *'Should Women Hold Office?'*, one which brought forth some sharp palavering by the lady debaters before it was carried by a narrow majority. In the resulting popular meetings among the most vocal members were Idris Perkins and David Gould.

Lectures, particularly those illustrated by *'limelight'* slides, attracted large audiences with subjects varying from *'Heroes of the Life Boat'* at the English Wesleyan Methodist vestry to that of *'The British Empire'* sponsored by the East Glamorgan Conservative Club at the Universal Hotel.

The Aber Valley United Choir won the Chief Choral Competition at Llanbradach Eisteddfod and staged many concerts. Many choristers joined the newly-formed Aber Valley Male Voice Choir also conducted by Edmund Evans. But in addition, such was the strength of choral music in the village that Ben Price was able to form not only a Senghenydd Male Voice Choir but the Orpheus Choir, a mixed choir of some fifty voices with Gwilym Marsden as accompanist. The Orpheus Choir held its first public performance on two successive nights in August at the Gwernymilwr Hotel. The programme opened with a miscellaneous repertoire which included solos by Miss Mary Price, daughter of Ben, and Idris Berkins, followed by the performance of Joseph Parry's cantata *'Ymgom Yr Adar'* (Conversation of the Birds). The main characters were played by Rees Jones (youth), Idris Perkins (Eagle), Miss Mary Evans (Cuckoo), Master Morgan John Davies (Robin Redbreast), Master J. Bevan (Wren), Miss Kate Williams (Thrush), Miss M.J. Morgan (Nightingale), Miss Thomas (Lark), Misses J. Jenkins and R.D. Perkins (Goldfinches), Misses Arianwen Jones and G. Bevan (Busy Bees). To enhance the atmosphere *'the Assembly Room was prettily decorated, the scene tending to represent the forest glade in which all the birds met to render their respective songs'*. It was a remarkable occasion.

Nor was music-making confined to choral expression in that the Senghenydd Brass Band was formed under the baton of Mr. G. Harding of Llanbradach with J. Rowe as Secretary and William Williams as Treasurer. Supported by a substantial donation from the Universal Company for the purchase of instruments, its first concert was held at the Universal Hotel in November when it was reported to have played with good effect. Shortly afterwards it embarked on its first turn-out through the village *'giving a good account of itself considering most of them are amateurs'*, a less than enthusiastic judgement which was remedied after its next venture by the reports that *'the playing showed a decided improvement and we are pleased that we possess a brass band which breaks the silence with sweet music'*.

Well-patronised were the *'Penny Readings'* held at Tabernacl vestry. Extensively popular throughout Wales, the title derived from the entry charge of 1d, their declared aim was that of *'improving the cultural and moral tastes of the working class'*. Open to children and adults, a session of six monthly meetings was held in the Winter and Spring months, concluding with a free tea for the children. The meetings took the form of a mini-eisteddfod with small money prizes offered to the best performers in competitions which could include solos, duets, recitations, instrumental performances, reading an unseen passage of prose from which the punctuation marks had been removed, an impromptu debate conducted by a pair of speakers and small choral groups. Acceptable as was the small monetary prize the greater value was attached to the embroidered bag in which it was presented, their accumulation becoming a source of prestige.

In March the first eisteddfod, albeit on a modest scale, was launched by the English Congregationalists. A more comprehensive one was organised in August by the Lodge of the Ivorites at the Gwernymilwr Hotel, and among the winners were the *'Senghenydd Minstrels'* conducted by David Jones (Mixed Choir competition), Morgan J. Davies (Boy's solo), Towyn Jones (Tenor solo), Idris Perkins (Bass solo and Music Sight-Reading), David Gould and Idris Perkins (Impromptu Debate). Another one was promoted at the same venue in September by the English Baptists in which local competitors figured prominently in the prize list and the choral prize was shared between the *'Senghenydd Musicians'* conducted by Ben Price and Salem Choir conducted by John Rees.

Whether the purpose was to raise funds or to conclude tea meetings, dinners or other functions the principal medium of entertainment was a concert. One presented at the Universal Hotel by the Caerphilly Minstrel Group was described as *'providing entertainment the like of which has not been seen at Senghenydd'*. Another, promoted by Tabernacl, included artistes from neighbouring villages and was hailed as *'One of the best yet held in the place'*. But invariably there was little need to go beyond the confines of the village to compose a programme derived from the galaxy of talent available - Ben Price's two choirs, chapel choirs such as those of Noddfa and Salem, various choral groups and gifted-individuals. However, the villagers did venture forth to Abertridwr for eisteddfods and concerts and eagerly anticipated was the journey by special train to Cardiff for the pantomimes at the Grand and Royal Theatres.

Both the Aber Stars Rugby Club and the Aber Valley Baseball Club were dominated by players from the village. The former, under the captaincy of Joe Meyrick, ably supported by such as Tom Gould, Windsor Morgan, Idris Williams and Henry Mathews was undefeated against other Junior teams by the end of the year, and in the latter Club the Captain was Idris Williams with Fred Loughor as the Secretary.

CHAPTER 3

The development of the colliery suffered a serious setback during the first half of 1897 due to geological problems and water seepage so that at one stage the number of shifts was reduced from three to two and many workers were laid off. It was not until August that the weekly output reached 1,000 tons, the *'big vein'* struck and the *'Cardiff Times'* reported that it was anticipated the output would reach 6,000 tons a week.

All the while the increasing militant attitude in the South Wales coalfield in opposition to the Sliding Scale and support for Unionism was being reflected at the colliery. Some miners had joined the Cambrian Miners' Association led by *'Mabon'* and in August he made his first visit to the village when he addressed a mass meeting at the Gwernymilwr Hotel in both Welsh and English. Such were his oratorical powers, accompanied by hymn singing, that the meeting voted to join the Association.

W.T. Abraham M.P. 'Mabon' 1st Lord Merthyr of Senghenydd.

However, although a Lodge was established the work force was deeply divided and by September only 110 out of about 300 workers had joined. This disunity became apparent later in the month over a rumour that the Manager intended to sub-contract work on the main seam. The Lodge Secretary was unable to seek a meeting with the Manager over this rumoured grievance because he did not represent a united body and in his words, *'the non-Union men are the masters'*. Consequently, operations were suspended and the work force came out on strike for the first time. It lasted eight days and was resolved only by the intervention of *'Mabon'* meeting the Manager who confirmed that the rumour was unfounded and had arisen from the Company's decision to operate a single shift in future which would entail some men being *'taken out'*. The Manager's explanation was accepted and work was resumed despite the threatened loss of jobs, an episode which did nothing to heal the rift between Unionists and non-Unionists.

As more seams were opened up in the latter part of the year so more workers were employed and the population increased rapidly from 1,755 in August to 2,500 by the end of the year, the origin of the newcomers varying little from the pattern of previous years, a substantial intake coming from the Cynon and Rhondda Valleys.

Plans were approved for another 43 houses, extensions to 14 others, a shop and bakehouse for John Thomas and three stables. Permission was granted to J.T. Evans of the Stores to partition part of his stable to serve as a temporary slaughterhouse, ironmonger Jacob Jones was licensed to store and hawk petroleum, Lotwick (Ludwig) John of Parc Newydd farm was registered as a purveyor of milk. In August there were 314 occupied houses and 126 under construction, very many for Senghenydd Building Club, and by the end of the year 416 houses were occupied and 58 under construction.

With the demand for accommodation exceeding the supply overcrowding was common. Houses were being occupied before they were certified as being fit for occupation as occurred in Stanley Street when builder Henry Williams was prosecuted. The secondary main sewer was extended but the Chamber of Trade was critical of what it deemed to be slow progress in the provision of an adequate system. In reply the Council criticised estate and houseowners for trying to avoid responsibility for connecting their properties to the sewer and served a Notice on the Colliery company to connect up their seventeen Huts. The inadequacy of the scavenging was attacked, and bitter were the complaints that *'parts of the village have no proper water supply of any kind to depend on'*.

A virulent epidemic of scarlet fever that extended from January to August necessitated the closure of the Infants' School for three weeks in March and again in April for a similar period.

A deputation from the village complained forcefully about the state of the main Parc Road as did the Senghenydd Building Club about the state of Gelli Road where it had built thirty-eight houses. In response to all complaints about the roads the Council insisted that it could not assume their care and authorise top-metalling until they had been prepared in accordance to specific regulations by the estate owners, housing clubs or builders. However, it agreed to widen the lower part of Gelli Road and metal it provided Lord Windsor ballasted it, and also to lay ashes on the footpath to Abertridwr. As to the vehement criticism that *'the whole place has been in total darkness this year'*, its appointment of a man to supervise the lighting of 13 oil lamps at a salary of 15/- a week seemed to promise better prospects.

With the Aber valley inhabitants still incensed that Councillor Edward Thomas was returned as a member of Caerphilly Town Ward and that no progress had been made towards separate representation other than a plan being prepared by the Surveyor in October another year passed in bitter recrimination. Towyn Jones, Secretary to the Chamber of Trade, expressed the general disaffection when he wrote to the Clerk, *'the inhabitants of this district feel they have not received due attention these last two years.'*

Provision for education remained unaltered during the first seven months of the year while two school buildings were being constructed. The number on roll at the Infants' School increased to over 160 with consequent over-crowding and Log Book entries such as *'the school work is carried on under considerable difficulties owing to the four classes being in the same room.'* Aggravating the situation was the emission of smoke and fumes from the stove so that the school was closed on two occasions as being *'unfit for occupation'*. Added to these tribulations was the drastic effect of the scarlet fever epidemic in March and April, and it says much for the dedication of the staff that H.M. Inspector reported, *'The school is exceedingly well-disciplined and its conduct as regards attainment is certainly creditable when allowance is made for the time lost through the epidemic and for the inconvenience of the premises.'*

Then in June and July the hot weather posed ventilation problems so that with the disruption caused by the construction of Noddfa Chapel in close proximity it must have been with a considerable sense of joy that when the school closed for the Summer Vacation on July 30th so Miss England wrote in the Log Book, *'School work will be resumed at the New premises on August 30th.'*

The long-awaited Infants and Mixed Schools, built by Joseph Howells, were formally opened on August 30th by the Chairman of the School Board and in the afternoon the scholars were entertained to a tea provided by the Board. However, because essential furniture and equipment such as blackboards had not been delivered, the pupils did not attend until September 6th.

Senghenydd Council School which was built in 1897.

There were no changes in the staff of the Infants' School which comprised Miss England (Head Teacher), Misses Margaret Evans (Uncertificated), Miriam Rowlands and Margaret Gould (Pupil Teachers). Later in the term Miss Evans resigned and appointed were Misses Mary Ann Jones (Uncertificated) at a salary of £45 per annum and Margaret Roberts (Candidate Monitress). The 180 pupils were organised into three classes and the term passed without any major problems.

Appointed as Head Teacher of the Mixed School, its motto that of *'Goreu Arf, Arf Dysg'* (*'The Best Tool is the Tool of Learning'*), was Mr. Daniel Lloyd at a salary of £80 per annum. Appointed to the staff were Misses Sarah Morgan (Certificated Assistant), Mary Rees (Uncertificated), Catherine James (Pupil Teacher) and Mr. Joseph Edmunds (Candidate Monitor). Later in the year Miss Mary Rees resigned and appointed were Misses Selina John (Paid Monitress) and Mary Miles (Uncertificated). The number on roll was 136, almost all transferred from Abermill School, and they were organised into seven Standards to form five classes. The statutory school-leaving age was twelve, but this could be extended for a further year if the scholar had not attained an established level of competence. Consequently it was a feature of all such schools that in practice the leaving age was thirteen.

The Master, who taught full-time as was the practice, was far from impressed with the level of competence of the intake in the 3RS which he noted as very weak and some Standards as in a backward state, and as the number on roll increased to 200 he also complained about the delay in appointing additional teachers. Nor was he happy about the quality of the staff which he recorded as *'very weak, to having no experience in teaching Standards.'*

He devoted particular attention to attendance, a major factor in the determination of the School Grant, and a frequent visitor was the Attendance Officer (*'Whiperin'*), the awesome figure of Mr. Joseph Millward, a chapel deacon and lay preacher. Fines were imposed on parents of children who were absent for unwarranted reasons but an entry in the Log Book that *'a new lad was admitted who had just left the Truant School at Quakers Yard'* signified the dreaded fate that awaited a persistent truant. Truancy was not yet a problem, nor was unwarranted absenteeism except on Mabon's Day which had become interpreted by many as a family holiday. Moreover, the Master adopted the universal play of closing the school when major functions such as religious services, tea parties and outings were held in the village.

Of these early days a former pupil wrote, *'Mr. Lloyd did not have a room of his own but sat in a classroom in such a position that he could see into every room. Discipline was very strict. Each teacher had a* "signal"*, a wooden stick which* "clicked" *and used instead of giving orders. Thus, for example, one click meant* "come to attention"*. When Inspectors came to the school we all stood up and saluted. Mr. Lloyd was a man of outstanding ability and personality and excelled as a musical director.'*

The pupils also stood up when the members of the Board visited the school to check the registers, all of whom expressed their satisfaction with the conduct and progress of the school in this initial stage.

It was another year in which the religious denominations were very active in raising funds by various means, some pursuing the objective of a permanent place of worship or building a chapel, some to pay off the debts incurred. Significant was the opening on February 25th; of St. Peter's Mission Hall, designed to seat 300 at a cost of £800, when sermons were delivered by Rector Henry Morgan, the Rural Dean of Caerphilly, Revs. J.R. Buckley of Llandaff and T.C. Phillips of Cardiff. The communion vessels were presented by Howell and Gwenllian Phillips of Craigyrhufan farm. Then in March Rev. David Jones was inducted as curate, a fervent Welshman like the Rector, who introduced a Welsh service on Sunday morning and held a Welsh class for monoglot English-speaking communicants.

Members of *'Noddfa'* were building the first chapel in the village. The English Baptists opened a *'vestry'* in Clive House and in December laid the foundations of *'Ebenezer'* vestry as a permanent place of worship. In August the first annual Demonstration of the United Sunday Schools took place, the scholars and teachers marching through the streets before being entertained to tea and then adjourning to Gelli farm for games.

The three hotels again applied for licences at the Caerphilly Brewsters Session with intense rivalry shown by the applicants amid an array of eminent barristers, solicitors and press reporters. In support of the applications the respective Counsels stressed the growth of population and the need to provide better facilities for the villagers and commercial travellers. Counsels on behalf of Josiah Morgan and Mrs. Miles emphasised the accommodation available at their hotels, the Counsel on behalf of Mr. Hurman in respect of the Parc Hotel stressing that although he owned the Universal Hotel the beer was supplied by Crosswell's Brewery. Ranged in formidable opposition were a Queen's Counsel representing the Pontypridd and Rhondda Temperance League, Rev. Tawelfryn Thomas who presented a petition signed by 600 inhabitants opposing the applications, the police, builder Henry Williams who had testified that he owned 36 houses and had not heard any complaint from the families as to the lack of licensed accommodation and Crosswell's Brewery on behalf of the Universal Hotel. Incredulity and dismay greeted the decision of the Bench to grant provisional licences to the Leigh and Gwernymilwr Hotels, and such was the resultant outcry, that as in the previous year, the decision was reversed by the Glamorgan Licensing Authority, much to the delight of the vast majority of villagers and to Robert Loughor of the Universal Hotel which was granted a renewal of its licence despite the accusation of Sunday drinking.

On October 1st the Parc Hotel, together with the *'message and parcel of land'* was conveyed by indenture *'between William Henry Mathias and Walter Herbert of the one part and the Caerphilly & Castle Brewery Ltd. of the other part in fee simple of a yearly rent charge of £10'.*

That the decision of the Bench was reversed was due in very large measure to the increased strength of the Temperance cause in the village which had been enhanced by the formation of a branch of the British Women's Temperance Association under the Presidency of Mrs. Sands. It was further strengthened by the establishment of the Star of Senghenydd Lodge of the Good Templars (Undeb y Templwyr Da), a Friendly Society in which they like the Rechabites, took a vow of abstinence and were dedicated to waging war on the *'demon drink'*, their meetings open to children and adults, religious in essence but included lectures and competitions. Further support came from the Education Board when Mr. R. Prys Jones gave an object lesson on *'Alcohol'* to the pupils in the Mixed School.

But powerful as was the support from the community at large for the Temperance movement it was unable to stem the increase in drunkenness and accompanying acts of violence or the continued practice of shebeening. Frequent were the press reports of the turbulent element embroiled in a fight, brawl, assault or domestic disturbance with headlines of *'Police Assaulted'*, *'Drunken Colliers in Fight'*, *'Husband Attacks Fight'*. Particularly sensational was the heading *'Alleged Cannibalism in Senghenydd'* conjuring up a gruesome picture. But happily this proved to be an example of journalese license when it was revealed to be nothing more than one drunken miner biting into the thumb of another drunken miner during a quarrel over a racing pigeon!

Meanwhile, Queen Victoria's Jubilee was well and truly celebrated in June, the occasion marked with the official opening of *'a bridge linking both ends of the village'* by Alderman H. Mathias and Josiah Morgan. The school children were granted a week's holiday and on the 25th, headed by the Colliery Band, they paraded the streets before being entertained to tea provided by Alfred Thomas, M.P. Other pleasurable occasions during the year were a *'picnic party'* outing to Weston-super-Mare organised by the Chamber of Trade and its first Annual Dinner.

Choral music continued to flourish with Ben Price taking over as conductor of the Aber Valley United Choir in addition to that of Senghenydd Orpheus Choir, the former holding a Grand Concert at Abermill School featuring the cantata *'The Ruler's Daughter'* in which bass Idris Perkins and tenor Towyn Jones played prominent roles. Active also were chapel choirs and various groups. A mini-eisteddfod was held in Tabernacl vestry, and among the many concerts was one juvenile organised on behalf of the Ambulance Class. Idris Perkins, juvenile Morgan J. Davies and David Gould were consistently successful in eisteddfods in surrounding areas and Thomas Wigley won the prize for the Singing on Sight competition at Llanbradach. But pride of place was accorded to Mary Price, daughter of Ben, a member of Madame Rees's Ladies Choir who made her debut as a solo artiste in a concert at the Park Hall, Cardiff, when it was reported that she distinguished herself above the ordinary.

Praiseworthy too was the improvement in the performance of the Colliery Band which had been reinforced by new-coming bandsmen.

The Debating Society and lectures remained popular. Another form of entertainment was introduced this year when Mrs. Emily Orton was granted a theatre licence for two weeks, renewable fortnightly for a period of three months, in respect of the *'American Pavilion'*, a temporary primitive structure of wood and canvas erected near the Leigh Hotel, to offer dramatic entertainment. The audience was seated on wooden benches.

The rugby players dominated the *'Aber Stars'* team and such was the enthusiasm for the game that there came the first signs of separation from Abertridwr when *'pick-up'* games were played on the Gelli fields.

On Christmas Day an eisteddfod on behalf of Noddfa Chapel was held at the Mixed School, the proceedings conducted by *'Tawelfryn'*. Among the individual winners were Idris Perkins singing *'Adsain o'r Gan'*, soprano Miss M. Jones singing *'The Holy City'*, David Gould for a poem and Miss A.M. Morris in the children's recitation competition. The Male Voice Choir competition, for which the test piece was *'The Sailors' Chorus'* was won by Rees Thomas's Party. The Chief Choral competition, for which the test piece was *'Addoliad'* was won by Noddfa Choir conducted by John Thomas, defeating the Senghenydd United Choir conducted by Ben Price.

On New Year's Eve the English Congregationalists organised a Grand Soiree and Supper at the Gwernymilwr Hotel before the gathering moved to the chapel for a service.

But as the year drew to a close it was at a time of unrest in the coalfield. Between 1890 and 1896 the price of large coal at Cardiff Docks had fallen from 13/- to 9/2d a ton, the result of a deliberate policy by the coalowners to sell cheaply. They were enabled to do so by keeping wages low and by the operation of the Sliding Scale which sustained their profit margin. As a result the miners' wages had been eroded so that now the estimated average weekly wage of the day worker was about £1-1-0 with the take-home pay between 17/- and 18/- after deductions for the doctor, Sick Fund and other items. In addition, the miners had been subjected to *'speed-up'* conditions to improve production and to haggling over payment for work in difficult places.

The anger had welled up in September at a conference of delegates from the entire South Wales coalfield. There it resolved to give six months notice as from October 1st for the withdrawal of labour in support of the termination of the Sliding Scale, a 10% increase in wages and a basic minimum wage. When this notice was tendered the response from the Monmouthshire and South Wales Coalowners Association, led by Sir W.T. Lewis, was utter rejection of these demands. Since both sides had remained intransigent and determined *'to face it out'* the prospects boded ill for the coming year.

January 1898 passed without any sign of a break in the deadlock between the South Wales coalowners and the work force. On February 26th, before the six months' notice had elapsed, the coalowners suspended all negotiations and declared their intention of imposing a *'lock out'* at the end of March unless the miners withdrew their demands. The work force remained implacable.

Daily life in the village continued on its normal course.

On February 19th the Chamber of Trade held its second Annual Dinner, a lavish affair by all accounts, numbering among its guests landowner and coalowner Major Lindsay, Edward Shaw, Councillor Edward Thomas,

Thomas Jones the Assistant Overseer of the Workhouse, solicitor Charles Goodfellow, Josiah Morgan, Vicar Henry Morgan and Dan Lloyd.

In March the opening of *'Ebenezer'* vestry by the English Baptists was doubly important. Not only did it provide another permanent place of worship but it marked the induction of the first resident Nonconformist minister in the person of Rev. David Roberts who combined this ministry with that of Salem vestry. A pious, thoughtful, sympathetic and caring pastor and an eloquent preacher, in the next thirty-five years he was to play a major role in all aspects of the community and was greatly revered. A matter of regret was the departure of David Harris, lay preacher to the English Congregationalists. Little interest was aroused by the County Council Election for the Caerphilly Division. William Thomas was elected as Treasurer of the South Wales Miners' Association. Builder Henry Williams was killed in an accident at his quarry.

At the infants' school, with 190 on roll, Misses Catherine Millward (Uncertificated) and Margaret Roberts (Monitress) were appointed to the staff but Miss England continued to complain that it was inadequate in qualifications and experience. At the Boys' School, with 200 on roll, Joshua Bowen (Uncertificated) was appointed to the staff, emphasis was laid on a uniform style of writing and Geography was included in the curriculum. In neither of the schools was Welsh taught and St. David's Day was celebrated only by the customary half-day holiday without any special programme. Attendance was high in both schools and steady progress was made.

House building continued but plans were approved for only eight houses, a bakehouse, two coach houses and a stable. As in previous years there was continual confrontation between Caerphilly Council and the landowners over the responsibility for connecting up the sewerage and drainage pipes from houses to the mains. There was a long and bitter dispute on this account over Parc Road, the estate agent Mr. Bruton insisting this was the responsibility of the Council and the Council threatening to undertake the work and charge the cost. The disputed question also arose when the Council deferred requests from the tenants of the Parc Newydd Estate and from the Secretary of Senghenydd Building Club to allow occupation of houses because of drainage difficulties. Notices for the Abatement of Nuisances in respect of blocked drains were served on Mr. Bruton, on the owners of three houses in Stanley Street and three shops in Parc Road, the Council resolving to execute the work and charge the cost if not remedied.

On the positive side, the salary of the scavenger was increased to £48 per annum plus £1 for each cesspool and the Council agreed to a request from the Chamber of Trade to provide two public urinals on Parc Road.

On March 31st, the day when the existing six-months' agreement expired, the Coalowners' Association, still refusing to negotiate, terminated its contract with the miners and the lock-out/strike became effective on April 1st.

On April 4th the Urban District Council elections were held and for the first time the voters were able to register their votes at a polling station in the Mixed School instead of having to journey to Caerphilly. Elected to serve the

Aber Valley was Manager David Thomas who defeated Robert Loughor of the Universal Hotel by 368 votes to 225.

By April 9th the lock-out/strike was complete throughout the entire coalfield, but the miners were ill-prepared. Whereas the owners were organised into a well-financed powerful unit the miners were represented by seven small disunited Unions, none affiliated to the Miners' Federation of Great Britain, without a co-ordinated organisation and lacking central financial resources.

With the *'strikers'* denied financial assistance from the Poor Law, the financial assistance from the small Unions was quickly exhausted. The result in Senghenydd as elsewhere was destitution and hardship, alleviated to some extent by efforts such as that by the English Wesleyans who used the money set aside for building a chapel to distribute food at the vestry each day while it lasted. So as early as May such was the resultant privation throughout the coalfield that a delegate conference voted to negotiate, but the response of the Coalowners' Association was to insist on the unconditional acceptance of terms which were more severe than those in existence.

Rejected by the miners, the lock-out/strike continued with prideful resolution. Some financial support continued to come from the Miners' Federation of Great Britain although it was not obligated to do so, but it was pitifully inadequate. The strike committee doled out a meagre weekly sum at the Universal Hotel and the Distress Committee by organising concerts and with the assistance of business people strove to help those families in greatest need.

By mid-June the situation throughout the coalfield was becoming so desperate with tales of harrowing suffering that another effort was made to open negotiations but the owners remained implacable, insisting on a return on their own terms. Later in the month, the government, concerned at the effect on the national economy, tried to intervene. The president of the Board of Trade nominated a conciliator under the terms of the Conciliation Act to effect a compromise and resolve the dispute, but Sir. W.T. Lewis contemptuously rejected the proposal as unwarranted interference and the attempt was rebuffed.

So July and August dragged remorsely on, the owners ruthlessly determined to starve the miners into submission. So it proved. On September 1st, no longer able to endure the suffering of their families, a meeting of the provisional Committee representing the miners throughout the coalfield decided to return to work on the terms imposed by the owners. By these terms the sliding Scale remained in force, wages were reduced and even *'Mabon's Day'* was abolished. Led by Sir W.T. Lewis the Coalowners' Association had won a complete victory. A week later the miners returned to work dispirited, bitter and angry.

During this harrowing period the community responded with typical resilience and unity of purpose. Priority of purpose was to shelter the children as far as possible from the desperate reality.

Only two references are made in the School Log Books to the dire circumstances, one an entry in May by Miss England referring to a comment by the H.M.I. that *'backwardness in some lower divisions will doubtless disappear when the district becomes more settled'*, the other entry by Dan Lloyd in July that *'The number of scholars less owing to several families leaving because of the Strike.'* But there is no indication that attendance was affected other than that associated normally with illness. The H.M.I. reported on the Infants' School that *'The teaching is satisfactory in many ways'* despite being critical of the unqualified staff. Of the Mixed school he reported, *'The results are very promising and the Master, who is a teacher of approved merit, is certain to raise the school to the highest level of efficiency when he has had time to establish his method'*, and he praised the introduction of Elementary Science into the curriculum.

'School as usual' was clearly the resolve of both parents and staff, much to the satisfaction of Rev. Tawelfryn Thomas and Evan Sherrah elected by the ratepayers at the School Board election in May.

There was no halt in house-building and plans were approved for another 25 houses and 14 cottages and extensions to 24 houses. By the end of August a total of 461 houses had been completed although all were not occupied and 58 were in the course of construction.

The Chamber of Trade was no less diligent, and it was as a result of its proposed change of name for some streets, endorsed by a meeting of rate payers, that for the first time all streets were officially designated in July. They were:

Commercial Street: formerly Parc Read and Windsor Road.
High Street: formerly Eleanor Road.
Caerphilly Road: formerly Gelli Road.

Commercial Street, Senghenydd.

Kingsley Place: formerly Kingsley Place and Cenydd Terrace.
Cross Street: formerly Stuart Road.
Stanley Street: formerly Stanley Road.
Station Road: the road leading to the station via the Gwernymilwr and Parc Hotels.
Windsor Place: block of three houses near the smithy.
Station Terrace: stet.
Parc Terrace: stet.
Grove Terrace: stet.
The Council also agreed that the houses be numbered.

A measure of satisfaction was derived from the Council's agreement to ballast and metal parts of Commercial Street, to share the cost with the Senghenydd Building Club for similar work on part of Caerphilly Road and to allocate a sum of money for the improvement of the mountain road to Nelson. William Evans was awarded the tender for lighting the street lamps and supplying the petroleum at a wage of 30/- a week.

Public health continued to be a major concern. Although more houses were being connected to the sewer and tenders had been accepted for the extension of the Main Aber Valley Sewer into the village, Towyn Jones, Secretary to the Chamber of Trade was constrained in May to complain that *'the present state of drainage is detrimental to the health of the inhabitants and we urge the Council to get on with the main sewerage scheme.'* Notices for the Abatement of Nuisances were served on house-owners in Station Terrace respecting foul and overflowing cesspits and on house-owners in Kingsley place respecting blocked drains.

But the *'black spot'* posing a health hazard was still Stanley Street, largely owned by the administrators of the Henry Williams Estate. In April the Sanitary Inspector reported a *'nuisance'* caused by *'inhabitants in the top position of the houses, which are occupied as double houses, emptying their slops on the road in front.'* In May the Council ordered the cessation of occupation of some cellar dwellings in that they did not conform to the Housing Act being lacking in proper privies, were in an insanitary condition and likely to have an injurious effect on the tenants. A lengthy acrimonious dispute ensued. The administrators were also instructed to ensure that the refuse thrown into their nearby quarry be discontinued and that it be properly fenced. In June a case of typhoid fever was reported in one of the houses *'condemned some time ago for want of drains'*, and in August two cases of diphtheria were reported *'in a house where typhoid fever prevailed'*.

The water supply was under constant scrutiny. In May the Medical Officer of Health attributed a case of scarlet fever to water drawn from an open well near the Parc Hotel which was polluted by sewage and a closing order was served against Crosswells Brewery, and in August the Universal Colliery company agreed to filter its water supply for drinking purposes before it entered the mains.

A new health hazard had emerged in May when four cases of scarlet fever were attributed to contaminated milk supplied by Ludwig John and as a consequence the Medical Officer recommended the distribution of posters and pamphlets with the instruction to boil the milk before consumption.

For a considerable time the Chamber of Trade had drawn the attention of the Council to the lack of any measures to combat house and property fires and the need for fire hydrants to be installed and for a supply of appliances. As a result the Council made an approach in May to the Universal Company seeking terms for the supply of hydrants and water.

Undeterred by the financial stringencies of the time and the decline in beer-drinking the three hotel-owners applied for licences at the Brewsters' Session. Mrs. Miles applied for the transfer of the licence from the Colliers Arms in Nantgarw to the Leigh Hotel, Mr. John Chivers for the transfer of the licence from the New Inn at Caerphilly to the Parc Hotel owned by Caerphilly Brewers. The application by Josiah Morgan was supported by a petition from 275 householders, an assurance that he would personally manage the Gwernymilwr Hotel and a reminder that he and his family had spent over £10,000 in building houses. Once again opposition came from the police, the Pontypridd & Rhondda Temperance Defence League, Rev. Tawelfryn Thomas and the proprietors of the Universal Hotel who pointed out that its weekly barrelage had been reduced to five as a result of the strike. In the event the Bench granted a provisional licence to the Gwernymilwr Hotel, a decision that was confirmed later.

Despite the drastic reduction in beer consumption yet *'shebeening'* was still practised and Anne James of 4 Stanley Street was sentenced in July to a month's imprisonment for this offence, having been fined many times previously at Barry. Nor deterred was the opening on August 20th of a Conservative Working Men's Club in premises adjoining the Gwernymilwr Hotel.

Normal services were held at the places of worship as were the Anniversary Services. Cause for celebration was the opening on May 1st and 2nd of the first chapel as opposed to a vestry. This was Noddfa, built for the Welsh Congregationalists to accommodate 700 at a cost of £1,800 by Joseph Howells of Caerphilly. The services were conducted by the renowned Rev. S.R. Roberts of Llanbrynmair, Rev. W.R. Bowen of Maesteg and *'Tawelfryn'* as the caring minister. Elected to the diaconate were Jacob Jones, Dulais Jones, Edward Davies and David Gwynne with G.D. Griffiths as Secretary and Evan Sherrah as Superintendent of the Sunday Schools.

Yet while some degree of normality had prevailed during the period of the lock-out/strike the struggle for survival had exacted a grievous toll not only on the family unit and the commercial sector. The religious, social and cultural fabric of the community had been deeply eroded. Halted were the building programmes of some denominations and all congregations struggled to discharge the interest on acquired loans. Discontinued were Sunday School treats and outings, the United Sunday School Demonstration, social teas and the promotion of cultural functions. Muted were the United and Orpheus choirs and the brass bands. Suspended was the Debating Society as was the promotion of eisteddfods although some concerts were organised to raise funds for the Strike Committee. The funds of the Friendly Societies were exhausted and every organisation was adversely affected.

Deep in debt, embittered by the distress inflicted on their families, angered and humiliated by being forced to surrender completely to the coalowners and faced with a reduction in wages, the miners returned to work. But they went back firmly resolved that never again would they be found in a similar position.

The lockout/strike proved to be a watershed in industrial relations in the coalfield. They had learned a fundamental lesson - the need for unity, and in October the seven minor Unions amalgamated to form the South Wales Miners' Federation. Under the presidency of *'Mabon'* its structure was composed of an Executive Council with the task of negotiating price lists for piece-workers and rates of pay for the day wage workers, terms of work and safety conditions, the coalfield divided into Districts under Agents with the colliery Lodge as the basic unit. Henceforth *'Mabonism'* based on the concept of harmony between employers and employed was dead, to be replaced by an era in which the miners demonstrated an increasing temper of militancy and industrial protest.

However, the rest of the year passed without any confrontation at the colliery and slowly with characteristic resilience the village began to resume some of its normal vigour.

House-building continued but there were no plans for additional houses. Progress was reported on the construction of the Aber Valley Main Sewer but in November the Council Surveyor reported that practically the whole of the subsidiary sewers had no means of flushing. In reply to criticism that the water supply was still inadequate and often polluted the Council offered the prospect of improvement by announcing that its provision was to be undertaken by the Rhymney and Aber Valley Gas & Water Company which would negotiate directly with the landowners and builders, the Council responsible for overseeing its purity. Notices for the Abatement of Nuisances were served on house-owners in Stanley Street, Commercial Street, Station Terrace and Kingsley Place in respect of clogged drains and overflowing cesspools.

A virulent outbreak of diphtheria in December which claimed four deaths and necessitated the closure of the schools for two weeks was suspected of having been caused by contaminated milk.

A request that the Council *'take over'* the back lanes was refused in connection with the Senghenydd Building Club houses, a request for a further 20 street lamps was considered and it was decided to set up a committee to examine sites for a public slaughterhouse.

At the Infants' School there were no staff changes and the months passed smoothly until December when it was devastated by the death of two children from diphtheria and the closure of the school.

Miss Lizzie Israel (Uncertificated) and Arthur Morgan (Paid Monitor) were added to the staff of the Mixed School where progress was halted also by the closure of the school. Cause for celebration was the Success of J.A. Roberts, son of Rev. David Roberts, in winning a scholarship to Pontypridd Intermediate School for Boys, the first scholar to do so. He later recorded, *'This meant walking over the mountain some three miles daily and the same back, there being no suitable trains, and buses were not in evidence'*. Subsequently he returned to the school as a Pupil Teacher in 1904, studied at Southampton University College in 1907 and 1908 before returning as a Certificated Teacher. Commissioned as a Captain in the First World War and decorated with the Military Cross, he was to succeed Dan Lloyd as the Headmaster of the Boys' School in 1925.

Nationwide, the provision for Higher Education was very strictly limited and in this district it was confined to Pontypridd Intermediate School and Lewis School, Pengam, for boys, with County Schools at Hengoed and Treforest for girls. Apart from some fee-paying places entry was determined by a very severe Scholarship Examination. But even with a scholarship, the working class parents could ill-afford the expense that would be involved over many years and consequently it was very rare for their children to be entered. Given the meagre family income, the expectation was that sons would contribute as soon as possible by joining fathers in the pit, a prospect welcomed by the mass of boys as heralding the proud status of being a wage-earner. As to girls, it was an age when higher education was not generally regarded as important and the traditional prospect was that their role was to help *'mam'* with the household chores and care of younger children, perhaps to work in a shop or enter *'service'* before early marriage.

Gradually the religious denominations and the various organisations resumed a vigorous commitment. Tabernacl Chapel was opened by the Welsh Calvinistic Methodists, Noddfa Chapel promoted an eisteddfod and the English Congregationalists provided an evening of lantern-slide entertainment. The Male Voice and Orpheus Choirs were once again in full voice and the colliery band in full sway. An orchestral band was formed and by the end of October it was reported as *'fast becoming a success and a credit to the village under the genial bandmaster Mr. Davies.'* The Good Templars and Rechabites organised an eisteddfod at the Gwernymilwr Hotel with soloists Idris Perkins, Morgan J. Davies, Lizzie Lewis, William Smailes and the Orpheus Choir among the winners. At Aberdare Hall the Good Templars held a social tea which was attended by over a hundred people *'who partook of the good things provided and tastefully laid out by the ladies'* before being entertained to a concert. Chemist M.E. Price and Mrs. Emily Orton, were licensed to sell fireworks.

Sixty students were enrolled for the Evening Continuation Classes at the Mixed School, the lighting supplied by lamps. The Senghenydd and Aber Debating Society was revived under the Presidency of the curate, Rev. David Jones, supported by Vice-Presidents J.E. Lloyd, T.J. Thomas, station master Thomas Nicholas and Secretary M.E. Price. Seventy members attended the first meeting *'where it was gratifying to note the active interest shown by the female portion of the inhabitants.'* Included in the programme for the session were debates on the motions *'Should Capital Punishment Be Abolished?'* and *'Socialism Versus Capitalism'*, and papers read on the subjects of *'Workmen's Libraries'* and *'Temperance'*. Mrs. Orton was granted a theatre licence for the *'American Pavilion'* for two weeks, renewable each fortnight for a period of three months.

Memorable if not universally welcomed was the official opening on December 1st of the licensed Gwernymilwr Hotel as *'a first-class Family and*

The Square Senghenydd pictured shortly after the opening of the Gwernymilwr Hotel.

Commercial Hotel under the management of Mr. Josiah Morgan'. Taken in conjunction with the recently-opened Working Men's Club and the continuing practise of *'shebeening'* it brought no comfort to the Temperance movement or to the police faced with drunk and disorderly behaviour, fights, assaults and wife-beating.

Memorable and universally welcomed was the formation of the Senghenydd Rugby Club separate from the Aber Stars, due in large measure to the support of Manager David Thomas. Will Davies was elected as Captain, a position he was to retain until 1902, and among the founder players were D. Davies, F. Fullalove, T. Gould, D. Jones, J. Jones, R. Jones, F. Meyrick, A. Morgan, P. Richards, D. Skym, I. Thomas, I. Williams and S.G. Worman. In the course of the season friendly matches were played on the Gelli fields against Caerphilly, Bedwas, Machen and Llanbradach.

At the close of a year which had witnessed desperate hardship and the decline in population from 2,583 to 2,211 the village was in a somewhat sombre mood as the diphtheria epidemic still raged. But the crowds which

The formation of Senghenydd Rugby Club (Senghenydd Thursdays).

assembled on the square each Saturday night to listen to the brass band conducted by John Bussell was an indication that this *'small but enterprising town'* was on the road to recovery and hopefully was an augury of more happy times in the coming year.

Although the miners remained embittered and strongly opposed to the Sliding Scale and the continued practice of employing non-Union labour the year 1899 was to pass without any serious confrontation between the Lodge and the management. More seams and districts were opened up, the manpower increased to 751 and production of the best steam coal in South Wales increased to 3,000 tons a week. Correspondingly the village returned to relative prosperity and the population increased to about 3,250. More houses were built and more occupied but that there were plans for only a further six houses, three shops and two stables indicated a slowing-down in demand.

It was the year when the struggle for separate representation for the Aber Valley on the Caerphilly Urban District Council reached a successful conclusion when an Aber Ward was created with a representation of three Councillors. As a result the election on March 27th aroused very great interest, the local Liberal Party Association holding a series of public meetings at the Gwernymilwr Hotel. There were five candidates - Manager Edward Thomas seeking re-election, Robert Loughor of the Universal Hotel, builder Eleazor Lewis of Glanffrwd House, John Lewis of Treharris (brother of Eleazor) and Edmund Evans of Abertridwr. Elected were Edmund Evans, David Thomas and Robert Loughor and with the active support of the

Chamber of Trade they brought renewed pressure to bear on the Council to accelerate the provision of basic utilities.

More houses were connected to the sewers, another two subsidiary sewers were installed, a resolution was carried to provide the sewers with Flushing Chambers and contracts were agreed for other subsidiary sewers and for an extension to the Aber Valley Main Sewer. All were encouraging signs, but due to the neglect of landowners, builders and property owners the problems remained of failure to connect houses to the sewers, of overflowing cesspools, choked closet drains and defective slop water drains. Particularly affected were Stanley Street and Station Terrace. Among the Notices for the Abatement of Nuisances were several served on Crosswells Brewery (Caerphilly Brewery) in respect of defective drainage and nuisance cause by the cattle at an outbuilding of the Parc Hotel which was kept as a cowshed by Ludwig John. A Notice was served on builder Thomas Williams in respect of property occupied by Dr. James for not providing a proper receptacle for the disposal of manure, and a similar notice was served on Josiah Morgan respecting a stable at the back of his hotel. In pursuit of the resolve to provide two public urinals an agreement was reached with Josiah Morgan to site one on his ground near the Leigh Hotel and a site for the other was being sought in Station Road.

The water supply continued to give cause for concern. In March the Rhymney and Aber Valley Gas & Water Company submitted plans to install water mains but in the meantime many houses in High Street were practically without a water supply in the drought of June and July when only a very small quantity was available from a spring. The Universal Company was threatened with proceedings in that the water fed from their reservoir into the public domain was not wholesome for drinking purposes and was only withdrawn when it agreed to construct a filter bed. The Caerphilly Brewery was ordered to close the well near the Parc Hotel which had been re-opened.

In addition to the health hazards posed by the sanitary and water supply problems the most serious threat came from contaminated milk supplied by Ludwig John of Parc Newydd farm who kept a cowshed also in an outhouse of the Parc Hotel. The continued outbreak of diphtheria in January was attributed to this source and on pain of prosecution he was ordered to sell milk only from Foelddu, Maesdiofal and Gelli farms. But he continued to sell his own milk, the number of cases increased and in February a fatal case of typhoid fever was reported *'in a house where diphtheria was prevalent'* and he was prosecuted. The virulent epidemic of diphtheria from September to December was also attributed to contaminated milk supplied by him and resulted in at least one death. Once again he was prosecuted and Dr. T.W. Thomas, the Medical Officer of Health, urged that all milk be boiled before drinking

As was the official practice for treatment of all infectious diseases every case of diphtheria had to be notified by the local doctor to the Medical Officer of Health and strict regulations were imposed on the movement of patients and contacts who were restricted to the home. But the regulations were often ignored. Prosecuted was a Mrs. Prosser of Station Terrace *'who, while suffering from diphtheria, a dangerous and infectious disease, did wilfully expose herself without proper precautions against spreading the said disorder by entering and travelling by train from Senghenydd to Caerphilly on 16th October, and that she also, being in charge of her child John Prosser suffering from the same disorder, did expose the said child in the like manner'*. Also suffering from the disease, Albert Fine left the village and was prosecuted, and Dr. James was admonished for not registering his name with the Medical Officer.

Still subject to many petitions from the residents was the poor state of the roads which one irate villager described as a disgrace and that *'it would require a genius to find a dry spot on the most important ones which are simply composed of mud and water and sorely in need of repairs and ballasting'*. Goaded by the local Councillors to respond, the Council approved plans for the Private Street Works to undertake work on Commercial Street, High Street, Caerphilly Road, Stanley Street and Station Road. Furthermore, Councillor Loughor proposed that parts of Commercial Street and Caerphilly Road be sewered, levelled, metalled, paved and kerbed by the Council. In addition, a tender was accepted for the delivery of limestone chippings to be laid on the road to Abertridwr. But demands for more street lamps brought no satisfaction. Successful however, was the application by Josiah Morgan to install an acetylene gas lamp outside his hotel and it shone like a beacon in the dimly-lit square.

At the Infants' School, with 190 pupils on roll, the staff was increased and comprised Misses M.J. Morgan (Certificated), M.A. Jones, A.A. Millward and Maria Davies (Uncertificated), M.J. Gould, M. Rowland and Mr. Roberts (Pupil Teachers) under Miss England, but as in previous years H.M. Inspector noted that *'the Mistress works hard and deserves every encouragement yet her efforts have been handicapped by a weak staff,'* nor was he happy that the fireplaces were small and the rooms barely warm enough on a cold day and that the smoke blew down the main room. With the adverse effect of the prolonged diphtheria epidemics it was a frustrating year, relieved only by the customary St. David's Day half holiday and the first school photograph.

At the Mixed School, with 290 pupils on roll, Miss Catherine James left for Swansea Training College and appointed were Mr. A.J. Williams of Abertridwr, an experienced teacher who was a highly competent musician, eisteddfodwr and sportsman, and Ernest Roberts as a paid Monitor. Under Dan Lloyd (£80 p.a.), the staff comprised A.J. Williams (£65 p.a.), Sarah Morgan (£65 p.a.), Lizzie Miles (£63 p.a.), Joshua Bowen (£62-10-0 p.a.), Mary Rees (£50 p.a.), all Certificated, together with Uncertificated Lizzie Israel (£35-4-0 p.a.), pupil Teacher Joseph Edmunds (£10 p.a.) and Monitors Arthur Morgan and Ernest Roberts on a salary of £7-16-0.

Attendance was affected by the diphtheria epidemics but it was a highly successful year marked by the introduction of an *'Open Day'* for parents held on two successive afternoons in July. Algebra was introduced into the curriculum, twenty seven scholars were presented with books by the Clerk to the Board to mark their excellent attendance record. Relief from the strict routine was afforded by the Master's occasional talks illustrated by lantern slides, the first school photograph, the St. David's Day half-holiday and the closures for village functions and outings. The H.M.I.'s report that *'The methods are thoroughly good and the discipline is highly satisfactory'* was well received by the Board members Rev. Tawelfryn Thomas (Vice Chairman), Evan Sherrah and Towyn Jones.

For Mr. Lloyd personally it was a significant year. In July he moved with his wife and family from Caerphilly to the designated school house and his son Reginald won a Scholarship to Pontypridd Intermediate School. Later, Reginald pursued a distinguished academic career at Oxford University as well as being awarded a *'Blue'*, but sadly died of wounds sustained in the First World War.

The religious denominations made renewed efforts to raise funds. Among the many functions were a *'coffee supper'* followed by *'various games indulged in by both sexes'* held by the English Congregationalists, a *'knife and fork supper'* followed by lantern entertainment organised by the English Baptists at the Gwernymilwr Hotel, a lecture and a concert at the Gwernymilwr Hotel promoted by the Welsh Wesleyans. Sunday School treats and Anniversary Services featured largely in the calendar and a Cymanfa Ganu was held at Noddfa Chapel. Once again the strong Temperance movement opposed the applications for licences made on behalf of the Leigh and Parc Hotels which were again rejected.

But for all that there was no diminution in the scale of social malaise associated with drunkenness and physical assaults.

The Orpheus Choir and Male Voice Choir were fully engaged, the latter competing in eisteddfods including that at Pontypridd, but without success. Successful eisteddfod competitors Idris Perkins, David Gould and elocutionist Marie Morris featured in concerts as did soloists bass Rees Thomas, tenor Thomas Thomas, soprano Miss Jones of Park House, W. Smales, T.F. Evans and violinist George Gould.

The Debating Society enjoyed a particularly successful session. It opened with a *'Conversazione'* at the Gwernymilwr Hotel when *'the Assembly Room was illuminated and decorated in an excellent manner, the table tastefully laid by the ladies, and after having done ample justice to the niceties of the table the company first listened to a few addresses before dancing until 11 o'clock, concluding one of the most happy gatherings ever held in Senghenydd'*. Included in the session's programme was a debate on the motion *'Should Ireland Have Home Rule?'*, a lecture illustrated with lime-light views by Dan Lloyd, an excursion to Minehead and a decision to set up a library, and the last meeting was attended by 160 people.

Well-patronised in January was a special train to Cardiff for the purpose of attending a pantomime, *'it rarely happening that Senghenyddites have an opportunity to visit Cardiff after dark because the passenger train on this branch is subject to the Early Closing Act'*. In March the Chamber of Trade held its Annual Dinner and the Good Templars organised a social evening when sixty people *'having done ample justice to the good things provided, indulged in various games such as* "Simon Says Thumbs Up" *until 11.00 p.m. exactly when everyone wended their way homewards, satisfied that a most pleasant evening had been spent.'* In June the Chamber of Trade embarked on its annual outing. In the same month the first Cricket Club was formed, registering a convincing

The first Cricket Club in Senghenydd.

victory over Abertridwr with a team comprising F. Lewis (Captain), C. Ball, T.E. Davies, J.R. Davies, D. Edwards, H. Jenkins, A. Lewis, B. Price, F. Sloggett, D. Thomas and S. Worman. In September preparations were made for the Evening Continuation Classes at the Mixed School. In October, Mrs. Orton was granted a theatre licence for the portable American Pavilion, renewable fortnightly for three months. Under the captaincy of Will Davies the Rugby Club was improving in skill and stature.

Along with the entire nation the village was aroused by patriotic fervour with the outbreak of the Boer War in October, and demonstrated by the names of Ladysmith, Kimberley, Mafeking and Pretoria being progressively assigned to districts in the Lancaster Pit.

December was a somewhat sobering month. The British forces suffered disastrous defeats and the diphtheria epidemic which began in November had not abated. Nevertheless it had been a year of great endeavour and to a large extent the village had recovered from the desperate trials of the previous year.

On Christmas Day, Noddfa Chapel held its annual eisteddfod.

In 1900 a new Manager was appointed to the colliery in the person of Edward Shaw, M.E., from Gadlys, Aberdare, with David Thomas retained as Manager responsible for the general administration. The development proceeded apace with a corresponding increase in the work force drawn as in the past from neighbouring areas, coal-mining areas in Glamorgan with a large contingent from the Cynon Valley, some from Monmouthshire mining areas, some from the slate quarry areas of North Wales, some from the rural areas of mid-Wales. By the end of the year it numbered 814 with 671 underground and 143 on the surface, producing 184,000 tons a year. The Senghenydd Sick, Accident and Funeral Fund was formed and a fairly good proportion became members, paying 3d a week. The Company made a profit of £25,752.

Edward Shaw, Manager and Agent of the Universal Colliery Senghenydd.

With wages still declining in the South Wales coalfield so the Union intensified its opposition to the Sliding Scale and launched a renewed campaign for a *'closed shop'*, and following the general pattern the Universal Lodge held frequent checks on the membership by organising *'show cards'*. One held in April had the desired effect when 67 new members were enrolled. Nevertheless, in May the Executive Council of East Glamorgan Miners' Association under President David Roberts of the Lodge resolved that *'in consequence of a number of men in the Aber Valley at the Universal and Windsor Colliery, Abertridwr, not having joined then consideration be given as to the advisability of tendering a month's notice on June 1st for the withdrawal of labour with a view to getting all men to join'*. In the event this threat was withdrawn when sufficient non-members were persuaded of the error of their ways by various means. Even so, the question of appointing an Agent for the Aber Valley was deferred for a year until the number of Union members increased.

Throughout the early months of the year the village joined the nation in celebrating the success of the British forces in the Boer War, that of the relief of Kimberley in February, of Ladysmith in March and Mafeking in May, the last occasioned by a school holiday.

The year passed without any progress in the demand for separate representation on Caerphilly Council for Senghenydd and Abertridwr, the

County Council remaining unresponsive. At the election in April both Edmund Evans and David Thomas were re-elected with Josiah Morgan as the other member. Then on July 3rd Josiah Morgan informed the Council of his intention to resign, and on August 14th the Council resolved that *'Josiah Morgan has become disqualified from holding the office of Urban District Councillor by reason of his having on or about the 25th day of July 1900 been adjudged bankrupt and that the Council now declare the office of Councillor lately held by the said Josiah Morgan to be vacant'*. This announcement came as a shock to the villagers who received it with disbelief and no little sadness.

By the end of the year the population was approaching 3,500. House-building continued but in so far as there were no plans for additional accommodation then the supply now seemed to satisfy the demand.

There was cause for optimism in respect of the sewerage system. The construction of the Aber Valley Main Sewer proceeded steadily so that in February the Secretary of the Chamber of Trade, Towyn Jones, wrote to the Council urging that the necessary connections to the village be made before the summer. In April the Council took over the upper portion of the sewer from Abertridwr and for the remainder of the year work continued on its extension into the village with some streets connected up.

The Council continued to be assiduous in pursuing property owners and builders who failed to remedy faults which posed a health hazard. Chief offender was builder-owner John Williams who was repeatedly served with a Notice for the Abatement of Nuisances re defective drainage involving thirteen houses in Stanley Street. Notices in respect of defective drainage and not providing proper receptacles for depositing manure in stables were served on builders John and Eli Lewis, the owner of a stable used as a slaughterhouse by John Edwards, the Universal Colliery Company, Josiah Morgan, John Williams of Treherbert and John Lloyd of Porth. Ludwig John was twice prosecuted, once for a nuisance caused by cows at the rear of the Parc Hotel, once for occupying premises at the rear of the Parc Hotel as a dairy or cowshed without it having been registered. In accordance with the Factory and Workshops Act Mr L. Jones was threatened with proceedings for neglecting to whitewash his bakehouse.

The scavenger was criticised by the Chamber of Trade for the indiscriminate tipping of refuse, not properly removing refuse from the back lanes and for over-flowing cesspools. Indignant was Mr. Elisha Thomas that he had refused to take away the fish heads from his fish-frying premises.

Progress was made towards the provision of a public urinal when a tender submitted by Andrew Harper for its construction was accepted and terms were being sought in October for the necessary pipes and water supply.

As to the continued criticism of the roads, most of the difficulties arose as usual because the Council would not assume responsibility for their upkeep until the landowners, Building Clubs and builders had first properly sewered, levelled, paved, metalled and channelled them. Now, increasingly the Council was prepared to take direct action when the owners proved uncooperative and when the *'Private Street Works'* carried out in August on parts of Commercial Street, Caerphilly Road and Station Road proved unsatisfactory, it determined to carry out the work and charge it to the owners. As to the inevitable complaints about the inadequate street lighting there was no improvement with only two additional lamps provided. Criticism of the lamplighter, paid 9/- a night, was rebutted by his complaint that boys were in the habit of climbing up the posts and extinguishing the lamps.

In the provision of education there were significant changes both nationally and in terms of post-Infants' School reorganisation in the village. The school-leaving age was raised to fourteen with exemption for early leaving granted only to those successful in what was termed the *'Labour'* Examination, one which assessed whether the pupil had achieved a pre-determined level of competence. On May 1st the Mixed School was reorganised to form separate schools for boys and girls.

Dan Lloyd assumed the Headship of the Boys' School, his staff was drawn from former members of the Mixed School and comprised A.J. Williams (C), Sarah Morgan (C), Joshua Bowen (U), Lizzie Israel (U), Joseph Edmunds (P.T.) and Arthur Morgan (P.T.), and it remained stable. Attendance was at a high level with regular attenders rewarded with lantern entertainment, a few pupils passed the *'Labour'* examination, cricket matches were played on the school yard, captained by members. of staff and the number on roll increased from 146 to 192. The H.M.I. reported, *'This is a very carefully conducted school. The Master aims at a high standard in both instruction and discipline and his success, considering the disturbing condition of the year, is most creditable.'*

Appointed as Head Teacher of the Girls' School was Miss Martha Davies of Caerphilly. Without any previous rapport with Senghenydd she faced a more formidable situation. Nor was it made easier by many staff changes which ultimately comprised Elizabeth Miles (C), Dinah Evans (C), Elizabeth Coleman (C), E. Shaw (P.T.), Elizabeth Gould (Cand. P.T.), Matilda James (Cand. P.T.), Margaret John (Cand. P.T.) and A. Jones (Monitress). Despite the staff being mainly unqualified and inexperienced the H.M.I. Reported, *'The discipline is very good and the teaching is likely to reach a high standard of quality judging by the present indications.'* A few passed the *'Labour'* examination and the number on roll increased from 155 to over 200.

At the Infants' School there was an important change when Miss England resigned in April as a consequence of her impending marriage to Mr. Fred Williams and she was succeeded by Miss Margaret Austin. As in the past there were many staff changes and at the end of the year it comprised Misses M. Rees (C), M. Marks (U), M.A. Jones (J.M. Rowland (P.T.), M. Roberts (P.T.), A.M. Morris (Monitress) and M.J. Lewis (Monitress). It was not surprising therefore that the H.M.I. reported, *'Too much teaching has been done by Pupil Teachers and Unqualified Assistants which probably accounts in part that the condition is by no means first rate.'* However, he added the optimistic note that *'Under the New Mistress and with recent improvements in the staff it it is probable that the present defects will be removed.'*

An entry in the Log Book in September records that *'Welsh is taken by Class 1 on the first lesson on Tuesday and Thursday'*, but there is no indication that Welsh was included in the curriculum of the other schools and in all three St. David's Day was celebrated only by the half-day holiday.

In June the Welsh Baptists opened *'Salem'* chapel, built at a cost of £2,000. The organ, together with the table and chairs for the *'Set Fawr'* (Big Seat) was donated by Josiah Morgan. It thrived under the ministry of Rev. David Roberts, the membership numbering 120. A matter of great regret was the departure of Rev. David Jones, the very popular curate who had contributed greatly to the cultural as well as the spiritual welfare of the community. He was succeeded by Rev. Henry Evans. Prominent in the calendar of all denominations were the Anniversary Service and the Harvest Festival. The Welsh Baptists journeyed to Tonyfelin Chapel in Caerphilly for the United Cymanfa Ganu and the Welsh Calvinistic Methodists journeyed to Pontypridd for their Cymanfa Ganu. In July a special train conveyed the Aber Valley Sunday Schools to Barry Island and in September the Methodist Sunday Schools departed for Penarth.

Salem Chapel.

The strong Temperance movement again played a major role in the rejection of ale licences for the Leigh and Parc Hotels, but undiminished was the scale of drunkenness, public disorder and assaults.

The Cricket Club increased its membership and in July the Chamber of Trade embarked on the annual outing.

Many were the concerts held throughout the year, but the most memorable was the one held in March at the Mixed School to raise funds for the purchase of a piano. Held on two successive evenings, chaired by Edward Shaw and Towyn Jones, it was performed by the pupils and staff of both the Mixed and Infants' Schools, and was supported by instrumental accompaniment provided by pianist Lizzie Israel, organist M.E. Price, and a violin section comprising Messrs. G. Gould, J. Davies, C. Dewar, C. Isaac, T. Hutchings and Miss E. Brace. Opening with the rousing chorus of *'Rule Britannia'*, the programme continued with solos, duets, trios, choruses, action songs, musical drill, recitations, dialogues and sketches. Sufficient funds were raised for the purchase.

Winifred Lewis of the Welsh Ladies Choir won the contralto solo competition at the prestigious Caerphilly Castle Eisteddfod. Idris Perkins, David Gould and elocutionist Marie Morris continued to compete successfully. Well-patronised was the Debating Society at the opening meetings of the 1900/01 session as was the American Pavilion under the management of Mrs. Orton.

Such was the strength of the Rugby Club with its two teams that it was admitted to compete in the Cardiff and District Union, and the fixture list included matches against Caerphilly, Bedwas, Machen, Rudry, Llanbradach, Maesycwmmer, Fleur de Lys and Penrhiwceiber. Captained by Will Davies, the 1st team included J. Bryant, D. Davies, T. Davies, W. Davies, T. Gould, D. Gwynn, W. James, D. Jones, T. Lewis, D. Prosser, J. Williams, T. Williams and F. Yendle. Captained by E. Jones the United team included T. Burrell, J. Evans, J. George, A. Gould, A. Griffiths, D. Hurley, H. Hyatt, D. Jenkins, J. Griffiths, C. Jones, T. Morgan, E. Thorne, J. Walters and J. Williams.

Over the course of the year the main cause for concern remained the social problem of drunkenness and physical assaults. The appointment of Edward Shaw as an Overseer of the Poor for the Eglwysilan Parish exemplified the fact that this was the age of the Poor Law and Guardians and that there were pockets of poverty, particularly affecting the aged, in Senghenydd as elsewhere. Infant mortality remained high and as in previous years a virulent epidemic of diphtheria raged through November and December. But it had been a year which had seen the village a vibrant and confident place in which to live.

CHAPTER 4

With 700 men and boys employed at the colliery and with production increased to more than 6,000 tons a week a general air of prosperity prevailed in the opening month of 1901.

This was reflected in the number of business premises which were concentrated mainly in Commercial Street. Here were branches of Lloyds Bank Ltd., London & Provincial Bank Ltd., the Senghenith Industrial Cooperative Society Store, the Refreshment Rooms of Thomas Lewis, M.E. Price's chemist shop (James Bros. & Co.), the sub-Post Office manned by Miss Jane Bussell, the surgery of Dr. Philip James and Dr. Thomas Everard.

Here were the general stores of W. Thomas Marshall, Mrs. Susannah Rowlands and William Bryant, the general stores and bakery of John Thomas, the shops of grocer and confectioner M. & F. Williams and of grocer and baker William Samuel. Here were eight grocers - Mrs. Louisa Jones, David Jones & Co., James Dunning, Evan Morris, Ithel Thomas, India Tea Co., Edward Kinsey and David Edmunds. Here were seven butchers - Joseph Edwards, Eastman's Ltd., John & George Gould, Philip Morgan, Evan Jenkins, Tucker & Lewis and Mrs. Winifred Lewis. Greengroceries were supplied by John Bailey and Benjamin Davies. Mrs.Jane Bray and Elisha Turner kept *'fish-frying'* shops.

Senghenydd and Aber Valley Co-operative Society committee when their new premises were opened in Senghenydd in the early 1900s. The manager, B.M. Williams, is standing in the centre.

Here were drapers Samuel & Thomas, Thomas Davies, S. & M. Edwards, John Morgan and Evan Perkins, tailors David Jones, Charles Pugh and William Evans, outfitter Charles Isaac, hosiers David Lewis and David Bowen, dressmaker Miss Mary Rowe, boot and shoe makers Towyn Jones, William Godwin, Edward Thomas and Bristol Boot Company.

Here too was the ironmongery, hardware and furniture store owned by Josiah Morgan, the ironmongery of Edward Jones, the hardware store of Philip Richards, the furniture store of Albert Fine, watchmaker Thomas Bussell, newsagent David Williams, hairdresser/tobacconist Peter Stephens and Gillard Spencer, the homes of painter/decorator George King and haulier David Lewis.

Along High Street were draper William Baker, grocer William Price, the china warehouse of William Williams, stationer and tobacconist David Charles, the general store of David Powell and baker Charles Jones.

Other general stores in the village were those of Mrs. Margaret Davies and Robert Clarke in Parc Terrace, William Davies in Grove Terrace, Jacob Jones in Stanley Street.

Registered as purveyors of milk were Ludwig John of Parc Newydd farm, Mrs. Louisa Jones and Robert Rowlands.

Also listed were quarry owners Harper & Agland, quarry owners and builders H. Williams and Son, builder and quarryman Mrs. Martin Snailham of Station Road, builders Eli Lewis and W.E. Davies, undertakers D.C. Jones and John Rees, carpenter and undertaker Joseph Williams.

The Gwernymilwr and Universal (Andrew Hanson) Hotels were licensed as was the Constitutional Club in Station Road. The Leigh Hotel and the Parc Hotel (owned by Crosswell's Brewery) remained as Temperance Hotels.

Bearing testimony to the deep religious commitment were the chapels of the Welsh Congregationalists (Noddfa), Welsh Baptists (Salem), Welsh Calvinistic Methodists (Tabernacl), English Baptists (Ebenezer), Welsh Wesleyan Methodists (Seion), English Congregationalists, English Wesleyan Methodists and St. Peter's Church for the Anglicans.

Mr. Dan Lloyd was the Head Teacher of the Boys' School, Miss Martha was the Head of the Girls' School and Miss Margaret Austin was the Head of the Infants' School.

Law and order was maintained by Sgt. John Davies of 32 Parc Terrace and a constable. Thomas Nicholas was the Station Master.

The epidemic of diphtheria continued to rage into January and there were a few cases of scarlet fever. The Annual General Meeting of the Miners' Lodge under president John Edwards and Chairman Ben Evans was a routine affair. The auditors reported on the exceptional good order of the financial records, secretary Tom John reported that £217 compensation had been awarded to workmen during the year, reports were given by Miners' Agent Hubert Jenkins and William Evans Chairman of the East Glamorgan Miners' Association and all the officers were re-elected. Towyn Jones, Secretary of the Chamber of Trade, complained to the District Council of inadequate street lighting and the poor state of the road to Nelson. Apart from the departure of Miss Elizabeth Gould from the Girls' School there were no other staff changes in the three schools which remained trouble free apart from the effect of the epidemic.

The main talking-point in the village this month was the continuing saga of Josiah Morgan. A public examination of his financial affairs described him as *'a bankrupt innkeeper'* with liabilities of over £18,000. Despite his counter-statement that there would be a surplus of assets over liabilities, that the final dividend would be 20s in the £1 and that steps were being taken to annul the bankruptcy the outcome was that his estate, including the Gwernymilwr Hotel, houses and store were sold to a Bristol gentleman. His departure in the last week was one of general sympathetic regret in view of his major contribution to the development of the village and his many acts of beneficence to religious organisations.

On February 9th, the day of Queen Victoria's funeral and national mourning, the colliery was closed in accordance with the decision by the South Wales coal-owners to suspend all work as a mark of respect.

Of greater importance to the village was the funeral on the 26th of Colliery Manager Edward Shaw. The Boys' and Girls' Schools were closed *'as a mark of respect'* and a cortege of over a thousand mourners attended to pay tribute to a very popular, respected figure and a devout member of the English Wesleyan Methodist Chapel. He was succeeded as Colliery Manager by his son, also named Edward, who at thirty years of age was one of the youngest in South Wales to hold such a position but had considerable experience as fireman, overman and latterly as Under-Manager. On his appointment Sir W.T. Lewis was reported to have told him that the Directors recognised that he was the youngest Manager in the coalfield and that he would have direct oversight of one of the most difficult of mines as it was dry and fiery but that they had every confidence in his ability. David Thomas continued as Manager of administration and soon afterwards W.T. Rees was replaced as Agent by Robert T. Rees, a mining engineer and Director of the Board of Examiners who lived and slept in the village for one or two days a week.

In March the Council Surveyor was instructed to prepare a report for the improvement of the water supply to the lower part of the village and Dan Lloyd was appointed as overseer of the poor for the Eglwysilan parish. Miss Elaine Morgan was appointed as temporary Head Teacher of the Infants' School (due to the illness of Miss Austin since early February. Among the cases tried at Caerphilly Magistrates Court was of a drunken collier charged with assaulting Sgt. Davies and P.C. Jones).

There were two memorable concerts. One was *'a miscellaneous and Juvenile Nigger entertainment'* performed on two successive nights by the pupils of the Boys' School. The other was the first concert by the newly-formed Aber Valley Male Voice Choir conducted by Harry Phillips. Held at Salem Chapel, the solo artistes were all local - soprano Mary Price (Royal Welsh Ladies Choir), contralto Winnie Lewis (Royal Welsh Ladies Choir) and bass Idris Perkins (London & Provincial Concerts).

The Nigger Minstrels at Senghenydd Junior School 1900.

In April the Chamber of Trade complained about the state of the roads, street lighting and the water supply. Miss Austin was still absent from the Infants' School. *'Bertie'* Roberts was appointed as a Paid Monitor at the Boys' School and a small number of pupils were submitted for the *'Labour'* examination. At the Girls' School, Miss Elizabeth Gould had resigned, Miss S.A. Ward appointed as a Monitress, Miss E. Shaw appointed as a Candidate Monitress and a few pupils were entered for the *'Labour'* examination.

On May 6th Rev. Tawelfryn Thomas (Vice Chairman), Evan Sherrah, Towyn Jones, Thomas Nicholas, J.F. Evans and William Davies of the Universal Villas were elected to the School Board. On the 22nd the press reported, *'Mr. Josiah Morgan, late of the Gwernymilwr Hotel, Senghenydd, has emerged from his financial difficulties. Owing chiefly to losses incurred by the construction of the hotel he filed his petition for bankruptcy in July of last year. He has now been able to pay off all his liabilities and has received formal notification of the annulment of his bankruptcy order. Mr. Morgan has moved to Porth where he intends to trade in hardware and home furnishing'.*

On Friday, May 24th, King Edward VII took the salute at the Trooping of the Colour to mark the anniversary of the birthday of the late Queen Victoria.

The schools were closed, but not for that reason. Recorded in the Log Book of the Boys' School was the brief, stark statement, *'Awful calamity at the Universal Colliery this morning at 5 o'clock. Terrible explosion. No school. Schools closed for the Whitsun Vacation.'*

At 4.30 that morning the night shift of 240 men comprising rippers, repairers, timbermen, wallers, hard-heading men, hauliers, ostlers, labourers, a few colliers and the firemen had started to come up the pit. Some remained below to finish their work. The day firemen had descended to prepare for the day shift.

By 5 o'clock most of the men had come up. Shortly afterwards, coming up in the Upcast shaft cage were fireman John Morgan, master haulier Dan Skym, John Davies, Daniel Lewis, William Lewis, David Morris and Edward Watkins. As it came to bank, all except Morgan and Skym left immediately and proceeded to the lamp room. Dan Skym stepped forward from the cage and then, as he said, *'In a second or two, before I had walked ten yards, there was an awesome report accompanied by a roaring cloud of dust and smoke coming from the shaft, the whole of the pit stage was blown up into the air and the noise was deafening. My poor butty was buried in the ruins.'* His butty John Morgan was stepping forward when the force of the explosion lifted the cage beneath him before it was blasted upwards into the winding gear, hurling him clear but pinned by timbers and debris. Banksman John Bailey went to help him. When the debris and timbers were cleared and Morgan extricated, it was found that he had escaped serious injury and was later taken home. Meanwhile, in the words of Daniel Lewis, *'We were going from the shaft to the lamp room when we heard a tremendous explosion. Upon coming round we saw pieces of timber flying round and to save ourselves from being struck we ran into the lamp. room. There were three reports'.* William Lewis gave a slightly different version. *'We had barely placed our lamps when we heard a tremendous report. We thought the boilers had exploded and we were so frightened that we crawled under the lamp tables. Then in a couple of seconds another report followed and we heard stones and pieces of timber falling upon the roof of the lamp room. When we went to the door we saw dense volumes of smoke coming from both the shafts and it was from the downcast shaft that the reports seemed to come.'*

In all there were three separate reports, the first two in rapid succession, the third after an interval of some seconds described *'as like the discharge of a heavy cannon each accompanied by a rumbling noise similar to that produced by an earthquake, and so deafening and fearful that they were distinctly heard on the Pontypridd road, a distance of 3½ miles away over the mountain and in Llanbradach.'* In the vicinity of the pit the ground trembled beneath the houses. Tom Jones of Caerphilly Road told a reporter, *'I was in bed when we heard the explosion. One of the family asked what was the noise. I said that I thought they were firing because it was the Queen's birthday.'*

Rudely awakened from their slumbers by the awesome sound, men, women and children poured into the streets, running helter-skelter to the pithead with terrible foreboding in their hearts.

Manager Edward Shaw was in bed but within minutes he was at the pit-head directing operations. There he viewed the scene of devastation, the upcast cage hurled into the headgear, the damaged plank staging at the top of both shafts. Fortunately only the covering of the ventilation fan was damaged and the fan was still working. A tally check at the lamp room indicated that at least seventy eight men had not booked in their lamps, but the precise number underground was uncertain. In fact there were eighty two.

From the outset the work of rescue and exploration was seriously delayed because of the difficulty encountered in being able to descend the pit. When Shaw tried to operate the cages of the downcast shaft he failed to do so because the cage at the bottom of the pit was jammed. The rope of this cage had then to be detached, and it was not until 7.30 that Shaw with a shift of men which included two day overmen began their descent only to be thwarted 18 feet from the bottom where the shaft was blocked by trams which had been blown into it by the force of the explosion. Leaving volunteers to shin down the guide ropes to clear the obstruction Shaw returned to the surface.

By this time news of the explosion had spread rapidly to all parts of the district and further afield, and as the gravity of the situation began to be fully realised so Managers, Under-Managers, mining engineers and hundreds of miners from miles around and all parts of the coalfield converged on the village to volunteer their services, together with doctors, nurses, members of the St. John Ambulance Brigade and Red Cross Society, policemen.

The team of volunteers, working heroically under David Thomas the colliery Engineer, had cleared the obstruction at the bottom of the shaft by 10 o'clock, five hours having elapsed since the onset of the explosion. Shortly afterwards the first descent was made by two parties led by Agent R.T. Rees and Edward Shaw, one to examine the East side, the other the West side of the colliery. The parties included Dyer Lewis (Assistant Inspector of Mines), T. Griffiths (Agent for the Windsor Colliery), Manager J.C. Tibbon (Treharris) and Manager T. Richards (Lewis Merthyr) together with other officials from neighbouring collieries.

As both parties inched and struggled their way into their respective areas so the full extent of the havoc was evident from the massive roof falls. However, the hope of finding survivors was awakened on the east side when haulier William Harris was found in almost a lifeless condition and badly burnt lying against the side of his dead horse. Dr. Burke of Llanbradach and Dr. McKenzie of Caerphilly went down the pit and restored him sufficiently to be brought up on a stretcher, but the hope of finding more survivors soon diminished with the discovery of the bodies of John Jones and Thomas Coombes on the East side and of George Warren on the West side.

By the afternoon a host of officials and miners had assembled from every quarter of the coalfield. Standing by were Dr. James, Drs. Burke and Lloyd (Llanbradach), Drs. McKenzie, Thomas and Dolman (Caerphilly), Drs. Thomas (Ystrad), Morris (Tylorstown), Davies (Penygraig), Jones (Mountain Ash), Joyce (Porth), units of St. John Ambulance Brigade and the Red Cross, a large contingent of Glamorgan Constabulary and a mass of reporters. Moving among the relatives and friends of the entombed men, now joined by hundreds from the surrounding area, were Revs. David Roberts, Henry Morgan, Tawelfryn Thomas, Henry Evans, members of the Salvation Army and other clergymen striving to offer some words of comfort. Said Rector Henry Morgan, *'I have never seen such terrible anxiety. It's a sad, sad business, waiting, waiting, hoping against hope.'*

As soon as the gravity of the disaster became known the Cardiff Postmaster had taken prompt action in anticipation of the mass of messages which would overwhelm the small ill-equipped office in the village by despatching a staff with Wheatstone apparatus and by 1 o'clock the special circuit was in operation. Sir W.T. Lewis, on holiday in the South of France, had been contacted earlier and required that he be informed with a progress report every four hours until he returned.

About 1 o'clock there was a deep feeling of gloom when the body of George Warren was brought to the surface, and then a sigh of relief as William Harris came up *'in almost a hopeless condition'*. Then followed the bodies of John Jones and Thomas Coombes.

At 2.00 p.m. the two parties, augmented by further shifts, returned to the surface, some having been affected by after-damp, by which time Mr. J.T. Robson, H.M. Inspector of Mines, and Mr. Adams, his assistant, had arrived. Together with Company Directors Sir Thomas Morel and H.W. Martin and Managing Director W.T. Rees they were briefed on the situation by Agent Rees and Shaw.

Then Robson and Adams, accompanied by two Colliery Managers, descended the pit where their inspection confirmed the worst fears of the exploratory parties, the violence of the explosion grimly evident. It had penetrated every district and passed through almost every working road and face, all filled with fire damp. The main haulage roads were damaged and blocked by falls of roof which Robson described as *'both higher and more continuous than I have ever seen after any explosion elsewhere.'* The heat was intense. Even at this very early stage it was apparent that there was little likelihood of any entombed men having survived.

The paramount task was to clear a passage over or through the falls for the exploratory parties and to allow ventilation to clear pockets of after-damp. All that afternoon, scorning all dangers, the work of exploration continued with feverish intensity. Said D. Watts Morgan, Miners' Agent for the Rhondda District, *'There's bravery here such as cannot be eclipsed. They came as volunteers to render what help they can to their fellow men locked in the dark depths of the pit. Many have been affected by after damp. They carry their lives in their hands. They seek no reward.'* But for all their endeavours little progress was made.

Among the messages of sympathy which had flooded into the Post Office was one from the Home Secretary which read, *'The King is deeply grieved to hear of the terrible disaster at the Universal Colliery. His Majesty commands me to express his deep sympathy with the families of those who lost their lives, also his admiration of the gallant attempts to save life. Signed. Ritchie.'* During the course of the day the Post Office dealt with over 800 telegrams as well as press releases.

Throughout the afternoon the crowds around the pithead had grown to mammoth proportions, marshalled by a large police force under the command of Chief Constable Colonel Lindsay. Hundreds of people had converged from the surrounding area and further afield, most on foot, some by carriage, some from the Rhondda and Cardiff by special trains from Caerphilly. Mingling with the crowd were Alfred Thomas, M.P. *'Mabon'*, members of the S.W.M.F. Executive and J.F. Charles, Chairman of Caerphilly Council. Present too were the local Superintendents of the Prudential, Refuge and other Assurance Companies to make arrangements for the payment of claims when deaths would be established.

'As the evening came on and the shadows of the hills deepened across the valley so the thousands of sympathisers turned sadly homewards. At the pithead the visible signs of the havoc wrought by the fiery storm were as nought beside the havoc in the bowels of the earth where over seventy miners lie entombed, whether dead or alive none knew. The anxious faces around were sadly eloquent that the worst is feared, for eleven hours have elapsed since the explosion and still no communication has been established with those below', wrote an *'Echo'* reporter.

As the evening drew into the night Mr. Robson said, *'I fear there is no chance of getting through to the entombed men tonight. There are a tremendous lot of heavy falls and the ventilation is very bad. On all sides one can see how terrible was the force of the explosion.'* Until then hearts which had hoped against hope became filled with black despair as little hope could be entertained of recovering alive any of the entombed men.

At 7.30 p.m. forty coffins were unloaded at the railway siding.

Around the pit-head some families had been persuaded to return home. Other families and friends began a sad vigil, watching the relief parties descend throughout the night, carrying with them the earnest prayers of aching hearts still clinging to a ray of hope. Down below the gallant work of exploration continued relentlessly, frequently halted by rock falls and concentrations of gas.

Earlier that day in the House of Commons the home Secretary was asked if he had any information as to the explosion. Mr. Ritchie replied, *'No sir. I am sorry to say that up to the present time we have no intelligence beyond that which has appeared in the public press. I am expecting news almost every moment and when it comes I will take care to find some means of communicating it to the House.'* Shortly after midnight he took that opportunity to read the contents of some telegrams which had been despatched by W.T. Rees. The first read, *'Regret to report explosion this morning about 5 o'clock. Seventy eight men supposed to be down at the time. Two have been brought up, one alive. Explorations are proceeding but up to the present moment the fate of the others is uncertain.'* The second, *'Ventilation is being returned as fast as possible, but many large falls are impeding rapid progress. No more persons have been seen. It is impossible to say when the workings will be thoroughly explored. Plenty of willing hands.'* The third, timed at 8.05 p.m., read, *'Mr. Robson, the Inspector of Mines, and three Assistants here. Every effort is being made to explore the underground workings which are very badly damaged. One man has been brought out alive and three bodies have been brought up. Have the greatest fear as to the fate of those still in the pits.'* The House received this news in sad and sympathetic silence.

The scene at the Universal Colliery after the explosion on 24th May 1901.

As dawn broke over the village on Saturday, May 25th, *'there were lights in the windows of nearly every home. The night had brought no rest. A silent crowd of grief-stricken men and women lingered around the pit top and awaited the day with anguish in their hearts.'* On this day hope of recovering alive any of the entombed men seemed to be abandoned. The colliery management, preparing for the worst outcome, had converted the pay office into a mortuary ,the floor laid with hay, where Dr. James had conducted the official examination of the three bodies. In the adjoining carpenter's shop men were busily constructing ambulance stretchers.

'The Welsh coalfield once more has been convulsed to its centre by one of those dreadful catastrophes. which seem inseparable from coal mining and often exacts such a heavy toll upon human life. Senghenydd is a new place and this is the locality's first rude awakening to the perils and occasionally the terrors which are connected with the miner's occupation... Happy mothers and children yesterday, they are widows and fatherless today with the breadwinner a mangled corpse, a mere shapeless mass maybe, beyond the recognition of the wife of his bosom', wrote the Editor of the *'Western Mail'*.

In the morning Mr. Bernard Reece, Cardiff and District Coroner, opened the Inquiry into the circumstances of the deaths of John Jones, George Warren and Thomas Coombes at the Gwernymilwr Hotel. The jury was composed of Rev. David Roberts (foreman), draper W.H. Baker, builder W.E. Davies, milk vendor Ludwig John, baker Charles Jones, ironmonger Edward Jones, boot merchant Towyn Jones, painter George King, builder Eli Lewis, stationmaster Thomas Nicholas, draper Evan Perkins, grocer David Powell, chemist M.E. Price, grocer W. Price, grocer Ithel Thomas and grocer Fred Williams. Composed almost entirely of business men, with no miner and only five with some knowledge of colliery work, it was greeted with indignant protests. Even the jurors felt uncomfortable and one was constrained to ask the Coroner whether it was possible to summon a new jury *'as we are all tradesmen and feel we are not in the right place'*, but the Coroner's response was that he could do nothing in the matter having instructed the police *'to get the best possible jury, men of intelligence and respectability, and if possible, acquainted with colliery work'*. Presumably none of the hundreds of miners in the village were deemed intelligent and respectable.

The Coroner stated that he proposed only to take evidence of identification, and after the bodies had been formally identified he adjourned the hearing until the following Monday.

By mid-day the crowds had reached several thousands. Sir. W.T. Lewis was still in France but his eldest son arrived from his castle residence in Pembrokeshire.

In the afternoon the Executive Council of the S.W.M.F. met at the Gwernymilwr Hotel under the Chairmanship of *'Mabon'*, supported by Secretary Thomas Richards and Treasurer Alfred Onions, to nominate which members would represent the Federation at the adjourned hearing. It also decided that in the event of applications for immediate relief to meet funeral and other expenses then advances of sums between £20 and £30 be given to bereaved families in anticipation of the compensation awards and so recoverable. Furthermore, certain members were delegated to form a Relief Fund committee to launch a public appeal for support.

A committee of Executive Officers plus other members together with local people was formed and later issued this letter of Appeal, dated May 24th

'An Appeal for Financial Aid on Behalf of 57 Widows and 230 Fatherless Children.

The South Wales coalfield has again been the scene of a disastrous colliery explosion causing the death by terrible means of 81 of our workmen, 57 of whom were married men, all taken away without a moment's warning, leaving 57 widows and 230 fatherless children to fight the hard battle of life alone.

The committee desire to place on record their gratitude for the spontaneous expressions of sympathy already received from all classes of the British community from King to peasant, and we now confidently appeal to them for financial assistance to assuage in some measure the lonely position of the widows and orphans by securing for them sufficient funds to provide the necessities of life until the children will have attained that age which will enable them to provide for themselves.

Signed Alfred Thomas, M.P., Chairman of the Relief Committee; W. Abraham, M.P., President; W. Brace, Vice President; Thomas Richards, Secretary; Alfred Onions, Treasurer, South Wales Miners' Federation.

All cheques, post office orders etc. to be made to Alfred Onions, Tredegar, and sent to Thomas Richards, General Secretary, Beaufort, South Wales.'

All that day the work of exploration continued. No bodies were recovered. Three dead horses were brought up and buried in quick lime at a site a short distance from the pit.

Late that evening Mr. Robson stated, *'It is impossible there can be anyone alive in the pit. There is no question but that the flames were carried right through, and not one of us can have any idea how it originated. The fact that it swept the whole of the mine shows that it was carried by coal dust.'*

At midnight there were no more than a hundred people in the immediate vicinity of the pit but lights still burned in most homes.

Sunday, May 26th. On this Sabbath day came the ultimate realisation that apart from William Harris there would be no other survivors. During the early morning seven bodies had been found, followed by another fifteen, and by mid day fifteen had been recovered with others to follow. All were in a pitiable condition, their features burnt into shapeless forms and impossible to distinguish. One body was identified only by the initials on his strap, one by his boots, one by his clothing, another by a surgical appliance which he wore. One body had been found lying partly in a tram, his silver watch and brass chain blown onto a ledge two yards away, the watch stopped at 5.10. So little remained of some bodies and so mutilated were others that after identification they were coffined immediately and later buried without the coffin being reopened.

Normal services in the chapels and church were suspended, but in the pulpits throughout South Wales and further afield many a reference was made to the sorrowful calamity and prayers offered for the dependants of the victims.

The hills surrounding the village were black with people as all day they came in their thousands on foot, by bicycle, horse-drawn carriages and special trains, blocking the roads, besieging the hotels for refreshments. Many wore a mark of mourning, a black arm band or a black tie. Only relatives were allowed near the pit-head *'where many distressful scenes were witnessed and everything was done that could be done to assuage the grief of the stricken ones.'*

By 6 o'clock nineteen bodies had been recovered, all borne home after dark. Three more truckloads of coffins arrived at the colliery siding.

By the morning of Bank Holiday Monday, May 27th, *'the village quieter and an agreeable contrast to the unseemly crowds of Sunday'*, the number of recovered bodies had reached thirty three. The *'South Wales Echo'* reported, *'The scene at the pit head during the darkness preceding the dawn was grim and solemn. Around the improvised mortuary stood small knots of anxious relatives. Ever and anon the cage would come to bank with the sad burden of a corpse and its bearers. The sorrowful watchers would then fall back in reverent silence, making a line down which the muffled ambulance workers - brave men, every one - tenderly bore the rude brattice stretchers to the* 'dead house' *in the yard below. There the bodies were examined by Dr. James who, with his assistants, has been constantly at his post since the explosion happened. In many cases the identity of the body would be shrewdly guessed once it became known where it was found, but Police Sgt. Brinson, who is in charge of the mortuary, insists upon identification by relatives or friends before permitting removal. Frequently the clue to identification is of the slightest description - a tobacco box, a mark on a garment being all that could be reliable. When authoritatively identified the remains are placed in a coffin and carried to the home during the night. For many weary hours the tramp of ambulance men engaged on this task was to be heard in several streets in the village. Several of the bearers were so affected by the horrible nature of their work that they fainted.'*

'If in Senghenydd there is not to be found those outward manifestations of general mourning usually associated with colliery disasters in South Wales, nevertheless there is much hidden grief and many heart-rending scenes have been witnessed. The sufferers have had no lack of genuine consolers and sympathisers and to this in part may be attributed the calm resignation of the many widowed ones whose grief is nevertheless poignant', reported the *'South Wales Daily News'*.

Messages of sympathy and offers of help flooded in. From Treharris Ocean Colliery, Ynysybwl Lady Windsor, Cymmer, Pontypridd Great Western, Wattstown National Collieries, Clydach Vale, Dowlais Llanbradach, Lewis Merthyr, Abercynon, Aberdare and many other collieries had come volunteers to assist in the arduous, dangerous task of exploration and rescue.

At the resumed Inquest the formalities were completed in respect of the identification of the thirty three bodies recovered by that time. The Coroner then said, *'We have now completed the matter as far as we can go, namely identifying all the bodies which have been brought up. Those that we have seen are really not in a fit state to be seen and they ought to be buried at once. Dr. James has told me that in the interests of health we ought not to see any more and ought to be buried forthwith. I therefore do not propose that you shall see any more,and I shall adjourn the Inquest for three weeks when we shall go on and get evidence showing the probable cause of the accident.'* The Inquest was adjourned until Monday, 17th June.

Several members of the S.W.M.F. Executive Committee visited various families to inquire into the cases of special need and authorised sums ranging from £20 to £30 to those where there was difficulty in defraying the funeral costs in the absence of insurances or other means. Characteristically, Officers of the Salvation Army also distributed sums for temporary relief.

By midnight another fourteen bodies had been brought to the surface, the remains swollen with the heat of the pit and decomposed, the explorers compelled to swathe mouth and nostrils in bandages steeped in disinfectant. Among the bodies were those of Thomas Fullalove and his son Joseph found lying face down, locked in each other's arms.

At 8 o'clock on Tuesday morning, May 28th, outside each of two homes in Commercial Street, one in Stanley Street, one in High Street and one in Caerphilly Road had gathered a sombre crowd of men. Inside the homes a brief service for a victim was being held. When the services were over the coffins were placed reverently in hearses or on black biers. At the *'rising'* no hymns were sung as was the Welsh custom. Family mourners formed up behind the coffins, bearers lifted the biers on their shoulders and the corteges moved slowly through the streets lined with sorrowing men and women towards meeting at the square before proceeding to the station. There the coffins of John Davies, George Griffiths, John Harvey and James James were entrained at 8.30 and that of George Filer at 9.30.

In the early afternoon the body of William Thomas Evans was conveyed from the Huts to Newbridge by hearse.

Later in the afternoon a mass funeral for six victims took place *'amidst scenes of the most grievous and touching kind'*. Following the *'rising'* at the homes of Edward Bennett, Thomas Coombes, George Griffiths, William James, George Warren and Llewellyn Llewellyn, where no hymns were sung, the various corteges converged at the square for the long journey via Abertridwr to Eglwysilan churchyard. *'The united procession of sorrow was heart-rending as the many mourners wended their way slowly through the streets lined with silently-weeping crowds, every blind drawn, every shop closed, and manifestations of sorrow and sympathy shown on all sides. The remains of three were conveyed by hearse and horse-brake, the others reverently borne by relays of workmen marching manfully under the hot sun up the mountainside to Eglwysilan Church, followed by a host of mourners, some on foot, others in brakes. At the gate of the church, to the sound of the muffled tolling of the bells the corteges were received by Rector Henry Morgan, curate Henry Evans and Baptist minister David Roberts. The service was deeply impressive and when the Baptist minister gave an address on the departed there was not a dry eye in the gathering, all being deeply moved. It was brought to a close by the favourite Welsh hymn* 'Bydd Myrdd O Rhyfeddodau'.

Probably with the best intentions, but not fully appreciative of the plight of the dependants such as a widow with eight children was the *'Western Mail'* editorial: *'This is the first great disaster since the Compensation Act came into force, and it is some satisfaction to know that hunger will not wait upon grief as in former disasters. All the leading representatives of the big insurance companies were early on the scene to meet any claim, and their prompt payments enabled the sorrow-stricken families to make their provisions for the funerals and for keeping their homes together.'* Not a word about the sums donated by the S.W.M.F. to families in distress.

All day the task of exploration and recovery continued with undiminished energy and heroism, extending throughout the night. By midnight another four bodies were located, bringing the total to fifty one.

At the pithead a small knot of relatives of unrecovered victims continued their vigil.

Early in the morning of Wednesday, May 29th, three coffins were entrained, one for Bristol, one for Dowlais, one for Caerphilly. Later, two coffins were borne to Abertridwr station, both bound for Treorchy.

In the afternoon a procession more than a mile long followed the corteges of fourteen victims, eleven for interment at Eglwysilan, two at Groeswen, one at Llanfabon. The shops were shut, the curtains drawn in streets filled with sorrowing villagers. At about 2 o'clock part of the sad procession left for the ancient churchyard of Llanfabon some four miles over the mountain, the coffins borne by relays of workmen. The main concourse proceeded on its mournful way to the other destinations. It was headed by two hearses bearing the coffins of fireman John. T. Evans and David James, both deacons of Noddfa chapel, and in front of this part of the cortege were some fifty members from the Aberdare Lodge of Oddfellows of which Mr. Evans was a member, all dressed in mourning regalia, some acting as bearers. Following were the eleven coffins, all covered with handsome floral tributes, borne on the shoulders of relays of fellow workmen.

On to Abertridwr through streets of drawn curtains and mourners. There the concourse divided, the two hearses bound by way of Penyrheol, Watford and Gwaun Gledyr for Groeswen burial ground. There an emotional service was conducted by the minister, Rev. Tawelfryn Thomas, assisted by Rev. James Jones, minister-elect of Noddfa chapel, *'the bodies having been reverently committed to the earth a Welsh hymn was sung, and the mourners and crowd returned slowly to their homes'*. The corteges following the eleven coffins wended their slow, dignified way to Eglwysilan churchyard where the impressive service was conducted by the Rector, assisted by the curate, *'the scene one never likely to be forgotten by those who were present'*.

By midnight another five bodies had been recovered, *'the process of identification becoming increasingly painful and difficult. Decomposition had long since set in, indicating the revolting nature of the task which falls to the lot of the brave explorers'*.

That day the Lord Mayor of Cardiff decided to start a Relief fund.

Once again on Thursday, May 30th, the funerals began early. Entrained were one coffin for Aberdare, another for Strata Florida. Then soon after 1 o'clock another procession, headed by the Sunday School children of the Calvinistic Methodist Chapel, followed the coffin of Benjamin Griffiths, Sunday School teacher and elocutionist, to the station, his remains bound for Clydach in the Swansea Valley. Later in the afternoon two victims were buried at Eglwysilan, two at Caerphilly, one at Ystrad Mynach.

The Lord Mayor of Cardiff distributed sums from his Fund to the families most in need. The local Relief Committee, chaired by Beynon Evans and attended by Alfred Evans, M.P., met to consider the means of providing relief funds. The view was expressed that there was an immediate need for aid in that compensation under the Workmen's Compensation Act would probably not be paid for two or three months and that the Federation could not continue to vote sums of £20 or so to families. Mr. Thomas stated that there was no need for large funds but there was need for something to be done at once and he was pleased to subscribe £50.

By the end of the day nine more bodies had been brought to bank bringing the total recovered to sixty five.

Friday, May 31st, was another day of sad and mournful processions wending their way through the village bearing the coffins of eleven victims, all of whom, as on the previous day, being interred as soon as possible after discovery, their bodies disfigured and decomposed, identified only by clothing or possessions. Three coffins were entrained at 9.00 a.m., one for Llanfihangel near Aberystwyth, one for Ferndale, one at for Abercanaid, two at 1.00 p.m., both bound for Aberdare. In the afternoon long corteges followed three coffins to Eglwysilan churchyard and three to Llanfabon churchyard.

Underground, following the break-through earlier in the week into the Mafeking District the work was now concentrated on the Pretoria District where *'the exploration was a most dangerous and trying task in getting through the falls and the workings filled with gas, afterdamp and the offensive effluvium from the bodies of men and horses.'* The exploration was now coming to the end.

The mass of the work force not engaged in clearance or recovery had now been idle for over a week and with no immediate prospect of returning to work some had already sought employment in other collieries or elsewhere.

Sir. W.T. Lewis was expected back from France *'in a day or two'*. The large police force of over 70 had been reduced to 15.

On Saturday morning, June 1st, Sir W.T. Lewis, Baronet, arrived at the colliery, accompanied by Managing Director W.T. Rees and his son Herbert. He held lengthy consultations with the H.M. Inspectors and mining engineers and *'after referring in feeling terms to the sad calamity which had befallen the village and neighbourhood and expressing his deep sympathy with the bereaved families he was gratified with the progress made.'*

'The son of Mr. Rees called on Mr. Harris and brought a bottle of chicken broth from his mother. Mr. Harris is still delirious at times and very weak but making progress. He is thoroughly well-nursed and in order that he may not be disturbed by the noise of traffic a supply of sawdust from the colliery is placed over the street and pavement in front of the house', reported the *'South Wales Daily News'*.

None of the eight bodies recovered that day included those of fireman Ebenezer Davies or his son David, and *'the condition of widow Mrs. Davies is a very sad one. She is in a very delicate state of health, her figure a pathetic one at the mouth of the pit almost every day and night since the accident occurred'*.

Tenby and Rattler, the sole survivors of the fifty two pit horses, were brought to the surface.

At a committee meeting of the Senghenydd Sick, Accident and Funeral Fund it was reported that 62 members had been killed, that funeral donations had exhausted the Fund so that the Society was now in debt and unable to fully pay the death claims. Moreover, a number of miners who were ill and without any relief under the Workmen's Compensation Act would have their payments stopped immediately unless more funds were forthcoming. Consequently an appeal would be made to fellow workmen throughout the coalfield, donations made to Treasurer W. Moss and addressed to Secretary William Thomas.

On this day the Home Secretary requested Professor W. Galloway, F.G.S. Professor of Mining at the University College of South Wales and Monmouthshire, to produce a Report on the circumstances attending the explosion. He also called for Reports from J.T. Robson, Inspector of Mines, and from S.T. Evans, K.C., M.P.

At 5 o'clock it was announced that the recovery of the eight remaining bodies could wait for twenty four hours and consequently that no further exploration would take place on Sunday.

By this time news of Senghenydd in the press was confined to brief accounts in back pages.

On Monday, June 3rd, renewed efforts were made to clear the falls, recover the remaining bodies and restore the pit to working order. Two coffins were entrained in the morning. The three schools reopened after the Whitsun holidays but were closed *'in consequence of the several funerals taking place today and together with the general gloom thrown over the neighbourhood causing few to be present.'* Further donations were made to the Lord Mayor of Cardiff's Fund and Tom John, Secretary to the local relief committee, inserted an announcement in the press conveying its thanks for the letters and telegrams of sympathy and expressing his regret that because they were so numerous it precluded an individual reply. Three bodies were recovered.

On Tuesday, June 4th, three coffins were entrained. The schools opened and remained so despite only a few more children present. The Log Book of the Infants' School records, *'In looking over the Registers it was found that 19 of the little scholars are rendered fatherless'*, and that of the Boys' School, *'Among the victims of the holocaust were 10 fathers who among them had 12 boys in this Department.'*

Continuing to work night and day to clear the falls and try to recover the remaining five bodies were over 120 men *'with W.T. Rees, Robert Rees and Edward Shaw conferring and directing operations on the best way of re-arranging the shifts and restoring the colliery. The village is now beginning to resume its normal aspect.'*

The Caerphilly Council resolved that the Sanitary Inspector under the supervision of the Medical Officer *'be instructed to disinfect the houses in Senghenydd where dead bodies had been'*.

Workmen continued to leave the village in search of work, some never to return. On Wednesday, June 5th, a meeting of those *'formerly employed'* at the colliery, held at the Gwernymilwr Hotel under President John Evans, decided to accept the management's offer that there was some employment available at Lewis & Merthyr Collieries until the pit was ready to re-open.

On Thursday, June 6th, the *'South Wales Daily News'* commented, *'All is so quiet in the village that it is difficult to believe that a fearful catastrophe has so recently occurred.'*

On Friday, June 7th, the body of fireman Ebenezer Davies was brought to bank in the morning, extensively burned and decomposed, identified only by a tobacco box and his boots, taken not to his home but placed in the engine shed and interred at Groeswen in the afternoon. At the Boys' School, Dan Lloyd recorded, *'The gloom and awful results of the explosion accounts for the lowest attendance this year'*, a report which was similarly reflected in the other schools.

On Saturday morning June 8th, the vast majority of the *'old workmen'* the bulk of whom were now employed in other collieries, assembled at the colliery office to receive their pay for the week of the explosion, this being the fortnightly pay. These engaged in the exploration and clearing of falls during the following week were paid the standard rate of 4/9d per shift plus percentage. These were the men of whom was written, *'The disaster has been accompanied by the usual display of heroism on the part of the rescue parties, and it has been suggested that such heroism should be specially recognised by some sort of decoration of equal merit to the Victoria Cross. But the miners do not require special incentives for these deeds of courage. For the Welsh miner it is sufficient reward for him to know that he did his duty and that what he did so others would do for him if he were placed in similar distressing circumstances.'*

In the afternoon the Lodge members met at the Gwernymilwr Hotel to pay their contributions, and transfer cards were given to those who had left or intended leaving for other districts. Secretary Tom John reported on the donations received for the Sick and Accident Fund and the Lord Mayor of Cardiff's Fund.

Late that night the very-disfigured and decomposed body of fireman Christopher Martin was found, his body later identified by a tobacco box and his time sheet.

The bodies of fireman Gwilym Jones and David Davies were recovered on July 30th. The last body, that of William Parker, was not recovered until February 24th, 1902.

With one exception the body of every person had been more or less burned, the vast majority sickenly mutilated, identified only by a piece of clothing, a tobacco tin, a pocket watch, a buckle, a metal button and the like. So little remained of some bodies that they were immediately coffined after identification, the casket never reopened. The many decomposed bodies were also coffined immediately and buried within hours of being brought to the surface.

Death for the mass of victims had been mercifully swift. Jacob Lewis was found sitting on his haunches with a drill in his hand. George Warren was found in a rubbish stall, his body upright, his head downward against a tram, seemingly in the act of loading rubbish into the tram which was half full. But from the reports of the recovery parties the agony of some others had been more protracted before they were overcome by the deadly after-damp. James and Joseph Fullalove, father and son, were discovered lying locked in each other's arms, their faces to the ground. One body was that of a ripper who had evidently ran about four yards from his place of work into a stall nearby where he sat down on his heels, as colliers do, leaning his head against the cog, hoping no doubt to escape the awful blast. Having lost his lamp and stick a fireman proceeded along in the dark until he was overcome, his body found in a sitting position with his eyes open. Another man had made a desperate run for his life, his lamp found hanging almost fifty yards from where he fell, overcome by the after-damp.

Left to mourn the 81 victims were 54 widows, 229 fatherless children and some dependant parents.

One victim lived in Bedwas, one in Newport, three in Caerphilly and thirteen in Abertridwr, leaving 8 widows, 43 fatherless children and some dependants. Mrs. Morgan of Caerphilly lost her husband and son, aged widower George Lower of Abertridwr lost his two young sons. The wife of victim William Lewis of Abertridwr died in hospital the same day, leaving three orphans to be cared for by her sister Mrs. Anslow of Abertridwr, mother of seven children and widowed by the explosion.

Sixty three victims lived in Senghenydd, 12 in High Street, 10 in Commercial Street and Caerphilly Road, 8 in Grove Terrace, 6 in the Huts, Station Terrace and Stanley Street, 4 in Parc Terrace, 1 in Kingsley Place. Four were between the age of 17 to 19, eighteen between 20 to 29, nineteen between 30 and 39, eleven between 40 and 49, eight between 50 and 59, two between 60 and 69, one age 72.

Left to mourn were 44 widows, 12 elderly orphaned children, 174 fatherless children and the parents of 17 single men. Mrs. Davies of 12 Grove Terrace, Mrs. Fullalove of 42 Stanley Street, Mrs. Lewis of 12 The Huts and Mrs. Rowland of 49 Caerphilly Road each lost a husband and son. Widow Mrs. Rowlands of Commercial Street lost her son who was working his last shift before leaving to help her full-time in her shop. Mrs. Sarah Evans of High Street lost her husband only two years after a son aged 14 had been killed in an accident at the Gwernymilwr Quarry. Llewellyn Llewellyn of 10 Parc Terrace had worked at the colliery for only three weeks, his wife and children still living in Ogmore Vale. Mrs. Thomas of 45 Stanley Street, mother of ten children, was left with five under the age of ten. But for all who were bereaved the grief and trauma was immeasurable.

Not only had the wives lost a dearly-loved husband but the wage earner, the provider, as had some parents with the loss of a son. True, there would be the official compensation, but it would be a considerable time before this would be determined and dispensed. Meanwhile, the haunting question was how to meet not only the funeral expenses but the ordinary everyday bills. Financial support was forthcoming from the colliery Sick and Accident Approved society, insurance policies and Friendly Societies but the picture was one of dire distress. Fortunately such was the response to the Federation's Appeal Fund and that of the Lord Mayor of Cardiff's Appeal that by June 2nd the Relief Committee had distributed £1,700 in addition to the sums dispensed by the Lord Mayor to families in the greatest need.

As the sense of grief and stupor began to assuage a little so the demand grew for answers to some questions. What caused the explosion? Why was the effect so devastating? To what extent was the management responsible?

On June 13th a sub-committee of the S.W.M.F.G.B. met at the Gwernymilwr Hotel to arrange for representation at the Inquiry into the circumstances of the disaster and to pursue compensation claims. Among those present were Lodge Chairman Ben Evans and Secretary Tom John, and it was reported that £500 had been advanced by the Federation to meet the needs of families.

On Monday, June 17th, the adjourned Inquest/Inquiry was held at the Gwernymilwr Hotel. The Coroner stated that all he had to do was to complete the evidence of identification and then adjourn the Inquiry until Professor Galloway was ready with his Report. Griffith David Griffiths, the colliery office clerk, was the only witness, submitting a full list of the names and descriptions of all the men who had lost their lives of which seventy eight bodies had been recovered. The Coroner then adjourned the Inquiry until July 22nd.

The Lord Mayor of Cardiff came to the village and met local representatives at the Hotel to inquire into the circumstances of each victim's family. Among those present were Managing Director W.T. Rees, Agent Robert Rees, Dr. James and Revs. Henry Morgan, David Roberts and Henry Evans. It was reported that £382 had already been dispensed from his Relief Fund and £142-10-0 was voted for immediate assistance to forty four families. It was agreed also that after temporary relief had been afforded the surplus would be handed over to the Local Relief Committee to be set up by the S.W.M.F. The Lord Mayor then met a deputation of Miners' Agents to explain the procedure which had been resolved.

On June 20th the Relief Fund Committee met at the Park Hotel in Cardiff when, under the auspices of the S.W.M.F., the following officers were appointed to administer it - Mr. Alfred Thomas, M.P. (President), the Lord Mayor of Cardiff and Mr. W. Abraham, M.P. (Vice Presidents), Mr. Thomas Richards (Secretary), Mr. Alfred Onions (Treasurer) and the Senghenydd Branch of the London & Provincial Bank (Bankers). It was reported that £353-17-0 had been received and a list was provided of additional contributions to the Relief Fund.

With the resilience characteristic of coal-mining villages, the bereaved supported by communal care and the solace afforded by religious faith, so Senghenydd had begun to resume the ordinary threads of daily life.

The schools had returned to a familiar pattern with particular attention paid to attendance. A few pupils left, their fathers having obtained employment elsewhere, some sat the *'Labour'* examination, and the only problem was posed by a shortage of water resulting from a long spell of dry, hot weather. The Aber Valley Main sewer was nearing completion and the Caerphilly Council was seeking sanction for a loan to implement Private Street improvements. On June 20th the Chamber of Trade embarked on its annual outing, warranting the closure of the schools. On June 30th and July 1st Rev. James Jones, a student at Aberhonddu College, was ordained as resident minister of Noddfa Chapel, the proceedings conducted by the caring minister Rev. Tawelfryn Thomas and attended by ten ministers.

In July the Chamber of Trade complained to the Council about the shortage of water as the drought continued, the Council sought a site for a public slaughterhouse and issued six Notices for the Abatement of Nuisances.

At the official annual visit of the three schools by the H.M.I. he prefaced his report by stating, *'The workings of these schools have been seriously interrupted in consequence of the disastrous explosion at the local colliery'* before proceeding to praise them all. Referring to the Infants' School he commented, *'This Department has been under a great disadvantage during the past year on account of the prolonged absence of Miss Austin but through the strenuous efforts of the temporary Mistress and the staff the efficiency of the school has been kept up.'* Of the Girls' School he stated, *'There is clear evidence of hard work and effective teaching in all the classes, the discipline deserving special praise'*, and of the Boys' School, *'The lessons are of a stimulating and intelligent character and the order and organisation are highly satisfactory.'* Criticism was levelled at the inadequacy of the building to accommodate 170 girls and 217 boys and the inadequate *'warming'* arrangements provided by the open fires.

On July 15th Professor Galloway submitted his Report to the Home Secretary in preparation for the scheduled resumed Inquiry on July 22nd.

In the opening paragraphs he refers to two photographs of mine waggons, an empty one and one loaded with coal in the usual manner. *'The first weighs between eight and nine hundredweight, the second about thirty-seven hundredweight. It will be observed that one end of the waggon is made of sheet iron while the other is open, but in the latter case, two strong hinged iron bars serve to prevent large pieces of coal from falling out on to the road.*

The inevitable result of piling the coal so high above the level of the sides and having one end practically open is that quantities of coal are strewn along the haulage roads all the way from the face to the bottom of the winding shaft, and that this coal being constantly trampled upon by men and horses and thereby crushed to powder, has produced a continuous train of coal-dust throughout the whole of the haulage roads in the colliery, that is to say, from every working place to the bottom of the winding shaft.

It will be seen that this train of coal-dust has been the means of carrying the explosion into practically every working place in the colliery.'

He continued to stress this aspect with such statements as *'Under the circumstances prevailing at the time it is impossible to prevent the workings from becoming dry and dusty without having recourse to some means of damping them artificially'*, that *'The whole of the workings of the Universal Colliery, with the exception of one or two small areas, were dry and dusty when the explosion occurred'*, and again that *'With few exceptions the explosion penetrated into the stallroads and working - faces in every district in the mine... Coal-dust when mixed with air played the part of an inflammable gas in the explosion, and must have carried the explosion.'*

As to the cause and origin of the explosion he acknowledged *'it is difficult to fix the actual starting point except by inference.The probability is that the initial impulse was given by a blasting shot, but up to the present time nothing positive has transpired in regard to the firing of a shot at the instant the explosion took place. In the absence of a better explanation of the origin of the explosion I am disposed to think that a blasting shot was fired which raised and ignited the coal dust, no effort having been made to lay the dust in that locality by watering.'* In an Additional Note he stated that it appeared the explosion started in the East District.

He then proceeded, *'The extension of the explosion from this or any other point in the mine at which it originated is easily explained. A considerable volume of flame having been formed, a sudden expansion of the air took place, creating an airwave which swept through the roadways in every direction, raising the coal-dust and mixing it with air as it passed. The flame followed closely behind the airwave, rapidly increasing the volume of heated air, and, consequently the pressure that was driving it forward from behind. The airwave sent off a shoot into each roadway as it passed where it found a sufficient supply of coal-dust to sustain the flame and in this manner the whole of the workings that contained coal-dust were rapidly traversed, and the explosion became an accomplished fact.'*

Turning his attention to the means of preventing coal-dust explosions he stated, *'There is conclusive evidence that dampness, whether natural or artificial, will prevent a great explosion from occurring at all, and will arrest it completely if it is anywhere else, providing the length of the damp part is so great that the flame is unable to cross it'*, proceeding then to enumerate the various devices used in collieries to produce artificial dampness or wetness.

Summarising, he wrote, *'There are two methods of preventing the occurrence of of great colliery explosions:*

1. *To lay the dust by watering it. This precaution has been voluntarily adopted by many of the colliery owners in the South Wales coalfield, but, as it is not made compulsory by Act of Parliament, and therefore cannot be enforced by the Inspectors of Mines, it appears to be frequently neglected, or done only perfunctorily, by some of the Managers.*
2. *To employ dust-tight waggons filled only to the level of the upper edges of their sides.'*

Professor Galloway concluded, *'The mining community, generally, has accepted the view that coal-dust and not fire-damp is the principal agent in all great colliery explosions. After having examined the scenes of several great explosions I have arrived at the conclusion that the mixture of coal-dust and air is itself the inflammable agent which initiates and carries on the explosion and that the fine coal-dust plays the part of a quasi-gas when intimately mixed with air'*.

Such was his verdict on the *'Circumstances attending an Explosion which occurred at the Universal Colliery, Glamorganshire, on May 24th, 1901'*. It was left to the Inquiry to make the final judgement.

At the resumed Inquiry on July 22nd the Coroner further adjourned it until October 21st because three bodies had not been recovered, including that of fireman Gwilym Jones which was of particular importance in the determination as to the cause of the explosion.

A considerable quantity of debris still had to be cleared in the Pretoria District and the Lodge was in dispute with the management over a reduction in the rates of pay of some day-wage workers.

On July 30th the bodies of fireman Gwilym Jones and David Davies were recovered, Gwilym Jones's watch had stopped at 5.05.

A few more families left the village in August, Sgt. Leyshon Williams replaced Sgt. Davies and for the eighth time the applications by the Leigh and Parc Hotels for an ale licence were rejected. The Secretary of the Universal Sick and Accident Society reported that such was the response from other collieries to the appeal for financial aid it was now able to provide funds to alleviate distress. At the colliery the dispute continued over the reduction in wages of some day-wage workers, and on August 24th the committee of the East Glamorgan Miners' Association resolved to send a deputation to protest to the management. When this meeting proved abortive the colliery work force came out on strike on September 1st, terminating after four days when agreement was reached. The Union paid strike pay.

In the course of September and October the Chamber of Trade requested more street lamps and criticised the scavenging, plans were submitted for a Constitutional Club, Miss Martha Davies resigned as Head Teacher of the Girls' School to be replaced by Miss Dinah Evans, John Bevan of the Boys' School came fourth in the *'Scholarship'* examination for entry to Pontypridd Intermediate School and W.T. Marshall, chemist M.E. Price and Mrs. Ainslow were registered to sell fireworks.

On Monday, October 21st, the long-awaited Inquest opened in the Miners' Lodge room at the Gwernymilwr Hotel when Professor Galloway's Report was available to the Coroner and jury. The proceedings lasted four days conducted amid an array of eminent barristers, solicitors, mining experts and witnesses.

It opened with the formal identification of the bodies of Gwilym Jones and David Davies before proceeding to establish the cause and origin of the explosion. It was dominated by the evidence submitted by Professor Galloway. Among others who gave evidence were Messrs. J.T. Robson, Dyer Lewis and Gray, Robert T. Rees, Edward Shaw, colliery officials and workmen.

In relation to the cause and origin of the explosion Galloway reiterated the probability that the initial impulse came from a blasting shot fired in the East District. The three Mines Inspectors were not unanimous in their opinion with Robson observing that *'there can be no doubt that shot-firing is a possible cause but I have failed to find that it was the most probable one.'* However, all were agreed in the criticism of the lax control over the distribution of explosives and of the persons authorised to use them.

In respect of the crucial question, that of the cause for the devastating effect of the explosion, there was complete agreement by the experts of Galloway's damning evidence that it was due to the inflammation of dry, fine coal-dust which was present in large quantities due to inadequate watering. Only the well-rehearsed voices of the Agent and the Manager stoutly maintained that the roads were well watered and comparatively free from dust.

Guided by the Coroner's summing up, the jury returned the following verdict; *'That George Warren, on 24th May, 1901, in the Parish of Eglwysilan, in the County of Glamorgan, at the Universal Colliery, met with his death by burns and suffocation by the afterdamp resulting from an explosion at the said colliery on 24th May 1901, but we are unable to locate the exact spot, or to form an opinion as to how it originated but agree that it was carried through the workings by coal dust.'*

It recorded a verdict of *'Accidental Death'*, but prompted by the Coroner in his summation, it added this rider: *'The jury considers that the colliery was not watered in a satisfactory manner, the system of watering by means of casks and allowing the water to run along the centre of the road is in any way sufficient... The jury strongly urges the Members of the British Parliament to make it strictly compulsory to have the bottom, sides and top of the roads of collieries so well watered as to make it impossible for coal dust to spread an explosion.*

The jury also condemns the present system of giving out the explosive, and considers that a correct record should be kept of all explosives issued, used and returned.'

The Report of J.T. Robson, compiled in conjunction with the Assistant Mines Inspectors, was submitted on November 15th. Reaffirming Galloway's assessment as to the reason for the widespread devastation he stated, *'The evidence shows that a certain amount of watering had been done daily, but I am decidedly of the opinion that insufficient attention had been given to the coal-dust on the sides and timbers, and that there must have been a considerable quantity of it to cause such an explosion.'* He concluded, *'With the final recommendation of the jury in its rider I entirely concur... It is now universally admitted that coal-dust is a* 'greater enemy' *than even fire-damp, yet it is undoubtedly a fact that sufficient attention is not always paid to the prevention of its accumulation.'*

The Report of S.T. Evans on December 12th agreed that the extent of the explosion was caused by the presence of coal-dust, that *'the provision for watering was quite inadequate and those responsible for the management either had not duly appreciated the necessity of these precautions or had failed to see they were observed'*, and endorsed the recommendations of the jury. Yet, he concluded, *'While there was some laxity upon the matters to which reference has been made, I do not think there was established any breach of statutory specific duties to which the explosion was due, and I do not recommend any prosecution.'*

His judicial judgement prevailed and no prosecution followed of management or coal-owners on the legal basis that there were no specific statutory duties laid down to control dust accumulation. But the tragic effect of what the learned Counsel described as *'some laxity'* in the matter was that 81 men had been killed in horrible circumstances. *'If the main road had been thoroughly watered the men on the east side would have escaped, and if all the main roads had been thoroughly watered then only a few men, not the whole of the men in the colliery would have been touched'*, declared Robson. Commented Evans, *'The grave importance of efficiently watering the roads will be realised when it is pointed out that in the opinion of the Mines Inspectors and others well qualified to form an opinion if the roads had been properly watered then the loss of life would have been very much less.'*

The possibility that a more terrifying scenario could have occurred was voiced by S.T. Evans when he stated, *'If the explosion had occurred when the 240 night men were all in the mine, or in the day time when about 450 men would have been below ground, it will be seen that upon the efficiency of the watering of the coal-dust might have depended hundreds of lives'*.

Out of this tragedy a clear lesson had emerged - that the dry, gassy conditions which prevailed at the colliery would always present a potential explosive scene unless vigorous precautions were taken to prevent the culmination of dry, fine coal dust. Would the lesson be learned or would the scenario envisaged by S.T. Evans become a reality?

For the widows and other dependants the Inquest and Reports did nothing to assuage their anguish and bitterness. Faced with a bleak, uncertain future what compensation were they awarded? Under the terms of the Workmen's Compensation Act of 1897 the financial entitlement for those who had been solely dependent on the victim was a lump sum up to a maximum of £300, calculated on his average earnings over the previous three years and the extent of the dependency. When the sum had been determined, a third was allocated to cover funeral and other expenses and the remainder invested by the Registrar to provide 2/6d a week for each child. For those partly dependent, the sum within the same limit was open to agreement or to arbitration if disputed. For a victim without dependants, such as a single man whose father was working, then a sum not exceeding £10 was awarded for reasonable burial expenses.

Fortunately, such was the response to the various Relief Funds now amalgamated into the *'Senghenydd Relief Fund'* under the Presidency of Alfred Thomas, M.P., that it allocated a weekly pension of 10/- for an adult dependant and 5/- for a child.

During the closing months of the year the colliery was in full production as it had been for some considerable time, but these were troubled times in the coalfield with basic wages still falling and the Federation retaliating by organising *'stop days'* to restrict production. Also, on the national scale, the Taff Vale Judgement by which employers could cripple the financial basis of any Trade Union involved in a strike meant that this weapon was now rendered powerless.

The Aber Valley Main Sewer was completed, the Chamber of Trade protested against the vagaries of the water supply, the state of the roads, street lighting and scavenging and criticised the Council for not declaring a right of way for the public and vehicular traffic to Nelson via Maesdiofal farm. Glawnant and Caermoel farmhouses were condemned as unfit for human habitation and once again a Notice for the Abatement of Nuisance was served on Ludwig John in respect of the cowhouse at the rear of the Parc Hotel.

There was an epidemic of scarlet fever in November.

Miss Margaret Austin returned to duty at the Infants' School only to be faced still with a very inadequate staff both in number and experience comprising Misses M.A. Jones (U), M. Rowland (U), M. Roberts (P.T.), A.M. Morris (Monitress) and Mary Jane Lewis (Monitress). The senior schools were overcrowded and continued to have problems related to heating and the lack of artificial lighting but were making good progress. In both schools the attendance reached peak performances, stimulated by the School Board's introduction of a monthly half-day holiday to schools attaining a specified percentage. Dan Lloyd offered further incentives to pupils such as lantern-slide entertainment, a free visit to Cardiff Museum and the award of books presented on *'Prize Day'* in December. The staffs remained reasonably stable and at the end of the year that at the Girls' School under Miss Dinah Evans comprised Ethel Rundle (C), Elizabeth Miles

(C), Elizabeth Shaw (U), Matilda James (P.T.), Agnes Jones (P.T.), Margaret John (P.T.) and S. Ward (Monitress), and that of the Boys' School under Dan Lloyd comprised Albert J. Williams (C), Sarah Morgan (C), Mary Rees (C), Joshua Bowen (U), Lizzie Israel (U), Joseph Edmunds (P.T.), Arthur Morgan (P.T.) and J.A. Roberts (Paid Monitor).

Religious commitment was as strong as ever, the choirs, the various Societies, organisations and sports clubs were again fully active but undiminished was the scale of drunkenness and assaults.

The decline in population had been halted at about 3,100 although it was still hundreds less than in 1900, and normality in the pattern of life had returned to the village if not to the bereaved families.

The Universal Colliery during the intervening years between two explosions. Eighty one died in 1901 and 439 in 1913.

CHAPTER 5

As the impact of the explosion faded so production increased in the colliery and there was no difficulty in recruiting labour so that by 1904 the work force numbered over 1,000.

On Monday, February 25th, 1902, the Home Office issued the official copy of the Reports on the circumstances attending the explosion. On the previous day the last of the victims had been recovered from the Pretoria District, the very badly decomposed body of William Parker brought to a temporary mortuary at the Leigh Hotel. A native of Bristol he would have been married shortly after the day of the explosion.

In the course of the year many widows and other dependants appeared before Judge Gwilym Williams at Pontypridd County Court to apply for an amendment to the original allocation of the compensation sum. Plus in respect of five cases where a family had suffered two deaths and an original grant of £50 allocated, their submission for a further one third of the total amount of the compensation was granted. Miss W., whose widower father had left eight children, applied for support in that she and three others had been dependant on him and was granted £50 on account. Granted was the application by Mrs. W. that she be paid the entire compensation now that the four children were earning and she needed the money to carry on her butchering business. Mrs. V. was granted an additional £20 to open a small shop, Mrs. E. granted £10 to enable her to apprentice her daughter as a dressmaker, Mrs. C. granted £10 to meet the expenses incurred by the illness and death of her child. Also granted was the application by a widow who had claimed originally for a child but now stated that it was a *'love child'* of her late husband and therefore asked that the part of the lump sum retained for its support be paid to her to pay off the mortgage. A grant of £10 was made to Mrs. L. who had received £100 out of the £300 compensation but had remarried. Less fortunate were the very many widows whose claims for the allowance of 2/6d for a child to be increased were rejected.

In December 1902 the work force of the South Wales coalfield celebrated a great victory when the hated Sliding Scale agreement was replaced by a new system whereby a Joint Conciliation Board was established to define a minimum and maximum scale of wages and with arbitration procedures in the event of disputes over settlements. But with wages continuing to decline and the Board failing to satisfy the work force in its negotiations so the period over 1903 and 1904 was one of increasing militancy and unrest.

The Federation waged a vigorous campaign to ensure a *'closed shop'*, one which received strong support from the Universal Lodge led by Hubert Jenkins the Miners' Agent and William Evans the Chairman of the

East Glamorgan Association of Miners. The strained relationship with the management came to a head one day in June 1903 when the Union members decided not to descend the pit in the same cages as non-Unionists and asked that two queues be formed. Manager Shaw, supported by Agent Rees, refused this request, the Lodge responded by withdrawing labour that day and the Company retaliated by issuing summonses against 403 workmen for breach of contract. In July, Caerphilly witnessed the spectacle of the workmen marching en masse to the Magistrates Court where 368 were each fined £2. This episode did not deter the Lodge from continuing to campaign for a *'closed shop'*.

Nor was the Lodge deterred from participating in the Federation's strategy of periodically operating *'Stop Days'* when the work force was withdrawn for twenty four hours to stop production as a protest against low wages. It also pursued other grievances as in September 1903 when a strike lasting a week successfully resolved a dispute over rates of pay for opening up new districts.

The mounting militancy in the coalfield had its repercussions in the political field, generating some disenchantment with its traditional ties with the Liberal Party and an attraction towards socialism and the Independent Labour Party. This was reflected in the village. It had given overwhelming support to Sir Alfred Thomas, Chairman of the Welsh Parliamentary Party when he was re-elected as Liberal M.P. in the General Election of 1902 but many miners were critical in that he was no longer prominent in the debates. on industrial affairs and was known to be averse to socialism.

At the local level of politics there was anger that Senghenydd and Abertridwr were still denied separate representation on the Caerphilly Urban District Council where the Aber Ward was served by Edmund Evans, William Thomas and Robert T. Rees.

By the end of 1904 the population had increased to about 4,000 and plans had been approved for another 112 houses. These included 60 for the Universal Colliery Company, 12 for T. Wood, 9 for A.J. Marshall, 8 for builders Davies & Lloyd and 6 for Lewis Morgan. Alexandra Terrace and Coronation Terrace were built so had other houses with temporary addresses such as *'New Houses'* and *'Back Row'*. Such did the demand for accommodation exceed the supply that on occasions the Council agreed to grant a temporary Certificate of Occupation to owners of houses which lacked a water supply on the understanding that it would be provided, a practice which was condemned by the Chamber of Trade.

Plans were approved for another bakery, four premises for the Co-operative Stores, shops for John Bailey and John Davies and five other shops. Mr. Shibko opened a pawnbroker's shop. John Morgan of Caermoel farm, R. Thomas of High Street and John Edgeworth were licensed as purveyors of milk and W.T. Marshall was licensed to store and hawk petroleum.

Overcrowding was very common. In 1904 a survey of 222 houses conducted by the Sanitary Inspector/Inspector of Nuisances revealed that they were occupied by 1,326 persons and that 47 were occupied by two families. In some cases the sleeping arrangements were made possible only because the men worked different shifts.

Much of the housing was sub-standard with families living in squalid conditions, and in the words of the Chairman of the Caerphilly Magistrates Bench, *'Many houses are unfit for the occupation of pigs'*.

A total of 343 Notices for the Abatement of Nuisances were served on landowners, house owners and builders in respect of choked, dilapidated closet and slop-water drains. Other defects enumerated were defective roof troughing, dilapidated floors, dampness, back lanes not properly paved, overflowing cesspools and no proper receptacle for manure in stables. In most cases the Notices cited a combination of *'Nuisances'*.

Stanley Street, where twenty-three of the twenty-seven houses were owned by the executors of the Henry Williams Estate, continued to be a source of major concern over the occupation of the cellars. A house-to-house inspection was carried in 1902 and 1903 with resultant proceedings taken in each case in respect of choked closet and slop-water drains, dilapidated floors, no proper roof troughing and over-crowding. Following another inspection in 1904 a Notice of Closure was served on twelve houses in that the cellar dwellings were unfit for human occupation, the Medical Officer of Health declaring, *'How the poor live is a puzzling question, and how these people can live in those dark, dismal chambers where scarcely a glean of sunshine enters the precinct is a mystery'*. The proceedings were withdrawn only when the executors agreed to meet all the Council's requirements and gave an assurance that in future the houses would not be occupied as double dwellings.

Other streets were also subject to house-to-house inspections. In 1903 Notices were served on the owners of 31 houses in Grove Terrace in respect of defective drains. In 1904 proceedings were taken against the owners of 15 houses in Station Terrace, the charge citing choked drains, damp walls and dilapidated back yards, and Notices were served on the owners of 20 houses in High Street in respect of deficient roofing, deficient drainage and dilapidated back yards.

Proceedings were instituted against the owners of Caermoel and Cefn Llwyd farmhouses with a view to closure as unfit for human occupation, and a Notice served on the owner of Caerllwyn farmhouse in respect of defective drainage and roofing.

The water supply also came under criticism. While the Chamber of Trade was gratified that the Rhymney and Aber Valley Gas & Water Company had laid mains in Caerphilly Road it expressed disappointment that mains were not laid in High Street as promised, and in general criticised the supply as not always adequate or properly filtered and sometimes cut off with out prior notice. But the overwhelming number of complaints was lodged against landlords for failing to provide their tenants with a sufficient quantity of water for flushing the closets or for bathing. During this period the Council issued Notices for the abatement of this *'Nuisance'* on the owners of 31 houses in Commercial Street, 21 houses in Station Terrace, 16 houses in Stanley Street, 13 houses in High Street and 6 houses in Caerphilly Road.

All matters that affected public health were the concern of the Chamber. Following its complaint about the insanitary condition of the brook the Council issued Notices against the adjacent landowners and resolved to erect steel-mounted notice boards warning persons against throwing refuse into the brook. As to its complaint that refuse was being deposited outside the front doors for collection, the Council resolved to request the villagers that it must be deposited in the back lanes, but it took no action in response to the complaint that mat-beating was carried out at all times of the day and requesting the Council to compel this be done before 8.00 a.m.

In response to the ever-recurring complaints about the state of the roads the Council instituted proceedings against the property owners of Station Road and Station Terrace and against the Park Newydd Estate in relation to part of Commercial Street, but the side roads were still unmade and there was no progress in opening up the right of way past Maesdiofal farm to Nelson for vehicular traffic.

As to the question of street lighting the Council adopted a policy in 1902 whereby the police were appointed to hold a watching brief and submit a monthly report. Consequently, Sergeant Williams was appointed to this post at a remuneration of £3 per annum after he had earlier rejected a previous sum. Even so, this did not prevent the complaints in the ensuing years concerning the quality of light, the inadequate number of lamps and the dereliction of duty by the lamplighter. Some comfort was taken from the Council's negotiations with the South Wales Power Company to supply the District with electricity and the suggestion that the Rhymney Valley Company be compelled to provide a gas supply to the Aber Valley. But by the end of 1904 nothing had changed.

Pleasure was expressed by the Chamber when the Council voted to provide eight fire hydrants and also to approach the Postmaster General to provide a Sunday mail service. There was general satisfaction that the Railway Company now provided seven daily journeys to Caerphilly except on Sunday, but both it and the postal authorities were condemned for continuing to use the spelling of *'Senghenith'*.

Laudable as were the efforts of the Council and the Chamber to maintain a healthy environment the infant mortality was high and the period was punctuated by epidemics of smallpox, scarlet fever, diphtheria and measles, a situation common throughout the land.

Early in August 1902 a case of smallpox was reported in Stanley Street and much to the credit of the Council, an emergency meeting resolved to purchase a temporary six-bed hospital construction from London and to erect it speedily on a site on Mynydd Mayo, Eglwysilan. Meanwhile the occupants were confined to the house with the Council agreeing to their demand that the men's wages be paid and food supplied until the infection was over. It also authorised a constable to watch over the house by night and day and appointed Nurse Taylor at a salary of £3-3-0 a week to undertake duties in preventing the spread of the disease. By September 12th the disease had spread to other cellars in the street, the Medical Officer commenting that *'the outbreak was not surprising taking into consideration the class of people who come into these districts and that it broke out in such an insanitary area where the drains are defective'*. It claimed another six cases, one of which was fatal, and the pupils living in the street were excluded from school for two weeks. With the temporary smallpox hospital not ready for occupation the occupants of the affected houses remained housebound, the Council paying the rents and £5 to each man kept from work. This arrangement continued until the outbreak was brought under control by the latter part of the month, the hospital still not open, and it was not until mid-October that a caretaker was appointed, there having been considerable difficulty in filling the post.

Meanwhile, an epidemic of scarlet fever which had begun in July was now rampant and raged throughout October and November claiming the lives of Ada (2) Essery, Elizabeth (15 months) Essery, William Herring (6 days) and Mary Neale (24) of the Huts and a pupil at the Girls' School. The schools closed for three weeks in November and exclusion measures against some pupils continued into December. It was not always easy for parents to conform to the statutory obligation to confine to the home the children suffering from the disease. Proceedings were taken against Mr. N. of Parc Terrace in that *'whilst being in charge of his daughter Myra, a person suffering from a dangerous infectious disease, did expose her on November 10th without taking proper precautions against spreading the disorder in a street or public place'*. On December 9th a mother was charged at Caerphilly Court *'for allowing her son to expose himself in a public place (playing in the street) while suffering from scarlet fever when she and others had been served with the customary notice as to the precautions to be taken as a notifiable disease'*. The Chairman of the Bench imposed a fine but remarked with some sympathy how difficult it was to isolate cases in small houses. By mid-December the epidemic had largely subsided.

In 1903 some cases of diphtheria were reported. In January of 1904 a few cases of scarlet fever were reported, but then between September and November not only was there a scarlet fever epidemic but a virulent outbreak of smallpox which spread from Stanley Street to Parc Terrace, Grove Terrace, Commercial Street, Clive Street and Caerphilly Road. The first case in Stanley Street was reported on September 20th when the patient was removed to the hospital on Mynydd Mayo and the the occupants of the house were vaccinated.

Understandably, this outbreak aroused considerable fear but so did the rumour that all school children were to be vaccinated, a procedure which the Medical Officer had long since recommended. On September 23rd Miss James recorded in the Log Book of the Infants' School, *'A large number of women came to the school yard at 3.00 p.m. to demand their children to go home as a rumour was about that all children were to be vaccinated. This was quite without foundation but they would not be pacified and several children were taken home'.* Earlier, Miss Evans faced a demonstration in the yard of the Girls' School. So had Dan Lloyd who faced a crowd in a militant mood in the Boys' yard and recorded, *'A rumour that the boys were to be vaccinated in school in the afternoon. As a result many women visited the school and refused to believe that it was unfounded. The police were asked to assist in keeping the peace. The more obstinate parents remained until the school dismissed'.* It was some days before the *'scare'* subsided. Pupils living in the affected areas continued to be excluded from School for a period of time and by mid-November both epidemics were under control and fortunately without any fatal results.

At the schools there had been a major change in management when from October 1st, 1903, the School Boards had been abolished and the administration of education was vested in Glamorgan County Council which appointed an Education Committee and set up Boards of Management for groups of schools. On the Board for the Caerphilly Group which included the Senghenydd Schools the only familiar Manager to be appointed was that of Rev. Tawelfryn Thomas. A further change which operated from 1902 was that Pupil Teachers attended part-time at a Centre in Cardiff.

For the Infants' School, where the number on roll increased from 250 to over 300, these were difficult years. Not only did the epidemics of 1902 and 1904 have a grievous effect but there were frequent staff changes, some periods when the staff was inadequate or insufficient and occasions when the main room was so inadequately heated that *'the children marched and drilled until they got warm'.* Yet the H.M.I. reported in 1902 that *'The Mistress has very good notions, the teaching is careful and the work is creditable',* and in 1903 that *'The teaching painstaking and methodical and satisfactory progress has been made notwithstanding the absence of the Mistress due to ill-health'.* Then at the end of August Miss Austin resigned on the grounds of ill-health and Miss Catherine James was appointed as Head Teacher. It was a popular choice, a Senghenydd girl who had been a Pupil Teacher at the Mixed School, had proceeded to Swansea Training College and then returned to teach at the Girls' School. But 1904 proved a very difficult year. Miss James was absent throughout the first two and a half months having been ordered to take complete rest, the staff was insufficient and weak in qualifications so that at times *'there was great difficulty in carrying on work in a satisfactory manner',* the school was often cold and the epidemics had a profound effect. At the end of the year the staff comprised Leah Davies (C), Miriam Rowland (C), Esther Thomas (U), Mary Jane Lewis (P.T.), Blodwen Thomas (P.T.) and Edith Jones (P.T.)

At the senior schools, in addition to the adverse effect of the epidemics the inadequacy of the shared accommodation became more apparent as the numbers on roll increased, the lack of artificial lighting continued to pose a problem in the winter months and the vagaries of the coal supply led to occasions when only some fires were lit or none at all. Relative to the curriculum, a major change was the introduction of Welsh in 1902 with the emphasis laid on the spoken word, but as yet St. David's Day was celebrated only by the customary half-day holiday.

Among the duties undertaken by the County Council to facilitate entry to Secondary Education was the provision of a system of scholarships to provide free education for the poor. But there is no evidence during this period of any boy or girl even being submitted as a candidate for entry to the County Schools. Instead the goal was to leave school as soon as possible via the *'Labour'* examination when 35 girls were entered with 16 successful and 41 boys entered with 18 successful, some of whom were aged 12. Less legitimate were other efforts to obtain early release, such as that of a lad whose Birth Certificate had been forged and had been employed at the colliery for some weeks before it was detected, and another case in which *'the parents by erasing, altered the date of birth on the boy's birth certificate from 1889 to 1888 so that he might be taken from school to work'*.

At the Girls' School there were frequent staff changes. Due regard was paid to discipline and the attendance was generally of a high order although there was concern over absenteeism attributed to the skin disease of eczema. In 1902 the H.M.I. reported, *'The new Mistress, Miss Evans, has reason to be greatly encouraged by her first year's work. The girls seem to be genuinely interested in their lessons, especially in the Welsh lessons which are given with considerable success'*, and in 1903, *'This school continues to be well-instructed and the discipline is thoroughly satisfactory'*. The *'highlight'* in the calendar of 1904 was the school concert in May to raise funds for the purchase of a piano which proved so successful that on June 9th the Mistress recorded, *'Piano arrived from Messrs, Waddington and Sons, Leeds, who are allowing us to have it for £26, £19 paid in cash and the remaining £7 to be paid in six months'*. The H.M.I. reported, *'The teaching is earnest and well-supervised, and the children are exceedingly well-behaved and attentive to lessons'*. At the end of the year the number on roll had increased to 260 and the staff comprised Phoebe Griffiths (C), Ethel Rundle (C), Lizzie Thomas (C), Matilda Jones (U), Agnes Jones (P.T.) Maggie John (P.T.) and Maggie Thomas (P.T.).

At the Boys' School there were staff changes including the departure of Sarah Morgan who was appointed Head Teacher of Caerphilly Girls' School, a Drawing Examination was introduced in 1904 as a result of a visit from an Inspector of Drawing and a visiting lecturer gave a talk illustrated by lantern slides on the subject of *'Alcohol'*. Although attendance was still good the rate of absenteeism and truancy gave some cause for concern. Two boys were committed to the Truant School but by January 1904 the Master was able to report that *'truancy is gradually being suppressed'*. More parents were being summoned and fined sums ranging from 2/6d to 15/-. That he found absenteeism on certain Monday mornings particularly exasperating was evident from such Log Book entries in 1904 as:

'May 9th. Fifty two boys absent. The Monday mornings after the fortnightly pay day is always so.

June 13th. The colliers having a stop day and a trip to Barry caused very few to be present. Consequently no school was held.

July 18th. Very many boys absent. No real excuse. There was no work at the colliery today and accounts for the indifference of parents.'

Discipline continued to be rigidly enforced by corporal punishment administered by the Master and teachers, and on one occasion Dan Lloyd suspended a male Pupil Teacher for a period *'on account of his inability to control himself'*. Punctuality and cleanliness were important with the latter checked by the Master by an inspection of all boys. Also, within the accustomed remit of the times, was the Master's responsibility for the behaviour of the pupils outside school hours, the Log Book recording *'The Master addressed all boys on decency and and swearing'* and *'Complaints against five boys for stone throwing. Have attended the matter'*.

The Log Book also noted that a cricket team was re-formed, some members of staff playing in the yard with the pupils during the dinner hour. It was also the practice of some members of staff to coach games of football in the winter months during this period, sometimes with unfortunate consequences. On October 24th, 1904, *'Mr. Arthur Morgan strained the muscles of his thigh in a practice game of football during the mid-day interval and was obliged to return home'* and was absent for two weeks.

The school continued to be praised by the H.M.I. In 1902 he reported that *'Generally speaking the teaching is earnest and very successful and the boys are thoroughly well-trained in the matter of conduct in school'*, in 1903 that *'This school is ably directed, good methods are prevalent, the progress of the school most marked and the discipline is excellent'* and in 1904 that *'The syllabus has been carefully carried out, the teaching is generally successful and the discipline is excellent'*. At the end of 1904 the number on roll was 320 and the staff comprised A.J. Williams (C), C.T. England (C), Mary Rees (C), Arthur Morgan (U), Sarah Major (U) and J.A. Roberts (P.T.).

All three schools combined to collect £1-10-11$^1/_2$ for the N.S.P.C.C., £1-5-0 for Dr. Barnado's Waifs and Strays and 10/- for Cardiff Infirmary.

Religious conviction and sabbatarianism remained a cornerstone of family life. In 1902 Rev. Frank Williams was inducted as minister of the English Baptists and in October 1904 Ebenezer Chapel was opened at a cost of £2,150. In 1902 Rev. Henry Evans was replaced by Rev. Llewellyn Davies as curate of St. Peter's Church but he left in May 1903 as did the much respected and popular Rector Henry Morgan. Rev. D. Lloyd Rees succeeded as Rector of Eglwysilan parish and in March 1904 Rev. E.C. Davies assumed the curacy of St. Peter's Church. In December of 1903 Rev. D.B. Evans of Welshpool was inducted as minister of the English Congregational Chapel, one he combined with that of Llanbradach, his diaconate comprising W.T. Marshall, Henry Angell, C.T. England (Secretary) and A. Howells. The minister of Seion Welsh Wesleyan Methodist Chapel in 1903 was Rev. Harris. At Noddfa Welsh Congregational Chapel, ministered by Rev. James Jones, the membership was 240, Messrs. L. Thomas, W. Morse, L. Lewis, W. Edwards and C. Davies were added to the diaconate, and Messrs. William Evans, D.A. Jones, Dulais Jones and E. Perkins held various offices. Thriving also was Salem Welsh Chapel ministered by the popular Rev. David Roberts as were the Welsh Calvinistic Methodists. All places of worship boasted large congregations and thriving Sunday Schools.

Anniversary Services and the occasional chapel Cymanfa Ganu were paramount in the calendar. The frequent Sunday School tea parties and the annual excursion to Barry Island brought joy to the children and memorable was the *'Great Demonstration'* held on Eglwysilan Mountain on July 15th, 1904, which culminated in a picnic. The choir of St. Peter's Church embarked on an annual excursion. Social teas, bazaars such as one held by the English Congregationalists which raised £100, concerts, competitive meetings and lectures were organised to pay off the interest on loans and to meet the running costs such as the ministers' stipends.

The end of the Boer War in 1902 was a cause for celebration, the euphoria mirrored by Dan Lloyd when he wrote in the Log Book on June 2nd, *'WAR AT AN END. PEACE DECLARED, JUNE 1st. No school held. Holiday given. Thanksgiving hymns sung before the boys left'*. Later in the month the Coronation of King Edward VII was also greeted with patriotic fervour and a grant by the Caerphilly Council of £20 to the Aber Ward *'for reasonable expenses for celebration'*. Among those who had cause for celebration were the school pupils who were granted a week's holiday and presented by the School Board with a book entitled *'King Edward's Realm'*.

Celebration of national events was but one facet of the capacity for enjoyment which was a characteristic of life in the village, featured by the Miners' Federation Demonstration, the Chamber of Trade's excursion and dinner.

Any pretext was sufficient reason to warrant a social tea. One such function in 1904 was reported in the *'Glamorgan Free Press'* under the intriguing headline of *'Bachelor Girls at Senghenith'* with the following article: *'A benighted bachelor was recently parading the streets of the above township when he was confronted with a conspicuous poster headed* "A Bachelor Girls Social Tea". *Cognisant of the definition of the word* "bachelor" *and the anomaly it bore to the word* "girls" *he felt constrained to put in an appearance at Salem, Senghenith, on the 29th of March, so as to arrive at a solution of the would-be strategy, because it was here where the novel solution was to be witnessed and realised.*

But cold feet intervened and denied him this much-coveted privilege. However, he has elicited that those human prodigies (bachelor girls) transpired to be no more than ordinary everyday young (?) ladies whose ages ranged from 8 to 75 years. It is presumed that the discriminative appellation of 'Bachelor Girls' *was assumed through no other motive than to arouse the curiosity of mere men, thereby inducing their presence by a strategical exhibition of speculative and enterprising artifices. Oh! the whiles of women.*

The chapel was illuminated and decorated in excellent manner with mottoes such as "The Hand That Rocks the Cradle Rules the World" *and* "Men Build Houses, Women Make Homes." *Miss C. James and Mrs. M.E. Price acted in the capacity of President and Secretary respectively. All the ladies were dressed in pale blue and pink which contrasted very prettily with the foliage and sweet fragrant flowers. The leaders are to be heartily congratulated on the successful issue of this, the first leap-year social held at Senghenith, and it is sincerely hoped by the hundreds present who partook of the varied supply of the delicacies that this is not the last. It is rumoured that the Registrar of Marriages will be busily engaged during the coming months'.*

Still active were the Aber Valley United and Male Voice choirs. Great was the joy when the Male Voice Choir won the prize at Groeswen Eisteddfod in 1902 with the test piece *'Comrade in Arms'* and at the Rhymney Eisteddfod in 1904, but it was unsuccessful at the Caerphilly Castle Eisteddfods. In 1902 the Tabernacl Chapel choir conducted by Towyn Jones gave a highly acclaimed performance of the cantata *'David the Shepherd Boy'*. Among other *'Grand Concerts'* were three in 1903, one held on two successive nights at the Infants' School to raise funds for the purchase of a piano, a competitive one held at Noddfa Chapel and one which included *'guest artistes of brilliant talent'*.

An eisteddfod of modest proportions was organised by the English Congregationalists in 1902. Then in 1903 the village launched its most prestigious event, the first *'Chair Eisteddfod'* held in a marquee on the Park grounds. Special trains were organised and it attracted competitors and visitors from a wide area. It proved so successful that another was held on July 11th, 1904. Special trains were again organised and the schools were closed. The main prize was an oak chair offered for a poem in Welsh or English on the subject *'Hopes of Youth'*. For the Chief Choral competition, in which the test piece was Handel's *'Then Round About the Starry Throne'* the prize was £15 and a gold medal for the conductor. A prize of £15 and a silver-mounted baton for the conductor was offered to the successful Male Voice Choir, the test piece being Protheroe's *'The Crusaders'*. Prizes of £10, £5, £3 and £1 were awarded in the Brass Band contest. The highly successful eisteddfod was followed in the evening by a miscellaneous concert when *'the marquee was lit by electricity through the good offices of the Manager of the Windsor Colliery'*. organised by Ithel Thomas, (Chairman), Thomas Nicholas (secretary) and Towyn Jones (Treasurer) the proceeds were donated *'in aid of building a cottage hospital in the district'*.

Welcome were Mr. Ebley's theatrical shows, the arrival of John Scullett's Show and the occasional circus which in April 1904 was greeted with such enthusiasm by the children that the high level of absenteeism caused the schools to be closed.

In the realm of sporting pastimes there was a keen interest in pigeon fancying and racing. Cricket and football were popular. But pride of place was accorded to rugby which attracted a great following. Two teams competed in the Cardiff & District Union, the 1st team captained by Will Davies in 1901/2, Tom Lewis in 1902/3, Tom Gould in 1903/4 and Jack Bryant in 1904/5. Among the players were T. Burrell, J. Dallimore, D. Davies, J. George, J. Griffiths, D. Gwynn, J. Heaton, D. Hurley, H. Hyatt, W. James, D. Jenkins, D. Jones, E. Jones, E. Lee, W. Meredith, T. Morgan, G. Olsen, T. Parker, T. Prosser, T. Sellers, J. Smith, E.G. Thorne, J.Walters, T. Williams, F. Yendle. There were also two other teams - the *'Senghenydd Scarlets'* and the *'Senghenydd Lilies'* captained by D. Thomas. But although this was a community basically strong in religious conviction and observance, one in which the primary bond was the family, the secondary bond that of civic pride and responsibility exemplified by a host of social, cultural and sporting organisations, yet there was a far less attractive facet to the quality of life.

Work in the dusty, gassy colliery was physically demanding and unrelenting. Still vivid was the memory of the 1901 explosion and ever-present was the prospect of an accident. Wages were barely above subsistence level and demanding thrifty house-keeping. Accommodation was often sordid. Infant mortality was high and life-threatening epidemics were frequent. An increasing proportion of the population was of a transient nature, some of it undesirable. All these factors combined to create a turbulent anti-social element. Relief from the harsh working conditions and the often unsavoury living conditions was sought *'in the cup that cheers'* and the camaraderie afforded by the hotels and Clubs. Not only was drunkenness a major problem but a sub-culture of violence was prevalent, a situation common throughout the South Wales coalfield and in industrial areas in the country at large.

The licence of the Universal Hotel was transferred to William Thomas in 1902 and the Leigh Hotel was finally granted a licence in 1905 despite the opposition of the police and the Temperance movement. The Parc Hotel was still denied a licence but a court case in 1903 in which two travelling showmen were charged with stealing two casks of beer from landlord Lodwig John and another case in 1904 in which *'Benjamin Corfield, a barman at the Parc Hotel, appeared as a witness against William Green, his fellow barman, who was accused of privately selling the pub's beer'* demonstrated that the law was being flouted. Illegal also was the supply of beer and spirits at the Workmen's Social Club stewarded by William Blagden. Then on February 24th, 1904, the Senghenith Conservative Club, under the presidency of Colonel Morgan Lindsay, was opened by Colonel Williams-Quinn, M.P for South Glamorgan with a membership of 150.

Drunkenness was rampant among men and so frequent was their appearance at the weekly Caerphilly Court charged with drunken and disorderly conduct that the press report was headed *'Senghenydd Usuals'*. Nor uncommon were reports such as *'Woman Drunk in Charge of a Child'*, *'Mother an Habitual Drunkard'* and a case in which a widow was sentenced to two weeks gaol on the charges of being drunk and disorderly and assaulting a policeman. No day seemed to pass without a report of a domestic assault, a street fight, a street brawl, and wounding or an attack on the police. A collier was charged with unlawfully wounding a neighbouring widow over the alleged theft of an ash bin. *'Fracas at Senghenydd'* headlined the case of a drunken collier jailed for fourteen days with hard labour for an assault on P.C. Bevan with such violence that it required the assistance of Sgt. Williams and another Sergeant to take him to the Police Station. In the evidence it was stated that the fracas occurred in a very rough rough quarter of the village and only one man in the crowd offered to help the constable. Another report

Senghenydd Conservative Club.

headed *'Street Fight in Senghenydd'* was of a fight in Caerphilly Road between two drunken men who then both attacked and seriously injured a bystander who went to see the cause of the disturbance. *'Cellar Man Assaulted'* reported the case of a miner charged with assault and battery on the cellar man of the Universal Hotel following an accusation of cheating at *'tossing the coin'* in the Hotel. Benjamin Corfield was gaoled for a month for *'creating mayhem'* at the home of a widow.

With other headlines such *'Five Colliers Assault Police'*, *'Man Dragged from his Home and Assaulted'*, *'Assault on Barman at Gwernymilwr Hotel'*, *'A Dangerous Neighbour in Senghenydd'*, *'Unlawful Wounding'* and *'Shocking Story from Senghenydd'*, the seriousness of the situation was reflected by a Chairman of the Caerphilly Bench when he expressed his sympathy with Sergeant Leyshon Williams and his constables carrying out their duties *'in such districts as Senghenydd'*.

In addition to deep concern about such criminality not all forms of sport met with general approval. Frowned upon was the *'noble art of boxing'* practised at the booth promoted by Mr. Stokes. Condemned was the enthusiastic following for rabbit coursing at Caerphilly as *'detrimental to the moral, social and religious life of society'* in its barbaric cruelty. But many miners were undeterred in rearing dogs for this purpose. In March 1902 a match was reported between *'Kruger'* a Senghenydd dog and *'Flo'* a Crumlin dog for a stake of £40 in which the latter won by 11 to 7 rabbits after 12 courses, and in

1903 a collier was charged with causing unnecessary suffering to a rabbit in a match.

The unsavoury nature of both boxing and rabbit-coursing was not the only reason for their being castigated. Equally criticised was the gambling which accompanied both, a practice regarded as sinful and feckless. Apart from the stakes and wagers laid on these matches, there were other forms of betting such as that on horse-racing via the illegal *'bookie's runner'*, gambling on *'tossing the coin'* and card games such as *'banker'*, also illegal in public places but actively pursued by various strategies to evade the arms of the law.

To the mass of villagers the incidence of boxing, support for rabbit coursing and all forms of gambling were another indication of a sordid malaise in the community.

In 1904 a new Police Station was opened in Station Road to serve the Aber Valley. It comprised a charge room with two cells, three bedrooms, a men's bedroom for the constables, a kitchen, parlour, pantry and wash house.

Such was Senghenydd in 1904. Booming and volatile, the tenour of community life presenting a confused picture of great endeavour based on moral principles but deeply troubled by social problems, it was fertile ground for the religious revival movement inspired by Evan Roberts which was sweeping through South Wales bringing a message of comfort, joy and hope with the reassurance of His abiding love both in this world and the next to all who accepted the Way of the Lord.

The first revivalist meeting was held on November 8th, and on Sunday, November 13th, Mr. Rowland Corbett, District Evangelist, started a mission at the Wesleyan Methodist Chapel. His nightly meetings increased in power and influence, culminating on the Saturday evening of November 19th. The session began at 8 o'clock with prayer meetings. Then at 10.30 a band of about forty workers turned out into the streets for an open-air demonstration before returning to the vestry where services were continued until midnight. On Sunday morning the services were resumed at 6 o'clock and a series of indoor and outdoor meetings were held until 9 o'clock at night.

Prayer meetings were also being held in other chapels and during the ensuing weeks the *'fire'* of the movement continued unabated so that *'several well-known characters were arrested by the Spirit's powers and have heartily thrown themselves into the work of the Revival'*. Many conversions were made, some were *'backsliders'* who returned to the fold but most were *'seeing the light'* for the first time. Particularly significant was the number of young people who embraced the faith.

Then, after visiting Caerphilly for two days, Evan Roberts, the *'Messiah'*, came to Senghenydd on Wednesday, December 7th, accompanied by evangelists Amy Rees and Mr. M. Taggart and singers Mary Davies and Anne Davies. Captivating the emotional feeling of young and old it was a visit hailed with joy. Less than half the pupils attended school that day. From near and far they also came, including a Welsh Member of Parliament and ministers from Portsmouth, Norwich, Radnorshire and Monmouthshire. On one train from Caerphilly the passengers in a compartment held a prayer meeting and soon *'from all compartments there echoed the strains of revival hymns until the valley resounded with divine melody'*.

By half past one, long before the arrival of Evan Roberts, Tabernacl Chapel was crowded to capacity and so great was the waiting congregation that an overflow meeting was organised at Salem Chapel.

At Tabernacl, the service first conducted by local ministers amid an outflow of prayers and hymns, the congregation was aroused by a young lady who rose from the gallery with the heartfelt words, *'I hope my brother is in this congregation. Will you pray for him?'*. Several prayers were offered in response to her plea. Ten minutes or so later a shout was raised from the far end of the gallery - it was her brother announcing his conversion. A mighty cry of *'Diolch Iddo'* arose from the congregation, which then burst into song with the hymn *'Songs of Praise I will ever give to Thee'*. Then an expectant hush fell upon the assembled multitude as Miss Rees of Gorseinon walked slowly to the pulpit. *'Are you here to see Jesus Christ or to see Evan Roberts?'* was her opening challenge. Then she proceeded to describe the extraordinary scenes at Tonyfelin chapel in Caerphilly on the preceding night. Up stood an elderly man to declare his conversion, followed by some young ladies from the village who volunteered solos, joined in chorus by the congregation in a crescendo of sound. Miss Rees pleaded and prayed with the waverers to confess their sins, and amid some pathetic scenes, men, women and children responded with readiness when the time came for public confession. Rev. Tawelfryn Thomas took the rostrum and enrolled about twenty-one converts.

Meanwhile, Evan Roberts, accompanied by the two singers and Mr. M. Taggart, had gone to address the overflow meeting. *'For a time the meeting was decidedly cold, so cold indeed as to affect the young revivalist with deep emotion. He prayed and asked others to pray for a downpour of the Spirit, and presently there was a warmer feeling and the response to the invitation to confess was numerous'*. Many stood up from the gallery. One young man spoke of his own conversion, that of his father and a pugilist friend and appealed to the young men not to waste their time in idle pursuits. The congregation responded in great earnestness by singing the hymn *'Throw Out the Life Line'*.

In the evening Evan Roberts and his singers were joined by local ministers at Tabernacl before a packed congregation in a memorable gathering. The service was conducted in a highly-charged emotional atmosphere occasionally bordering on hysteria, punctuated with prayers, Sankey and Moody hymns and solos, all accompanied by shouts of *'Diolch Iddo'*, *'Bendigedig'*, *'Allelujah'* and *'Dyma Gariad'* from the congregation. When called upon to repent, many men and women made open confession and amid an aura of exultation sought forgiveness and salvation with the plea of *'Maddeu I Mi Nawr'* (*'Forgive Me Now'*).

So the visit of Evan Roberts came to a glorious end. But the impetus of the Revival continued long after his departure. On Boxing Day thousands of men, women and children paraded the streets singing hymns. By the end of December the Harvest of converts numbered 186 - 70 English Wesleyan Methodists, 44 Welsh Congregationalists, 33 Welsh Calvinistic Methodists, 15 Welsh Baptists, 14 English Baptists, 6 Welsh Wesleyan Methodists and 4 English Congregationalists. All were Nonconformists, both the Church of England and the Roman Catholic Church standing aloof.

Significant as was this statistic it does not reflect adequately the profound effect emanating from the Revival. Apart from the converts it strengthened the belief of those already committed, permeated family life and many facets of community life. Chapel membership and attendance soared. Services, prayer meetings and hymn-singing sessions were not confined to the chapels but conducted in the streets and elsewhere. At the colliery, prayer meetings were held at the pit head and even at the coal face, with absenteeism and bad language sharply reduced. Manager Edward Shaw told how at Christmas time many of the worst characters had asked for *'subs'* which formerly would have been spent on drink but now to be used for buying presents for the children or to buy clothes for them to go to Sunday School. Young men vowed never to take part in idle pursuits and so many renounced the game of rugby as wicked and sinful that the Club was forced to disband, not to be fully restored for some years. Such was the decline in drunkenness and criminal offences that the press was able to report. *'Matters are very quiet at the Caerphilly Police Court. There is no doubt that the Revival meetings in Senghenydd and the district have to a great extent lessened the charge sheet'.*

In the words of the *'Cardiff Times'*, the Revival had brought a remarkable spiritual awakening to the village, uplifting the moral and social ethos of the family and community.

CHAPTER 6

In 1905 Sir William Lewis bought out the existing owners of the colliery and amalgamated it into the main Company, the Lewis Merthyr Consolidated Collieries Company Limited, but this had no effect on the management. The colliery prospered and by 1906 the work force numbered 1,207, of which 1,002 worked underground.

With the coal trade prospering in general throughout the coalfield so a new agreement was reached between the South Wales Federation and the coalowners by which the wages were increased marginally. But this was no more than a truce as Maboniam was being undermined by the growing strength of the Independent Labour party with its evangelical crusading spirit and chapel-style Nonconformist ethos. Led by young militants it was determined to achieve fundamental changes in the industrial, economic, social and political processes.

On the national scale the Trade Unions were strengthened immeasurably by two Acts of Parliament in 1906. The Workmen's Compensation Act embraced all workers for the first time and covered industrial diseases as well as injuries, enacting a payment of 50% of the average weekly wage for partial capacity and a sum not exceeding £300 for death. The Trades Union Act reversed the Taff Vale Judgement by enacting that a Trade Union was not liable for a wrongful act committed by one of its agents or for losses sustained by employers in consequence of a strike. It also enacted that peaceful picketing was legal.

All the while the campaign waged by the Federation to attain a *'closed shop'* grew in intensity and bitterness. At the colliery, with the Lodge fully committed to the message *'Unity is Strength'* proclaimed the annual Demonstration, so there was increasing rancour not only in its relationship with the Colliery Agent but also with the non-Unionists who were brought under increasing pressure to join by threats of strike action and other measures.

With the village still denied separate representation on the District Council so the Chamber of Trade, supported by Councillors Edmund Evans, Miners Agent Hubert Jenkins and Colliery Agent Robert Rees, continued to press for action in respect of overcrowding, the water supply, scavenging, the road surfaces, street lighting and other issues.

To cater for the increasing population plans were approved for 25 houses in 1905 and for 89 houses in 1906, of which 68 were submitted by the Colliery Company and 20 by the Gwernymilwr Club. Even so, overcrowding remained a problem with that at Stanley Street still the most intractable despite the many previous proceedings taken against the owners. An inspection of one house in the street revealed the cellar kitchen occupied by a family composed of a husband, wife and six children who slept in an adjoining room which was damp, badly lit and ventilated, the upper part of the house occupied by three families, a husband, wife and child, a husband, wife and child, a husband, wife and four children, the sleeping arrangements not easily apparent. Once again proceedings were taken for the immediate cessation of the cellar dwelling occupation, and subsequently similar proceedings were instituted in respect of two other houses and five cellar dwellings in the street. Two underground rooms in Commercial Street were also subjected to the same occupancy restrictions.

In response to criticism that the water supply was often inadequate sometimes of poor quality and occasionally shut off without prior warning, the Council responded by making representations to the Rhymney Water Company, threatening proceedings against the Gwernymilwr Estate in respect of its reservoir, sending samples of water for analysis and in one instance distributing leaflets stating that the water should be boiled before drinking. It also issued Notices on the owners of 72 houses to provide a sufficient supply of water for the adequate flushing of the closets. Nevertheless, the complaints continued.

Attention was also devoted to household drainage and the system of scavenging. Notices were served on the owners of 81 houses in that the closet and slop water drains were deficient or defective. The scavenger, contracted at a salary of £95 per annum plus £1 for each cesspool, came under constant criticism because of the accumulation of mud and filth in the back lanes, rubbish in the brook and the insanitary state of the field behind the Parc Hotel where he had deposited household rubbish close to houses. Proceedings were taken against six villagers to abate the nuisances caused by keeping pigs in styes which were without proper drainage and a Notice was served on the proprietors of a travelling show to abate the nuisances caused by the lack of a public urinal. Welcomed was the erection of a two-stall public urinal on a site secured from the Colliery Company.

Such efforts to promote improved living conditions and a more healthy environment may explain in part the absence of smallpox cases, scarlet fever and diphtheria epidemics during these two years. But the picture was marred by an extremely virulent epidemic of measles from September to December in 1905 which claimed seven deaths, the victims all of school age and necessitated the closure of the schools for three weeks, the extent of the epidemic due in no small measure to the failure of parents to control the movement of their children suffering from the disease.

Faced with the inevitable confrontation with the property owners over responsibility for the road, the Council took over Private Street Works on Station Road and Station Terrace, the cost charged to the property owners, and resolved to carry out similar work on Parc Terrace, Grove Terrace and Lower Commercial Street. In respect of the inadequate street lighting, the prospect of replacing the oil lamps by electric lamps seemed to come a step nearer when the Council made a draft agreement with the South Wales

Power Company to cover the District. In the meantime, Police Sergeant Leyshon Williams continued to present a monthly report.

The agitation to supply the police with fire-fighting equipment came to a successful conclusion when eight fire hydrants and other appliances were delivered and a storage shed was erected near the Police Station. Sergeant Williams was appointed to hold a watching brief over the equipment at a remuneration of £3 per annum together with two constables each paid £1.

There were over 900 children of school age, each school with more than 300 on roll and encountering varying problems relative to overcrowding and staffing. A major change in the curriculum was the introduction for the first time of the systematic teaching of Welsh.

In 1905 Miss Catherine James was faced with daunting difficulties of gross overcrowding, staff changes and a staff which was weak in qualifications and insufficient. Also, one classroom was out of commission for three months due to a *'stench'* coming from beneath the floorboards so that classes had to be taken in the yard or cloakroom, and in the winter months the heating was often inadequate so that *'a great deal of physical exercise has to be taken to keep the children warm'. 'The school is so overcrowded that it is very difficult for the teachers to secure due attention and a heavy strain is imposed on their energies. The Mistress and staff do their work in a cheerful spirit. The staff is weak and two additional teachers should be engaged'*, commented the H.M.I. but no such teachers were appointed.

The situation became even more fraught in 1906, evident in Log Book entries such as *'School is often overcrowded with two classes crowded into one room, so discipline suffers', 'The staff is insufficient, making it impossible to follow the Time Table in the 1st Class with 80 on books and the 2nd Class with 85 on books', 'The 3rd Class is very large with 104 on books, average over 90, making it very difficult for the Uncertificated Teacher who has no one to help her', 'All classes are very large and are a great strain on the teachers'.*

At the end of 1906 Miss James's staff comprised Miriam Rowland (C), Mabel Ann (C), Mary Gay (U), Hetty Davies (U), Mary Jane Lewis (F.T.), Blodwen Thomas (F.T.) and Edith Jones (P.T.). It says much for the dedication of the Mistress and teachers that she was able to report that *'General Progress has been made'*, and that prior to the Christmas Vacation that there were three Christmas trees in the school, the classrooms decorated with crayon mottoes in straw frames with concerts held and gifts distributed on the closing day.

The Girls' and Boys' Schools shared the common problem of overcrowding, the lack of artificial lighting and the occasional shortage of coal for heating. Innovative was the prescribed Welsh syllabus and greater significance was attached to St. David's Day. Greater importance was attached to *'School Hygiene'* in view of the prevailing skin diseases such as scabies. Empire Day was celebrated on May 26th, 1906, when *'Lessons were given on the formation of the Empire and patriotic songs were sung'* at the Girls' School, and at the Boys' School *'Special lessons were given, followed by an assembly when, after the boys had saluted the Union Jack and given three hearty cheers for the King, they sang patriotic songs'.*

At the Girls' School the staff remained stable in 1905 and in July the H.M.I. reported, *'There is ample evidence of unremitting and intelligent application to duties on the part of the Mistress and staff with lessons carefully prepared'*, and steady progress was made. But in 1906 Mistress Dinah Evans was granted leave of absence from the beginning of the year *'To recruit her health'*, and until her return in May Miss Ethel Rundle was placed in charge. Also, throughout the year the problem of overcrowding was exacerbated by frequent staff changes. However a huge success was a tea and concert held at a neighbouring chapel in October to raise money for the final payment on the school piano and from the proceeds not only was it made but some library books were purchased.

The staff under Miss Evans at the end of 1906 comprised Ethel Rundle (C), Catherine Williams (C), Winifred Thornley (C), Maggie Bowen (U), Agnes Jones (U), Sarah Lloyd (U), Maggie Thomas (P.T.) and Catherine James (P.T.)

At the Boys' School there was overcrowding but it was not excessive and the staff remained reasonably stable. When there was an occasional shortage of coal, Dan Lloyd invariably found the solution, typified by the Log Book entry on November 10th, 1905, *'No fires lit. A few boys got eight buckets of large coal from home and soon fires were in the grate'*.

'Temperance Instruction' was included in the curriculum, the Master gave lessons to the senior pupils on the Metric System and Decimal Coinage, taught them to sing in three parts a Chorus from Schuman's *'Faust'*, and on August 30th, 1905, *'The classes received a special lesson on* "The Eclipse of the Sun", *the boys coming with coloured glasses and saw the eclipse'*. Although two boys were committed to the Truant School the attendance continued to be of a very high order, encouraged by the presentation of *'Award Cards'* and lectures illustrated by lantern slides as rewards to pupils achieving specific targets. The Master kept a stern eye on *'troublesome'* late comers, noting that *'The mothers in most cases do not get up in time to send them'*, and also conducted periodical cleanliness inspections *'some parents sending their children not as clean as they should'*.

David John Evans (age 12) and William John Owen (age 13) won County Probationer Scholarships, five pupils passed the Proficiency (Labour) Examination, a subscription was sent to Cardiff Infirmary, and there was much delight when the newly-formed rugby team defeated Caerphilly Boys' School.

The H.M.I. Reported in July 1905 that *'This Department continues to maintain its character for thorough efficiency and sound discipline'*, a judgement which no doubt would have been endorsed in 1906 when the staff comprised C.T. England (C), A.J. Williams (C), Miss Mary Rees (C), Miss Matilda James (C), J.A. Roberts (U) and Harry Bowden (P.T.)

The religious fervour generated by the visit of Evan Roberts continued undiminished into 1905 so that by the end of January the *'Harvest'* of converts had increased to 437 and to 526 by the end of February. This deepening sense of commitment was reflected throughout the year and into

1906 by increasing congregations at all places of worship - Noddfa Welsh Congregational Chapel ministered by Rev. James Jones, Salem Welsh Baptist Chapel ministered by Rev. David Roberts, Tabernacl Welsh Calvinistic Methodist Chapel, Ebenezer English Baptist Chapel ministered by Rev. F. Williams, the English Congregational Chapel ministered by Rev. D.B. Evans, Seion Welsh Wesleyan Methodist Chapel, the English Wesleyan Methodist Chapel and St. Peter's Church which under the curacy of Rev. Gwilym Rees boasted 74 choristers, a Sunday School of over 200, a Church Lads' Brigade and a Bugle Band by 1906. All were fully engaged in the usual round of organising concerts, social teas, bazaars, Sunday School teas and treats and the annual outing to Barry Island or another resort.

Such was the pervading moral ethos and strength of the Temperance movement in the early months of 1905 that the level of drunkenness and crime was relatively low. But this proved only a temporary phase because by the mid year, and increasingly thereafter, the hotels and Clubs Social plied a roaring trade again. The Social Democratic Club in Station Terrace was *'struck off'* for a year, charged with the illegal sale of beer and having no proper register of members, only for the premises next door to be opened as the Workmen's Constitutional Club, registering as a *'bona fide'* Social Club. So, once again a violent atmosphere prevailed around the hotels, Clubs and streets. Typical were these cases at the Magistrates Court in 1906: January - John Booth and John Jones fighting in Commercial Street; March - Harry Bowen and Richard Morgan, stripped to the waist, fighting in Stanley Street, watched by a large crowd; May - J. Mead and J. Reed, fighting in Commercial Street; July - James Smith and William Osmont fighting in High Street; September - John Jones and John Gough in Commercial Street; October - Thomas Donaghue and William Jones fighting in Commercial Street. Such fights were all too common as were brawls, assaults, attacks on the police, more serious crimes of wounding and domestic incidents, much of it attributable to an aggressive, anti-social element in the population which was transient.

The Aber Valley Mixed Choir, conducted by Tom Williams of Abertridwr, won 2nd Prize at Bargoed Eisteddfod and 3rd Prize at Caerphilly. The Senghenydd and Aber Valley Male Voice Choir, conducted by Harry Phillips, competed at Caerphilly, Abertyswg and Rhiwderin, albeit unsuccessfully. The precocious talent of twelve-year-old David John Evans was demonstrated in 1906 at a United Cymanfa Ganu at Caerphilly where he accompanied on the organ a hymn tune which he had composed. Edward Ebley continued to offer *'theatrical'* entertainment at his portable Olympic Theatre, and others who were granted short-term licences for portable theatres were Walter Haggar and Reuben Allworth. Welcome was the annual visit of John Scullett's Show as were the visits of a circus on two occasions in 1906.

Still affected by the aftermath of the Religious Revival only a few friendly rugby games were played under the captaincy of Jack Bryant in the 1904/5 season. A few more games were played in the 1905/06 season under the captaincy of Will Jones, but it was not until the 1906/07 season that the playing strength was sufficiently restored to re-form the Club.

Cricket was unaffected, the combined Senghenydd and Abertridwr Club continuing to play matches at Eglwysilan, unbeaten by August 1905 when it played against *'Riverside'* at Cardiff Arms Park. Among the players on that occasion were D. Davies, E. Eligman, F. Gingell, M. Peregrine, D. Thomas, D.R. Thomas, S. Worman, D. Watkins and M. Watkins. Other team members during the 1905 and 1906 seasons included H. Bennett, J. Davies, Hillman, L. Jarman, F. Lewis, Meredith, T. Nicholas, B. Price, G. Rees and B. Walters.

With industrial peace in the coalfield and the colliery having been further developed so the village enjoyed comparative prosperity. This was reflected in Kelly's Directory of 1906. Listed in Commercial Street were the Universal Hotel (Edward Evans), Leigh Hotel (Obadiah Meredith), Gwernymilwr Hotel (David Lewis), Lloyd's Bank and London & Provincial Bank, both open on Tuesday, the surgery of Dr. James, M.R.C.S., L.R.C.P., chemist George Starkey and the Post Office (Miss Jane E. Bussell). Here too were shopkeepers William Bryant, Philip Cooper, Richard Davies, George Gingell, William T. Marshall, Mrs. Edith Parker, Thomas Picton, Mrs. Susannah Rowlands, the Senghenith Industrial Cooperative Society Ltd., Thomas R. Thomas, Thomas Wynne; grocer and confectioner Frederick Williams; grocers and tea dealers Thomas E. Evans, William T. Jones, Howell Lewis, Alfred E. Taylor, Rees Williams; grocer and earthenware dealer David Jones & Son.; grocers Mrs. Louisa Jones, John Ithel Thomas; confectioner Harry Angell; ice-cream makers Bracchi Bros.; butchers Eastman's Ltd., Joseph Edwards, John Gould, Mrs. Winifred Lewis, Thomas Watts, Enos Williams, Thomas Williams; fried fish dealers Mrs. Maud Corfield, William Jones, Frank Ostler; greengrocers John Bailey, Edward Evans, Eli Howells; boot-makers Peter Halewood, Towyn Jones, Herbert Williams; boot and shoe maker Frank Yendle, shoemaker Edward Thomas; boot and shoe dealers Bristol Boot Co., Cash & Co.; outfitters Charles Isaac, Jones & Co.; drapers Thomas Davies, John Dixon, John Morgan, Samuel & Thomas; tailor David Dulais Jones; milliner George Davies; newsagents Miss Jane Bussell, David Williams; the Universal Furnishing Co. managed by Albert Fine ironmonger Charles Allen; hardware dealer Philip Richards; china and glass dealer Mrs. Elizabeth A. Pool; pawnbroker and outfitter Abraham Shibko; hairdresser and tobacconist William Lewis, hairdressers Griffith Jones, Peter Stephens; painter and decorator George King.

Along High Street were grocer Evans & Sons, greengrocer John Evans, butcher Mrs. Elizabeth Tyler, wine and spirit merchant David Lewis. Elsewhere were shopkeeper Robert Clarke in Parc Terrace, shopkeeper William Davies in Grove Terrace, baker and shopkeeper Mrs. Martha Snailham in Station Road, plumber and gas fitter Frank Slogett in Stanley Street, quarry owners and builders E.Williams & Sons, carpenter, builder and undertaker Joseph Price Williams.

Less than half the above-named proprietors were in business in 1901 indicating a high rate of *'turn over'* in the preceding years.

CHAPTER 7

During the period from 1907 to 1910 the work force at the colliery continued to increase and by 1908 was 1,600. Correspondingly, the population approached 5,000 by 1910, the majority still drawn in the main from the local areas and Glamorgan, much of it of a transient nature. But all was not well in the coalfield or in the colliery as the relationship between the owners and the work forces deteriorated even further. These were troubled times.

Re-echoed was the South Wales Federation's clarion call of *'Unity Is Strength'* and for a *'closed shop'* as the Lodge members and their families marched each year to a mass rally, headed by a brass band and with banner flying. It was a message which the Lodge pursued relentlessly under the leadership of Miners' Agent Councillor Hubert Jenkins, now a member of the Executive Council of the Federation. Generally the tactic of threatening strike action was sufficient to persuade non-Unionists of the error of their ways. The only exception occurred in 1908 when a strike was called on June 1st. Two days later, having been issued with summonses for breach of contract, over 300 miners, led by Hubert Jenkins, marched in protest to Caerphilly, calling en route on non-Unionists. On the day of the hearing they again descended en masse on the Magistrates Court when the bench, as expected, imposed a fine on every striker. This defiant action, coupled no doubt by a level of intimidation, proved successful in its aim, because work was resumed on June 14th, the Lodge Secretary having reported almost total affiliation to the Union.

Great jubilation was expressed by the South Wales miners in 1908 when its Federation was affiliated to that of Great Britain and when the Coal Mines Regulation Act established an eight-hour working day which came into force in December. Up lifted by this added strength they envisaged greater success in their struggle against the owners.

But they were soon disillusioned in 1909. With productivity in the coalfield in decline it was reduced still further by the operation of the Act. In order to maintain production the owners had to increase the work force, so adding to the cost. To recoup the potential loss in profit their Association retaliated by demanding a reduction in wages, the acceptance of a double-shift system and other concessions. A protracted and bitter struggle ensued with the Federation demanding a minimum wage as already the value of the wages did not match the increase in the cost of living. A mood of unrest pervaded the entire coalfield with threats of strikes countered by those of lock-outs. Nor was the situation improved by the *'Osborne Judgement'* which limited the powers of Unions to engage in political, educational or municipal affairs.

At the Universal Lodge a series of mass meetings declared its wrath not only in support of a minimum wage but in protest against the operation of the double-shift system, the rates of pay for working in abnormal places and payment for small coal.

The tempo of strife increased in bitterness in 1910 when the work force at a Penygraig colliery refused to accept the price list of 1/9d per ton of coal demanded by the owner of the Cambrian Combine in that it would not provide a living wage. On September 1st the owner declared a lock-out at the colliery and by November the entire Combine's work force of 30,000 in the Rhondda came out on strike, joined in support by miners in the Cynon Valley. The result was an industrial battlefield, leading first to sporadic disturbances, escalating to the *'Tonypandy Riots'* involving hand-to-hand battles against hundreds of policemen drawn from the Glamorgan and Metropolitan forces in which one miner was killed. Subsequently some infantry brigades and detachments of cavalry were drafted in so that the Rhondda Valley and some neighbouring villages came under a degree of military occupation. This was the position at the end of the year, the coalfield remaining in a volatile state, in a mood of tension, unrest and conflict.

The Universal Lodge was not directly or indirectly involved in this struggle but as elsewhere in the coalfield it shared the anger felt at the outrageous treatment afforded to their comrades and families. It also had immediate causes for bitter concern. For four days in October the entire work force had been withdrawn to allow the disposal of a heavy discharge of gas resulting from a rock fall in the Mefeking Level. Also four miners had been killed that year bringing the number of fatalities to fourteen since 1907.

This had not been a happy period in industrial relations and the state of unrest had its repercussions in the political field, both nationally and locally, with the increasingly militant miners seeking to improve their working, economic and social conditions via socialism, the ballot box and legislation. The affiliation of the Miners' Federation of Great Britain to the Independent Labour Party in 1909 was a demonstration of such an intent. Nevertheless, the I.L.P. struggled to make a definitive impact on the national ballet box against the entrenched traditional support for the Liberal cause despite misgivings as to its effectiveness in support of mining communities.

In Senghenydd, as elsewhere, Parliamentary Elections were fought with passion, accompanied by intensive canvassing and mass meetings. Particularly memorable were those of 1910. At the General Election in January, Sir Alfred Thomas (Liberal) was re-elected, defeating F.H. Gaskell (Unionist) by 14,721 to 5,727 votes. Subsequently, he was elected to the peerage and the House of Lords with the title of Lord Pontypridd. At the resulting By-Election for the East Glamorgan constituency in December the candidates were Clement Edwards (Liberal), F.H. Gaskell (Unionist) and C.B. Stanton (Labour), a miners' leader from Aberdare. Apparently Mr. Gaskell received a scant welcome in Senghenydd. It was reported that he was addressing a small crowd one Saturday evening on the square when *'towards the end of his speech an itinerant auctioneer set up his boxes and began to sell his wares. He was prevailed upon to postpone his auction but the meeting came to an end when a band appeared on the scene and began playing.'* The result was: Edwards 9,088; Gaskell 5,063; Stanton 4,482. To what extent the Universal miners voted for Stanton is not recorded, but this By-Election was a landmark in that for the first time in this constituency a Labour candidate had challenged the Liberal hegemony.

County Council and Urban District Council elections were conducted with equal vigour, and there was great satisfaction when Hubert Jenkins, standing as a Labour candidate, was elected to the Glamorgan County Council as the member for the Aber Valley in 1907.

Renewed efforts were made by the Caerphilly Council, the Chamber of Trade and other organisations in the campaign for separate Wards for Abertridwr and Senghenydd, and late in 1909 the County Council recommended such a provision with each Ward to be represented by three members. In January 1910 the Caerphilly Council resolved to recommend to support this proposal but it was rescinded in February over the question of boundaries. As a result the County Council decided to hold a local Inquiry and the year passed without any change.

The members representing the Aber Ward also remained unchanged Colliery Agent Robert T. Rees (Independent) who lived in Aberdare and was Chairman for the year 1908/9, Hubert Jenkins (Labour) of Abertridwr who was Vice-Chairman for the year 1910/1911 and Valentine Williams (Labour) of Abertridwr, a foreman blacksmith at the Windsor Colliery and nominated by the Lodge. Significant was an election in 1908 when Thomas James (Labour), nominated by the Senghenydd Lodge, opposed Robert T. Rees. Although he was unsuccessful this was the first time the representative of the colliery management and ownership had been challenged.

Between 1907 and 1910 the Council approved plans for a further 78 houses, including 37 for the Universal Building Society, 20 for the Universal Colliery Company and 16 for the Senghenydd Building Club. Phillips Terrace, Woodland Terrace, Graig Terrace and Brynhyfryd were built and more houses in Cenydd Terrace to accommodate the increased population. There was still a measure of overcrowding but only Stanley Street caused serious concern.

Pathways were often unmade but welcomed were the Private Street Works undertaken at Kingsley Place, Parc Terrace, Grove Terrace, Cross Street, High Street, Stanley Street and parts of Caerphilly Road and Cenydd Terrace. Even so, with the surface composed of compressed limestone chippings, the roads were dusty and easily rutted, and a common sight was that of a worker, contracted at 1/- an hour, watering them from a water cart. It was not until 1910 that a steam roller was made available for new streets taken over by the Council. Promise of a further improvement came in the same year when for the first time an estimate was sought for tar-spraying the main road from the Universal Hotel to Tabernacl Chapel.

Up to 1910 there was no change in the street lighting. Many more oil lamps were installed as was a 1,000 candle power Kitson Lamp on the square but the complaints of inadequacy continued. In the meanwhile the Council had been engaged in negotiations with the South Wales Power Company for a supply of electricity to the Aber Ward and in October 1909 it was granted permission to erect overhead wires. At the same time negotiations had been opened with the Rhymney and Aber Valleys Gas & Water Company for a gas supply and in August 1909 it had been granted permission to lay gas mains. By the end of November both Companies had completed the work and the Council resolved that the oil lamp pillars be taken down in both Abertridwr and Senghenydd. But at the end of the year it had not decided which supply to favour.

It was on February 23rd, 1910, that the Council resolved that the streets be lit by electricity. A formal agreement with the Power Company was signed at the end of May and work began on the installation of lamps from Thomas Street in Abertridwr to the Universal Hotel in August. Great was the joy when by early September the lamps had been installed at Commercial Street and the Square with the Company's promise of a supply to the side streets *'as and when the poles would be erected'*. On October 18th the Surveyor reported that the lighting consisted of 9 electric lamps and 50 oil lamps. Thereafter, the Company's assurances to give early consideration to the side streets did not materialise and bitter were the complaints at the lack of progress when no additional lamps were installed by the end of the year.

Reassuring was the Council's commitment to update the supply of fire-fighting to the Fire Station and its commendation of Sergeant Richard Walters and other police officers in dealing with a fire at the Cooperative Stores in March 1908.

Far from reassuring was the provision of an adequate and good quality water supply, the subject of continual petitions and complaints against the Rhymney and Gwernymilwr Water Companies.

Complaints against the Rhymney Company, the main supplier, included the supply being cut off without notice, an incident in Station Terrace when parts of a decomposed frog were found in the drinking water and occasions in June 1910 when the supply to some houses in lower High Street was limited to an hour a day. The Council made representations but no proceedings were taken in view of the Company's satisfactory response.

Far different was the Council's approach to the Gwenymilwr Company which over the years had proved intransigent to all threats of prosecution resulting from constant complaints over the supply from its reservoir to most of High Street and the schools. Proceedings were instituted in February, March and July of 1908 and again in June and July of 1909 in that the water was not only in short supply but unfit for drinking purposes. Pressure was also exerted on its customers by serving statutory Notices on fifty house-owners in High Street to effect a proper supply by negotiating with the Rhymney Company, but when the Gwernymilwr Company promised to *'put right'* the filtration system and other defects the house-owners ignored the Notices.

It had long been evident that the Gwernymilwr Company either did not have the financial resources or the will to remedy the situation and at one stage in 1909 it asked the Council to take over the reservoir, an offer that was rejected.

The situation deteriorated still further in May and June of 1910, partly due to a drought, the shortage of supply was very great, none on some days and the water that was supplied was unfit for drinking. Once again the Council intervened. An inspection of the reservoir by the Medical Officer and the Sanitary Inspector revealed that it was not equipped with filters, that the quantity of water was practically nil and the supply liable to pollution by the presence of sheep within the enclosure. Once again the Company was threatened with proceedings unless a filtration system was installed and the enclosure fence repaired within a certain period, and statutory Notices served on the house owners in High Street to connect to the Rhymney Company. Whether any palliative measures were taken is not clear but at the end of the year the Company was still in operation and the householders remained as customers.

In the commitment to eradicate any threat to public health, measures were taken to deal with complaints about the scavenging and 87 Notices for the Abatement of Nuisances were served in respect of dilapidated/clogged closet and slop water drains. In 1909 the Sanitary Inspector conducted a house-to-house survey in the village of the sanitary provisions and proceedings were threatened against the owners of 71 houses (32 in Commercial Street, 16 in Stanley Street) which were without flushing apparatus, and Notices served on the owners of another 45 houses (16 in Commercial Street, 16 in Caerphilly Road) where the flushing tanks were defective. Deficient roofing and troughing was another reason meriting a Notice as was a dilapidated and filthy back yard. Notices were served on Thomas Arnold who kept swine in a garden behind the Leigh Hotel and on Frank Ostler who kept swine in a field behind the Parc Hotel in that the styes were without proper drainage. Bakeries and farm cowsheds were rigidly inspected.

Apart from a virulent epidemic of measles in March 1910 which resulted in the closure of the Infants' School for three weeks there were only isolated cases of scarlet fever during this period.

In 1907 County Councils were authorised to levy rates so that school children might be medically examined and from 1908 all three schools were paid an annual visit by the Schools' County Medical Officer. The infants were weighed and measured. At the senior schools, pupils who were defective in sight or hearing were referred for treatment and all were examined prior to leaving. The cases referred for treatment were followed up by County Nurse Vaughan with visits to the parents, as was the procedure when Head Teachers referred cases of pupils with skin diseases. The Medical Officer also paid occasional visits such as that to the Infants' School when he examined the face, hands and neck of every child and the clothing of most.

In January 1910 a handkerchief and orange were distributed to each child in the three schools, a New Year's gift from Dr. & Mrs. James.

The Infants' School was excessively overcrowded with 340 on roll in 1907 because yet again the pupils who should have been transferred to the senior schools were retained as Standard I. Some relief came in 1908 when this Standard was accommodated in an overcrowded Noddfa vestry and also at Salem vestry later. Even so, typical Log Book entries were, *'Very crowded. Impossible to do any work in some classes'*, *'In Class II, a room for 60 children, there are 90'*, and on June 26th,*'The weather is very hot and over 100 children in Class III room. It is impossible to remain and while the hot weather lasts it will have afternoon lessons in the open in a field nearby.'* Pressure was relieved in January 1909 with the opening a newly-built classroom, but by 1910 the number on roll was 357 so that both the building and Noddfa vestry were overcrowded.

Adding to the strain of overcrowding was the fact that there were 34 staff changes during this period.

Not only did the children and staff suffer during hot weather but also in cold weather on occasions, testified in the Log Book with entries such as *'Heating inadequate. Staff and children have indulged in healthy romping games in between lessons'*, *'Temperature low. Marching taken in all classes'* and *'No coal. Some borrowed from parents.'*

Apart from the virulent epidemic of measles in March 1910 and the consequent closure of the school for three weeks the attendance was of a high order and steady progress was made.

Popular with parents, the school pervaded a happy atmosphere, featured by the annual *'Mother's Day'* with its choral items and a display of clay models, paintings and paper flowers. A concert in 1907 cleared the debt on the school piano. Each May Day was celebrated by the election of a May Queen, crowned in the yard, followed by Maypole dances and songs. Special was St. David's Day with a service of Welsh Hymns and prayers, followed by songs and games in the classrooms and concluding in an assembly with more songs and the Welsh National Anthem. Empire Day was celebrated by patriotic songs, marching and *'Saluting the Flag'*. Rambles were frequent, bulbs were potted, games were enthusiastically played and occasional tea parties were held to illustrate particular lessons. Christmas was well and truly celebrated - rooms decorated, cards made, a decorated Christmas tree in each room, plum puddings made and boiled in the school, a cake made and baked free of charge. Annual donations were made to the Children's Ward of Cardiff Infirmary and the N.S.P.C.C.

In June 1910, after criticising the overcrowding, the H.M.I. reported, *'The main needs of infant education are thoroughly understood. Probably the most interesting feature of the school is the attempt by the Mistress to revive some of the old Welsh games, entered into by the children with great enjoyment. Her efforts are much commended. Mother's Day is a most useful institution forging a link with staff and scholars'*.

On September 30th, 1910, Miss Catherine James resigned as Head Teacher prior to marriage and was presented with a silver tea service on behalf of the scholars and staff, together with a letter of appreciation from the Managers.

On October 31st the Headship was assumed by Miss Edith John who thereafter conducted an examination of each class, the results of which were not always to her satisfaction. Absent from the Log Book are any entries of Christmas festivities although presumably they continued. Her staff comprised Miriam Rowlands (C), Fanny Ford (C), Mildred Coles (C), May Adams (C), Edith Jones (U), Esther Phillips (U) and Supplementary Teachers Alice Fletcher, Emmie Hargreaves, Gertrude Thomas.

As with the Infants' School, the Girls' and Boys' Schools faced the same difficulties which had affected them in previous years.

At the Girls' School the number on roll averaged 340 and at the Boys' School it was slightly less. Overcrowded in 1907 and 1908, relief came in January 1909 when the building was extended to provide each with an additional classroom but in June 1910 the H.M.I. reported that the Girls' School *'is on the verge of being overfull and two teachers have more than 60 in their classes'* and the Boys' School *'is again nearly full.'*

The frequent scarcity of the water supply from the Gwernymilwr reservoir gave rise to serious concern, particularly so on the occasions when there was no supply as occurred in July 1908, throughout June and July, 1909 and again in July 1910, so posing a serious health hazard because the water closets could not be flushed. Unavailing were the efforts of the County Medical Officer and the Council Sanitary Inspector to secure any improvement.

The heating was often inadequate and on the occasions when no coal was delivered *'boys obtained coal from their homes to light fires'*. There was still no artificial lighting.

With greater emphasis placed on the teaching of Welsh the Education Authority greater importance was attached to St. David's Day celebrations and on that day in 1910 Dan Lloyd opened the morning session with an address followed by a programme of Welsh hymns, songs, choruses and recitations. A similar type of programme was presented at the Girls' School. Also observed in May 1909 was Empire Day. Miss Lloyd recorded, *'Patriotic songs and recitations. Lessons throughout the week will bear on the notable deeds which have won our Empire, our Colonial Cousins etc.'* At the Boys' School, *'In the morning the Master gave a short address. In the afternoon the lads were taken into the school yard and then marched in procession bearing flags, shields etc. to the hill east of the school where patriotic songs and the National Anthems were sung.'*

The staff at the Girls' School remained reasonably stable and very commendable progress was made. Notable was the opening in May, 1909 of a Cookery Centre located in the basement of the building and thereafter groups of older girls attended on three days a week over a ten-week session under the instruction of visiting Domestic Science teachers. Further joy came in May 1910 when a sewing machine was delivered which *'the older girls will be taught to use to facilitate the making of garments.'* Nurse Vaughan gave annual talks on *'The Care and Management of Infants'* and *'The Prevention of*

Diseases'. Donations were made to the Children's Ward of Cardiff Infirmary, Dr. Barnado's Homes and the N.S.P.C.C.

Another interesting feature was introduced in 1910 when the senior forms were allowed a small portion of the playground *'for gardening, the girls working after school - seeds, plants etc.'*

Attendance was of a high order five pupils proceeded to Hengoed County School, nine passed the Proficiency Examination and in June 1910 the H.M.I. reported, *'The work is thoroughly well supervised. The girls are well behaved and take a great interest in all lessons.'* The staff under Miss Dinah Lloyd at the end of the year comprised Matilda James (C), Ethel Rundle (C), Catherine Williams (C), Mary Jones (C), Maggie Thomas (C), Katherine James (U), Ellen Scott (U), Sarah Heritage (U) and Ellen Jones (U).

In the Log Book of the Boys' School on October 28th, 1909, was this simple entry. *'School closed. Funeral of Mrs. Lloyd, wife of the Headmaster.'* The other schools were closed also.

There were many staff changes at the school. In 1907 John Roberts left for Southampton University, returning in 1909, A.J. Williams and Matilda James left for Training College in 1909, Charles England left to take up a Headship in1910 and was presented with a gold-mounted pen.

New syllabuses were introduced for Physical Education and Dramatised History and for lessons on Temperance. Homework was given to candidates entered for County Scholarships. In 1907 Clifford Lloyd and and Trevor Shaw proceeded to Lewis School, Pengam, and in 1908 and 1909 six pupils passed the written examination but there is no record of how they fared in the subsequent Oral Examination. Fifteen pupils passed the Proficiency Examination. Groups of pupils visited the Museum, an Art Exhibition and the Welsh National Pageant in Cardiff. Noted in the Log Book on March 29th, 1907, was the entry *'most boys wore the oak leaf'*, *'Lady Day'* on March 25th, 1908, and St. Patrick's Day in 1909 and 1910. The attendance record remained high although there was cause for concern in that ten boys were committed to the Truant School, more parents were being fined and absenteeism on Cooperative Stores Quarter Days was deplored.

In June 1910 the H.M.I. reported, *'The discipline is excellent, the school is carefully and vigorously conducted and the general efficiency is well maintained'*. At the end of the year Dan Lloyd's staff included John A. Roberts (T.C.), Agnes Jones (C), Mary Rees (C), Francis Marshall (U), Benjamin Morgan (U), David James (U) and Harry Bowden (P.T.), a recent pupil.

For the pupils of all three schools the most memorable occasion during this period was that associated with the visit of King Edward VII and Queen Alexandra to Caerphilly on July 13th, 1907, when on the previous day they were presented with a commemorative medal by the Chairman of the Managers and his wife and granted a half-day holiday. The upper standards of the senior schools also enjoyed the unforgettable experience of journeying to Caerphilly Castle on the next day to join with those of other schools in presenting musical items before the King and Queen.

For the Head Teachers and staffs the most welcome news came in December 1910 with the announcement that a Junior School was to be built near to the present schools. At last the prospect of solving the problem of gross overcrowding was in sight.

In 1907 the Salvation Army rented Olive House in Caerphilly Road and subsequently purchased it for £180. In 1908 Rev. Richard Thomas was appointed as minister of the English Wesleyan Methodist Church for a year. At the Easter Vestry of St. Peter's Church, presided over by Rector D. Lloyd Rees, it was reported that the debt on the church had been repaid due to the energetic efforts of curate Gwilym Rees, and G.T. Starkey was elected as Honorary Secretary, Thomas Bailey as Rector's Churchwarden, Fred Williams as People's Churchwarden. In the course of the year an out-building was erected to relieve the pressure on the accommodation and the Welsh-speaking communicants launched a Fund for a separate building. In 1909 the St. Cenydd Welsh Anglican Church was opened with the Rev. Price Hughes, a fervent Welsh patriot, inducted as curate. The English Congregationalists replaced their iron-structured chapel with a stone, building to accommodate 500 and Rev. Thomas Jones was inducted as minister. In 1910 the Ebenezer English Baptists inducted Rev. D.M. Jones as minister, a commanding personality, a powerful preacher and politically active. A Free Church Council was formed with the professed aims of *'bringing closer together the various denominations and to try to improve the social conditions of the people'*.

Capacity congregations welcomed visiting evangelists such as Mrs. Jones from Morriston who preached at Salem Chapel and Rev. D. Griffiths, a blind preacher from Welshpool who came to Ebenezer Chapel. The occasional *'Cyrddau Mawr'* and *'Cymanfa Ganu'* aroused a similar response.

Large congregations remained the norm for the Sunday services and well-attended were the various mid-week services and meetings. Attendance at Sunday School remained the norm for most children. Many chapels also held Band of Hope for older children on mid-week evenings. There the proceedings included instruction in sight-reading music based on the tonic solfa method with the aid of Curwen's Modulator Chart and individuals were encouraged to sing and recite. In addition, a few chapels held mid-week meetings designed to prepare children for external examinations in Scripture Knowledge, and in 1907 it is recorded that Noddfa Chapel entered twenty-four candidates for the Welsh Congregational Union Scripture Examination in which Emrys Evans and Irene Champion were awarded 1st Prize in one category and David John Evans the 2nd Prize in another category. Eagerly awaited was the Sunday School outing, invariably to Barry Island, as were the *'treats'*.

Social evenings, bazaars, concerts, mini-eisteddfods, lectures and other functions were forever being organised to raise funds. Paramount too was the importance attached to the tradition of fostering choral music as witnessed by the prestige attached to the position of Arweinydd y Gan/Precentor, pride in the quality of hymn-singing and the performance of the choirs.

Still powerful was the support accorded to the Temperance Movement as represented by the Women's Temperance Association, the Rechabites and

Good Templars. Typical was a meeting convened by the Association in 1908 to demand that a local veto clause be inserted into the Parliamentary Bill dealing with the opening hours of public houses when rousing speeches denouncing the evil of drink were interspersed with musical items by Miss Bussell and others who were accompanied on the piano by David John Evans. Equally strong support was expressed for the Lord's Day Observance Society and vehement was the agitation in 1910 against a proposal to repeal the Wales Sunday Observance Act.

Yet the scale of drunkenness, physical assaults and other criminal acts continued to increase. The three hotels and the Conservative Club, extended in 1909, plied a roaring trade. The Workmen's Constitutional Club at 2 Station Terrace, masquerading as a bona-fide social organisation, was *'struck off'* for the illegal sale of intoxicant liquor in 1908 but re-opened in 1909 as the *'Working Men's Club'*. Facing intimidatory and often torrid street scenes, particularly on Friday and Saturday nights, were Sergeant Richard Walters, successor to Sergeant Williams whose death in 1907 was much-lamented, and two constables based at the Police Station.

Indicative of the aggressive and violent atmosphere that prevailed in the hotels was the employment of barmen/bouncers such as the well-known pugilist Ben Corfield and William Petty an ex-Grenadier Guards boxing champion. In 1907 ex-bailiff George Nicholas, the new landlord of the Leigh Hotel, issued a summons for assault against the previous landlord ex-Police Constable Michael Fahy. Frequent were the press reports such as *'Street Fighting in Senghenydd'*, *'Wounding Attack'*, *'Police Attacked'*, *'Landlord Assaulted'*, *'Bailiff Attacked'* and *'Domestic Affray'*. On December 27th, 1908, the headlines read *'Senghenydd Sensation: Tragic Orgy; Fatal Razor Clash'*, and *'A Squalid, Bloodstained Drunken Tragedy.'* On the night of Boxing Day Sergeant Walters and P.C. Smith were called to the home of engine driver David Morgan at 19 Brynhyfryd Terrace. There in a pool of blood lay lodger Edward Williams, a haulier known as *'Ned o'r Bell'*, his throat slit with a razor by Morgan following a quarrel. He died the following afternoon. It transpired that both had indulged in heavy drinking on Christmas Day and after tea on Boxing Day, all the time quarrelling over their prowess in their *'fighting days'* with Williams taunting Morgan until on Boxing night it culminated in a violent struggle with tragic results. Charged at Caerphilly Magistrates Court on January 3rd, 1909, Morgan was committed to the Assizes in April when the Crown Prosecutor described the brutal murder as *'a squalid drunken tragedy of a character unhappily associated with certain districts in South Wales'* and he was sentenced to seven years penal servitude.

In November 1910 the Urban District Council passed a Notice of Motion *'That the Chief Constable consider means of giving extra police protection in the Aber District'.*

While the press, as its want, gave full coverage to episodes which portrayed the village as a *'rough area'*, less publicised were the positive features engendered during this period. In 1908 the Parc Hotel was rented

Universal Workmen's Library and Institute.

from Crosswell's Brewery to serve as the Senghenydd Universal Workmen's Library and Institute with David Bevan as Secretary. Financed by the miners' weekly contributions, it provided a library, a reading room and a venue for indoor games such as draughts and dominoes. A Cymmrodorion Society devoted to the promotion of the Welsh language and culture was formed by Rev. Price Hughes, curate to the Welsh Anglican Church. The prestigious *'Chair'* Eisteddfod was revived in 1909, a festive occasion when the business premises were closed and special trains ran from Caerphilly, and among the local winners were Albert Bailey (Pianoforte solo under 14 years of age), D. James (Boy's Solo) and D. Thomas (verses on the Eight Hours Act). Repeated in 1910, not only were the business premises closed but a holiday was declared at the colliery. Another festive occasion was the first Flower Show, accompanied by a Dog Show and Carnival, held in 1910.

Functioning successfully were the Aber Valley United Choir, renamed the Aber Valley Harmonic Society in 1910, conducted by Dan Davies of Abertridwr, and the Aber Valley Male Voice Choir conducted by Harry Phillips then by Evan Rowlands. David John Evans continued to be acclaimed as a composer, pianist and organist. Acclaimed also was mezzo-soprano Miss Winifred Lewis, a pupil of the celebrated Madame Clara Novello Davies, who won the solo competition at the 1908 National Eisteddfod and also competed successfully in the duet and quartet competitions. Consistent eisteddfod winners were bass Idris Perkins, tenor Idriswyn Humphreys, boy soloist John Morgan Davies, boy pianist John

Evans Richards and elocutionist Miss Thomas. Maggie Davies won the Girl's Solo competition at Llanbradach in 1909.

The village boasted three brass bands, the Senghenydd Brass Band, the Wesleyan Silver Band and the Senghenydd Temperance Band conducted by W. Turner. Many of their instrumentalists were also members of the Aber Silver Band which won 2nd place in Class A at the Mountain Ash Eisteddfod in 1908 and 3rd place at the Caerphilly Eisteddfod in 1909.

Added to the many formal concerts were *'Smoking'* Concerts held at the Conservative Club. Annual visits were organised to Cardiff theatres, and in 1908 *'Some sought pleasure at the Drury Lane pantomime, a cheap train being run, when they thoroughly enjoyed their fleeting visit to the Metropolis.'* Each year until 1909 Ted Ebley was granted a three monthly licence for his *'Olympic Theatre'*. From January to April 1910 a licence was granted to a Mrs. Breamer, Alexandra Theatre, Cwm, to erect a portable theatre. Then in June a new form of entertainment was introduced when Walter Haggar, Castle Theatre, Caerphilly, was granted a licence to erect a theatre on the fair ground for a Bioscope Show, the precursor of *'moving films'*. To the fair ground also came John Scullett's Show and the occasional circus.

By the 1906-07 season the re-formed Rugby Club was restored in some strength and achieved full stature in the 1907/8 season with the new title of *'Bluebells'* and fielding two teams. Captained by Will Willacombe and then by

The Bluebells Rugby Club which was formed in 1907-08.
Back row: E.H. Thomas (Hon. Secretary), Jim Herring, Bert Hyatt, Will Jones, John Morgan, Will Fullalove, Dai John, Tom Smith. Middle row: Charlie Thomas, Peter Ross, Dai Lewis, Will Willicombe (Captain), Willie Walters, Will Warner, Phillip Skym. Front row: Edward Davies, Herbie Powell, Will Hyatt (Vice Captain).

The victorious rugby team, winners of the Ninian Stuart Cup and League in 1911-12. Front row: M. Jones (Trainer), F. Ward, A. Roberts, E. Magee, H. Davies. Back row: Will Crook, J. Jones, Will Fullalove, J. Gould, J. Herring, Will Willacombe, T. Marshall. Seated: Jim Dallimore, Jack Walters, Peter Ross, Will Pedro (Captain), Phil Skym, Will James 'Hero', J. Davies, T. Jones. Note: Will James known as 'Hero' with the Club Mascot a fox on his lap.

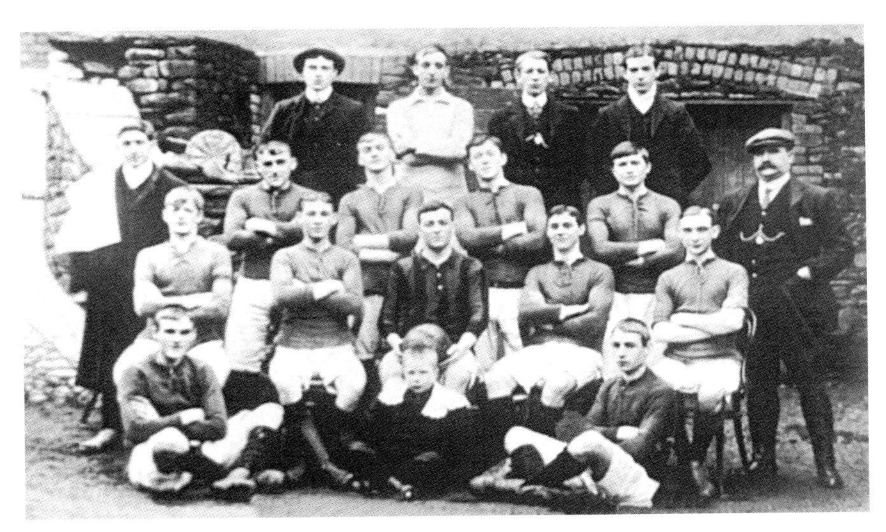

Senghenydd Albion A.F.C. 1909-10.

Will Hyatt, the 1st team included Edward Davies, Will Fullalove, Jim Herring, Bert Hyatt, Dai John, Will Jones, Dai Lewis, John Morgan, Herbie Powell, Peter Ross, Philip Skym, Tom Smith, Charles Thomas, Bill Walters and Will Warner. Such was the enthusiasm again for the game that in addition to the two Club teams another team, named the *'Scarlets'*, was formed, and the sight also of eager schoolboys climbing the mountain to play on the Goldref field bore eloquent testimony to its popularity.

Representing the other code was the *'Senghenydd Albions'* A.F.C. but little has been recorded of its progress other than a few match results in the press.

The combined Senghenydd and Aber Cricket Club continued to function until 1908 when the Senghenydd players then formed their own Club, playing on the Gelli fields and competing in the Second Division of the Glamorgan League. The composition of the team varied considerably. In July 1909 when the team was badly beaten by Cardiff Electrics at Cardiff Arms Park it comprised; A.H. Williams, W. Williams, T. Gingell, D. Davies, M. Peregrine, Prosser, C. Davidson, J. Williams, E. Evans, A. Davies and F. Northey in order of batting. Other regular players during the period from 1908 and 1910 were Jake Davies, Tom Davies, S. Hoare, W. James, Edwin Jones, D.H. Jones, Ted Jones, Fred Lewis, A. Shaw, John Thomas, M.E. Thomas, H. Tocknell, Bill Walters and R. Williams.

Cause for great concern to the Clubs was that as a result of tipping operations by the Windsor Colliery the Gelli fields were becoming increasingly under threat as the venue for play. Fortunately, due to the good offices of the Lewis Merthyr Company an alternative site was being excavated near the Universal Colliery in 1910. At the same time pressure was brought to bear on the District Council to provide a public recreation ground.

Boxing remained a popular sport with many a pugilist such as Albert Thomas featuring in contests at Virginia Park in Caerphilly.

Although this period had been one of industrial unrest and there was an anti-social problem yet there were many positive elements and Kelly's Directory of 1910 listed ninety three commercial enterprises, an increase of twenty since 1906.

Along Commercial Street were the Gwernymilwr Hotel (David Lewis), the Leigh Hotel (William John Evans), the Universal Hotel (Edward Evans), Lloyd's Bank, London & Provincial Bank, Senghenydd & Aber Valley Cooperative Society, Dr. James's surgery chemist and druggist George Thomas Starkey, the refreshment room of Bracchi Bros., ice-cream makers and confectioners; shopkeepers Cornelius Bishop, Thomas Evans, George Gingell, John Jehu, Edward Jones, W. Thomas Marshall, Mrs. Susannah Rowlands, Mrs. Mary Thomas, Daniel Williams, Frederick Williams and Herbert Williams grocers Charles Bailey, Danish Butter Co., L. & B. Evans, India & China Tea Co., Wm. Thomas Jones, Alfred Taylor and John Thomas; butchers Joseph Edwards, Eastman's Ltd., Albert Heal, Charles Parker, Alfred Taylor and Thomas Watts; greengrocers/fruiterers Enoch James, Edward Jones and Walter Swaithes; baker Thomas Thomas; confectioners Stephen Davies, D.W. Evans and William Hilbourne; dairyman Roger Thomas; fried fish dealers Benjamin Corfield, W. Organ & Son and Mrs. Alice Ostler; outfitters Louis Curity & Co., David Davies, David Evans, Charles Isaac and Jones & Co.; drapers Mrs. Anne Dixon, D. Edwards & Co., Benjamin James, L. Jenkins & Co., John Morgan and T. & R. Samuel; hosier John Moss; the fancy repository of James Watkins; boot and shoe makers Henry Gay, Towyn

Two early forms of transport in the town with W.T. Marshall's horse and cart, closely followed by what was probably the first motor car to be seen here.

Jones, Edward Thomas and Francis Yendle; boot dealers Cash & Co., William Davies and Mrs. Edith Harold; the Universal Furnishing Company; ironmongers/hardware dealers Charles Allen and Mrs. S.M. Richards; chins and glass dealer Mrs. Margaret Jones; newsagents Daniel Jenkins and Mrs. Catherine Williams; hairdressers Joshua Davies, William Lewis and Peter Stephens; watchmaker Thomas Bussell; herbalist Richard Pritchard; pawnbroker Abraham Shibko; undertaker, builder and quarry owner David Caesar Jones; painter and decorator George King; carpenter Thomas Williams.

In High Street were Post Mistress and stationer Miss Jane Bussell, the dining rooms of William Davies, ironmonger George Davies, greengrocer John Evans, butcher John Morris and hairdresser Alexander Spencer.

In Caerphilly Road were butcher John Davies, costumier Mrs. Sarah Shell and grocer Mrs. Lavinia Williams.

Elsewhere were builders Davies & Lloyd and baker Richard Wall in Station Road, quarry owners Agland Co. in Station Terrace, shopkeeper David Lloyd in Cenydd Terrace, shopkeeper Henry Sands in Coronation Terrace, shopkeeper William Davies in Grove Terrace, shopkeeper Sidney Morgan in Parc Terrace, shopkeeper John Kydd in Stanley Street, shopkeeper Mrs. Anne Lewis in Station Terrace and blacksmith Alfred Perry in Windsor Terrace.

Add the purveyors of milk, other bakers, street vendors and the auction mart to this list then the impression emerges of a thriving economy. But although comparative prosperity did prevail the decline in value of the colliery wages demanded thrifty house-keeping. Significant too was the very

This is a typical scene from the 1900s when there was a selection of shop premises doing plenty of business in the town, this particular shop was located in the Square.

high level of the *'turn over'* in business ownership, only thirty nine remained unchanged since 1906.

To what extent Dan Lloyd and Hubert Jenkins were called upon to discharge their roles as *'Overseers of the Poor'* is not recorded, but the Relieving Officer and bailiffs were frequent home visitors and the pawnshop flourished. Happily, many old people were released from the poverty trap when the Old Age Pensions Act came into force in January 1909 with the award of a non-contributory pension of 5/- a week to all persons over 70 years of age provided their income did not exceed 12/- a week or were not in receipt of Poor Relief.

CHAPTER 8

In 1911 the population was recorded as 5,895. The work force at the colliery approached 2,000, many travelling from neighbouring villages and towns, and production was high. But this year and the next were to prove troubled ones in the South Wales coalfield.

It opened with the Cambrian Collieries owner continuing to reject arbitration, a stance that continued month after month with resulting sporadic disturbances in the Rhondda and elsewhere. When, in September, the miners were forced to capitulate by stark necessity, the entire coalfield was racked with bitterness and anger. The inflammatory and violent atmosphere of the strike left a deep impression - the massive police force, the *'military occupation'* and the unrelenting determination to starve out the miners. So unrest and tension remained, the militant mood hardened with more support for the Labour Party and syndicalism, mounting pressure for a minimum wage and the *'closed shop'*.

Not recorded is the reaction of the Lodge and the community to the elevation in 1911 of Sir W.T. Lewis to the peerage with the title of Baron Merthyr of Senghenydd. Welcomed, however, was the Coal Mines Act which had particular significance in the context of the 1901 explosion, incorporating recommendations by a series of Reports from a Royal Commission on which Lewis had played a prominent role with reference to Coal Dust explosions, Control of Coal Dust and other related subjects. It enacted that unless the floor, roof and sides of the roads were naturally wet then the following measures were to be taken to prevent dust accumulation:

(1) The floor,the roof and sides of the roads shall be substantially cleared, as far as practicable, to prevent the accumulation of coal dust.
(2) Systematic steps, either by way of watering or otherwise, shall be taken to prevent explosion of coal dust occurring or being carried along the roads.
(3) The roads shall be examined daily and a report (recorded in a book for that purpose kept in the mine) made on their condition as to coal dust and steps taken to mitigate the danger arising therefrom.
(4) Tubs should be constructed and maintained so as to prevent, as far practicable, coal dust escaping through the sides, ends or floors, but any tubs not so constructed may be used for another five years.

Important in the event of fire or explosion, it was also enacted that all collieries provide means of reversing the air current by January 1st, 1913. But in the case of the Universal Colliery this date was extended to September 30th, 1913, because of particular difficulties.

By 1912 the South Wales Federation, urged by the younger generation of miners, was moving still further away from *'Mabonism'* towards hostility against the owners. At a time when shareholders in the South Wales Colliery Companies were receiving dividends of 20% and a labourer was paid 4/6d a shift, 27/- for a week of six shifts, the main campaign was now directed towards the establishment of a minimum wage.

In January, largely as a result of pressure from the S.W.M.F., the Federation of Great Britain conducted a national ballot on the question of submitting a notice of the withdrawal of labour in support of the demand for a minimum wage. The Universal Lodge voted in favour of strike action, a decision which echoed that of the miners throughout the country.

The coal owners flatly rejected the demand for a minimum wage, and when the government intervened with a plan to secure for the miners *'the power to earn a reasonable living wage'* this also they rejected. As week followed week with little hope of agreement so they began to draw up *'battle plans'*. On February 26th the proprietors in Glamorgan applied to Colonel Lindsay, the Chief Constable, for a special police force to protect their pits and premises, and it was reported that he was drawing up contingency plans for the deployment of 200 infantry and 50 cavalry to cover the Rhymney Valley, Caerphilly and the Aber Valley.

March 1st, St. David's Day, saw the biggest demonstration of Trade Union power ever seen in the country when every coalfield came out on Strike, all united for the first time in withholding their labour. Within a week coal prices rose, rail services were curtailed and serious inroads made in the national economy.

With both the miners and the owners standing firm, the government, becoming increasingly concerned at the economic effect, resolved to intervene and introduced a Minimum Wages Bill on March 19th. It became law on March 29th and the Federation of Great Britain called a national ballot on the question of return to work. The Universal Lodge voted by 351 to 83 to return, a decision in keeping with the national response. On April 6th the M.F.G.B. instructed a return to work, but it was not until April 14th that the Universal work force returned, the delay caused by the enginemen and stokers who were members of their own Association.

The villagers faced the Strike with their usual resilience, making every effort to conduct day-to-day affairs as normal as possible, but with Strike pay a meagre 8/- a week for men and 4/- for boys there was inevitable hardship and distress. On March 8th Dan Lloyd wrote in the Log Book, *'The coal tips open from 9.00 a.m.to 1.00 p.m. for the inhabitants. 39 boys absent picking coal'*, and on March 16th, *'17 boys here this morning who have had no breakfast'*.

A Relief Committee was formed, its priority being the welfare of the children such as setting up *'Soup Kitchens'*. Miss Dinah Evans recorded in the Log Book: March 18th: *'Owing to the Coal Strike the local Federations have organised a Committee to provide meals to all necessitous children. For today such children are being fed in the Cookery Centre here but henceforth will be provided at a capacious room in the unlicensed Parc Hotel. Two meals provided daily and teachers from all schools have volunteered their services between 12.00 and 1.00 p.m. and between 4.40 and 6.30 p.m.'*

Cooks and ancillary staff who worked at Senghenydd School canteen.

March 29th : *'Informed that the* 'Provision of Meals Act' *is now in force and that care be taken in the registration of children having meals'.* This meant that although the Committee was still responsible for the purchase and preparation of food, the cost was now borne by the County Council.

April 20th. *'Soup Kitchens closed today. The teachers have assisted at these every day.'*

There was undoubted travail in the community but morale remained high, and unlike some other villages in the district there were no *'blacklegs'*. Nor were there any serious disturbances. Gradually it returned to full vigour.

The miners had won a great victory, but the Act had laid down only the general principles, the precise implementation of the basic minimum rates left to be determined by Joint District Boards comprising employers and workers. The District Board for the South Wales coalfield met on April 27th, the Federation submitting its claims, the owners countering with lower offers. Not until July 13th was a conclusion reached with the standard shift rates for men ranging from 3/2d to 4/7d and for boys ranging from 1/6d to 3/- plus 51% in both cases. Far short of the Federation's demands, many men were still left without *'a reasonable living wage'* as the Act envisaged, so leaving a sense of betrayal.

The Strike dealt the *'death blow'* to Mabon's policy of conciliation and he resigned as President of the S.W.M.F. With the *'Fed'* industrially militant the period of *'Great Unrest'* continued, and at the Universal there were continual disputes over payment for operating new seams.

Meanwhile, on the domestic front the long campaign for separate representation on the Caerphilly Urban District Council had come to a successful conclusion in 1911 when Senghenydd and Abertridwr Wards were secured, each allocated three members. As a result the subsequent election in April aroused very great interest and was fought with vigour. There were five candidates - John Davies (Liberal), Thomas James (Labour), Towyn Jones (Liberal), G. Parker (Ratepayer) and Edward Shaw (Independent). Elected were Shaw - 619 votes; James - 400; Davies - 346. In the following year only John Davies was up for election and he defeated G. Parker. Not surprising was the election of Edward Shaw, a circumspect choice which followed a general practice in the coalfield apropos owners and management. The election of Thomas James demonstrated the ever-growing support by the miners for the Labour Party. That of butcher John Davies, a Vice-President of the East Glamorgan Liberal Association, indicated that the traditional Liberal support was still strong with the newly-opened Liberal Club boasting a membership of 845.

The need to provide accommodation for a population now approaching 6,000 had been largely satisfied. Some building was in progress and School Street emerged but no plans for additional houses were submitted in 1911 or 1912. As in the past years a feature of the housing market was the frequent change in ownership, the sales affording rich profits for the speculators and a valuable return for the purchasers by way of rents. Quoted, for example, was the sale of ten dwellings, each rented at 6/8d a week, for £1,450. Sold for £595 were five dwellings in Station Terrace, each yielding a rental of 5/-. Sold for £550 were three houses in Stanley Street, rental of 7/-. In 1912 there was a tentative project initiated by the District Council to build *'workmen's dwellings'* throughout the district but although the Senghenydd Councillors identified a possible site the project was not pursued.

While the overall accommodation appeared to have been judged as adequate the housing was often sub-standard. Over the years the conditions had improved but the Council still faced problems which endangered public health. Overcrowding was not uncommon and a watchful eye was kept on the basement rooms at the lower end of Caerphilly Road and in Commercial Street as well as the Huts. But continuing to be of major concern were the houses in Stanley Street where an inspection in December 1911 resulted in Notices for the Abatement of Nuisances being served in respect of six overcrowded cellar dwellings, nuisances in ten houses *'caused by the basement rooms being occupied as cellar dwellings'*, two damp cellar dwellings and four houses with deficient roofs and damp walls. As in the past, time and time again the cellar dwellings were condemned as unfit for habitation and closure orders imposed on the owners and tenants. But time and time again great difficulty was experienced in removing the tenants and even when this was accomplished the cellar dwellings were soon re-occupied. It was an intractable problem made more difficult by the many owners.

Caerllwyn and Cefn Llwyd farmhouses were condemned as unfit for habitation and closure orders imposed in July 1912, but by the end of the year they were still occupied.

In the course of the two years the number of Notices issued for the Abatement of Nuisances totalled 332, of which 135 were in respect of deficient/dilapidated closet and slop water drains and 132 in respect of deficient/dilapidated roof troughing. Other quoted reasons included dilapidated backyards, damp walls, dilapidated kitchen walls and four cases in which *'the closets were without proper ventilation and not provided with windows'*. Periodically, an entire street of houses was inspected. Thus for a variety of reasons the owners of 57 houses in Caerphilly Road were served with Notices in June 1912, and in October the owners of 34 houses in Station Terrace were recipients of Notices. Bakeries and cowsheds were subject to rigorous inspection.

The scavenging continued to be contracted out to Robert Alfred Bussell, tenant of Caermoei farm, and included the collection of household refuse and commercial rubbish, keeping clean the backyards, emptying the cesspools and finding tipping sites. Not surprisingly there were complaints, mainly on the state of the backyards.

Serious as was the concern about *'nuisances'* caused by housing defects the greater danger to public health continued to come from the inadequate and poor quality of the water supplied by the Gwernymilwr Land Company. From March and throughout the remainder of 1911, particularly during a period of drought from July to September, the schools and houses in High Street and School Street were very frequently left without a proper supply or no water at all. Time and time again proceedings were taken against the Company, notices served on house owners and the Education Authority to secure a supply by approaching the Rhymney Valley Water Company and closure orders served. All to no avail. The Gwernymilwr Company was either reluctant or financially unable to improve its supply and the Rhymney Company which supplied the rest of village was not geared to offer the additional necessary supply. The Rhymney Company itself was finding it difficult to cope with drought conditions and at one period it had to enforce rationing of the water supply to one hour a day. So the year ended with no solution vis-a-vis the supply to clients of the Gwernymilwr Company.

The situation remained unchanged from January to the end of June in 1912 with the inevitable proceedings against the Gwernymilwr Company, notices served on the householders and the Education Authority followed by closure notices. So desperate did the situation become in the schools that they were closed on June 3rd for three weeks. But happily a solution was now in sight. On April 30th the Gwernymilwr Company went into liquidation and undertook to negotiate with the Rhymney Company to supply its clients. By May 6th the Rhymney Company declared its intention to lay a water mains to High Street, and by June 25th its arrangements were almost complete for taking over the Gwernymilwr mains. By the end of July all had been accomplished and apart from some initial minor difficulties the rest of the year passed without complaints. Henceforth the entire village was supplied by the Rhymney Company and a major health hazard which had existed for almost eighteen years was now removed.

Happily, despite the problems posed by the water shortages and sub-standard conditions in some houses, there were no epidemics during these two years and only a few cases of scarlet fever, none of which proved fatal. The infants mortality, however, remained high, a factor which was common throughout the land.

Private Street Works were undertaken at Windsor Place, the approach road to Brynhyfryd and at Brynhyfryd. For the first time the main road to Abertridwr, Commercial Street, Station Road and High Street were tar sprayed, so vastly improving the surfaces. It was planned to tar-spray Caerphilly Road but all other roads were to remain surfaced with compressed limestone chippings, periodically water-sprayed from a water cart.

As to street lighting, still under the supervision of the Police Sergeant, the process of replacing the oil lamps with electric lamps continued throughout 1911 amid mounting criticism of the tardiness of the South Wales Power Company in doing so and of the inadequacy of the number of lamps installed. Although the latter criticism was remedied to some extent the Company's promise to complete equipping the side streets by the end of July and then by the end of November did not materialise and at the end of the year there were still nine oil lamps in operation. More lamps were installed in the early months of 1912 and in March all streets were lit by electricity and another long-term source of complaints was largely removed.

The provision of additional fire-fighting equipment was accorded greater importance, particularly after a fire in Commercial Street on August 25th, 1911, fought and extinguished by Sergeant Walters, his constables, Colliery Sergeant James, aided by Sergeant Evans and constables from Abertridwr, together with some villagers. As a result Sergeant Walters was officially appointed a fireman by the Fire Brigade Superintendent, more hydrants were installed, and sanctioned were the purchase of a Telescopic Fire Escape Ladder and the erection of a pole to dry the hose pipes. Unhappy were the men from the village who helped to put out the fire when the Council was unable to accede to their request for payment to replace affected boots and clothing.

There were further developments in 1912. Police Constables Charles James and John Davies were appointed firemen at a salary of £1 a year, a public meeting in October was chaired by Councillor Shaw with a view to selecting a Voluntary Fire Brigade in the village and in December the Council approved the draft conveyance of a strip of land adjoining the Police Station as a site for a Fire Brigade Station.

The search for a site for a public Recreation Ground continued. In 1911 two sites were recommended but in neither case was the landowner prepared to sell or lease, and by the end of the year so little progress had been made that the Senghenydd Traders' Association was urging the Council to obtain a site by compulsory purchase if necessary. In 1912 negotiations were opened with Mr. Creed, Agent to the Windsor Colliery, re a vacant site between Commercial Street and the railway line but no conclusion had been reached at the close of the year.

Nor was the Council any more successful in its pursuit of land for allotments. Sites to the rear of Station Terrace and High Street were recommended by the Senghenydd Councillors but with the landowners not prepared to lease no progress was made.

A sign that the motor vehicle had arrived in Senghenydd was the licence to store petrol granted to ironmonger Philip Richards in 1911. There was even a remote possibility that the villagers might not have to rely solely on the criticised rail service for public transport when a group of Caerphilly businessmen sought Council support to provide a *'motor omnibus'* service between Caerphilly and Senghenydd, but although encouraged the project was not pursued.

The schools were subjected to very serious difficulties as a result of the inadequate water supply from the Gwernymilwr Land Company throughout 1911 but particularly during the period of drought. Very frequently the Log Books noted *'No water'* so that the water closets could not be flushed and posing a health hazard. Continual visits were paid by the District Council's Sanitary Inspector and Medical Officer of Health as well as the School Inspector, and on three occasions the District Council issued notices of closure unless the situation was remedied. But the notices were never enforced and apart from a very few occasions when the firm of Davies & Lloyd was engaged to pour water into the tanks the year ended with no improvement. The situation deteriorated even further in 1912 and ultimately on the insistence of the Medical Officer of Health the schools were closed from June 3rd to July 8th, and to *'make up for the time lost'* the normal summer holiday in August was cancelled, much to the disappointment of the pupils. Happily the Rhymney Valley Water Company took over the supply in September and thereafter there were only minor initial complaints.

Very difficult also was the period of the Strike in 1912. Typically, normal school routine was maintained and every day from March 18th to April 30th the staffs assisted the Canteen Committee by supervising the children at the *'Soup Kitchens'* in the Parc Hotel. They also made donations to the Relief Committee.

But the years were not without happy events. Very welcome was the installation of gas fittings on April 1st, 1912 which ensured gas lighting in the ensuing winter months. The Coronation of George V in June 1911 was celebrated by a week's holiday and on the day the children were entertained to tea and presented with a Coronation mug, both provided by the District Council. In celebration of the Investiture of the Prince of Wales on July 30th, 1911, the children were presented with a commemorative medal donated by Baron Merthyr of Senghenydd and a book donated by the County Council. On the day, the schools were closed and sports held on the Gelli fields, prior to which a massed choir from the three schools sang *'God Bless the Prince of Wales'*, the Welsh National Anthem and the National Anthem.

Great was the general satisfaction and parental pride when some pupils were selected to attend the Caerphilly Higher Elementary School which opened on December 2nd, 1912, offering an alternative opportunity for further education. It was designed to provide a three-year course to selected boys and girls between the ages of twelve and fifteen which would further develop the education given in the Elementary School together with special instruction and preparatory training for employment available. The curriculum included Practical Science, Woodwork, Metalwork, Home-Making, Needlework, Shorthand and Typewriting as well as the traditional subjects. Entrance was by annual examination but in this initial entry the pupils were selected by the County Inspector. It is recorded by the Higher Elementary School that with further entries sixteen pupils came from Senghenydd. Sadly, it is also recorded that very many failed to complete the course, leaving at the end of the second year when they attained the statutory leaving age of fourteen because of financial reasons or domestic demands.

Apart from the Noddfa vestry still in use, there were no complaints of excessive overcrowding, but Mr. Lloyd, Miss Evans and Miss John were faced with continual staff changes. Occasional visits to the schools were made by the County Inspectors and Managers Councillor Thomas James, Rev. Tawelfryn Thomas and Alderman J.P. Evans. The reports of the Ministry Inspection in 1911 are not recorded and for the first time there was no Inspection in 1912.

Attendance at the Infants' School was at a high level, the *'Open Day'* was a success and St. David's Day was celebrated, but there is no record in the Log Book of May Day or Christmas celebrations. At the end of 1912 the staff comprised Misses Mildred Coles (C), Enid Hughes (C), Fanny Ford (C), Olive Greville (C), Gladys Wakeley (C), Edith Jones (U) and Carbetta Morris (P.T.) Only Misses Coles and Ford remained of the staff in January 1911.

At the Girls' School, of major significance was the development of the Cookery Centre when in July 1911 the school was chosen as one of six in the County to establish a Domestic Science Centre offering *'Home-Making'* instruction in Health, Needlework, Cookery and Infant Care. An instructress was appointed, and the school's senior pupils attended the Centre on three days a week with girls from Abertridwr School attending on two days. In 1912 the Courses were further developed, the Cookery instruction benefiting from the installation of a gas stove, all of which were highly praised by the County Inspectress of Domestic Subjects. The senior pupils attended two days a week with girls from Cwmaber and Abertridwr Schools attending on three days.

Attendance remained high. There is no record of any pupils leaving for a County School or as a result of passing the Proficiency Examination but seven left for the Higher Elementary School. At the end of 1912 the staff comprised Misses Eleanor Bradbury (C), Catherine Williams (C), Florence Lloyd (C), Daisy Jones (C), E.J. Bull (C), Laura Bryant (U) and Irene Jones (U). Only Miss Williams remained of the staff in January 1911. Attending on one day a week as Pupil Teachers were Margaret Rees and Winifred Lewis, a former pupil, both attending Hengoed County School.

Attendance was high also at the Boys' School although three pupils were committed to the Truant School and the Master was irritated by absenteeism on Cooperative Quarter Days. Brinley Jenkins won a County Scholarship to

Pontypridd Intermediate School and two pupils passed the Proficiency Examination but there is no record in the Log Book of pupils who departed for the Higher Elementary School. Noted was the St. David's Day celebration, that of Empire Day in 1911 and also the morning of April 17th, 1912, when *'the staff and scholars came provided with smoked glass to view the partial eclipse of the sun.'* Welcomed was the return of A.J. Williams from College, but J.A. Roberts left for Cwmaber School in 1912 and Miss Mary Rees, who had taught at the schools since they opened, resigned prior to marriage. At the end of 1912 the staff bore little resemblance to that of January 1911.

The Schools County Medical Officer continued to make an annual inspection of Infants, school-leavers, pupils with defective eyesight and those reported with infectious skin diseases. Nurse Vaughan, designated now as County Medical Nurse, then visited the parents of pupils who required treatment.

Undiminished was the strength and commitment of the chapel and church congregations. Following the departure of the very popular Rev. Gwilym Rees Rev. Henry Campbell Davies was inducted as curate of St. Peter's Church. Memorable was the Thanksgiving Service held by the Wesleyan Methodists which was accompanied by their Silver Band and extended over four days. So was the occasion when the Welsh Baptists went to Caerphilly to participate in the United Cymanfa Ganu. The traditional Sunday Schools outing to Barry Island aroused the usual excitement. Concerts, teas, bazaars and other fund-raising functions were promoted. Strong was the support for the Temperance movement and the Sunday Observance Society.

Undiminished also was the scale of drunkenness, the associated violence and criminal acts of a general nature. The Workmen's Constitutional Club in Station Road was *'struck off'* for contravening the licensing laws. Among the spate of Court cases heard in 1911 was that of the well-known fried-fish dealer and ex-pugilist with twenty-seven previous convictions who was sentenced to a lengthy term of imprisonment having been found guilty of assault, wilful damage and theft. In May, Police Constable Preece was shot twice in the arm when he tried to apprehend an intruder at the back of Mr. Shibko's pawnshop. He would not have subscribed to the press headline of the episode as *'Senghenydd Constable's Exciting Adventure'*, nor would it have been appreciated by Sergeant Walters who led a posse of constables in a vain search for the assailant.

The community's deep concern that the strength of the police force was insufficient in relation to the population was again expressed when in August the President of the Senghenydd branch of the Association for the Suppression of Evil wrote to the District Council to seek support for a deputation to meet the Chief Constable to request an increase in the force for the Aber Valley. The Council was in full agreement and named Councillor John Davies as one of its two representatives on the deputation but the Chief Constable was unable to accede to its request.

The charge sheet at the Caerphilly Magistrates Court in 1912 in respect of Senghenydd defendants continued to be dominated by drink related offences. Among the unrelated cases was that of a collier charged with assaulting a colliery official, an offence which received a measure of sympathy from fellow-workers but not from the Bench. Regarded as unfortunate were the fourteen miners charged with gambling, a very popular if illegal *'recreation'*. Playing *'cards'* on the Gelli fields, they were not sufficiently fleet of foot to escape the clutches of the arms of the law despite a warning from the *'scout'* of the approaching constables. Symptomatic of the judicial system was the sentence of fourteen days hard labour imposed on a miner found guilty of stealing a pair of shoes valued at 2/11½d.

Both the Aber Valley Philharmonic and Male Voice Choirs were active in concert performances and the occasional eisteddfod, the former awarded third prize at the prestigious Caerphilly Castle Eisteddfod in 1911. The annual eisteddfod held in 1911 was highly successful, the Senghenydd Brass Band particularly pleased by the award of second prize. Notable also was the eisteddfod organised in 1912 by the English Congregational Chapel under the Presidencies of Rev. D.M. Jones, Dr. James and Dan Lloyd. Once again young David John Evans demonstrated his prodigious talent when he was awarded the prize for his composition of a hymn entitled *'St. Vincent'* at an open competition held in Cardiff in December 1912. Still consistently successful in eisteddfods were bass Idris Perkins the champion soloist at Senghenydd and Abertridwr, tenor Idriswyn Humphreys, boy soloist Morgan John Davies a winner at Caerphilly and Llanbradach, pianist John Evan Richards a winner of the Junior Competitions at Caerphilly, Mountain Ash and Abertridwr. The Misses Rowlands and Humphreys won the duet competition at Llanbradach.

There was a development at the Parc Hotel which housed the Workmen's Library and Reading Room when on March 1st, 1912, the hotel and land was conveyed from Crosswell's Brewery, Cardiff, to a group composed substantially of businessmen which comprised Frederick Williams, Alfred Edward Taylor, William Thomas Marshall, Philip Richards, Charles Isaac, Benjamin Evans, William Davies, Samuel Price (Abertridwr) and Aaron Harris (Abertridwr).

In August 1912 the Senghenydd and Aber Valley Horticultural Society under the Presidency of Councillor Edward Shaw held a Flower and Vegetable Show. Allotments and back-gardens having been zealously cultivated there was an excellent display, one proud winner being Sergeant Walters. Featured were prizes offered to schoolchildren for collections of flowers and for drawings.

In March 1911 Mr. C.F. Waddon was granted a theatrical licence to give cinematograph entertainment on three nights a week at the Parc Hotel with the provision of compliance with safety regulations. In July a similar licence was granted to Mr. W. Haggar in respect of a theatre to be erected provided the plans were approved by the surveyor, particularly in regard to exits.

Then on September 19th a plan submitted by the National Picture Palace Company for a *'Public Hall'* was not approved by the District Council. On

October 3rd a revised plan was approved and work began on the building. On December 2nd an amended plan was approved.

By March 1912 the building was completed and on the 16th Mr. Charles Isaac applied for a seven-day Cinematograph Licence in respect of the Park Hall. But insofar as the Council had received a letter with a deposition from various chapels and churches in the valley which opposed granting of a seven-day licence to public halls and places of entertainment, it approved only a six-day licence. But after a while the *'Senghenydd Cinema Company'* devised a method to try to breach the six-day licence by submitting requests to hold Sunday concerts on behalf of *'good causes'*. Thus in July it was granted permission to hold a sacred concert on behalf of the Red Cross. In September it was permitted to hold a concert for the benefit of a resident. On this occasion there was no reference to it being a sacred concert. On December 10th it was not a concert but a cinema performance for the benefit of a resident which was granted. Then, despite vigorous opposition on religious grounds the Park Hall Picture House was permitted to hold cinema performances, including a matinée, on Christmas Day!

The Park Hall Picture House.

The Cricket Club increased in strength in 1911 and was able to field a 2nds team. Among the first-team players were S. Hoare, W. Jenkins, W. James, T. Jones, D.H. Jones, S. Lake, S. Lewis, H. Powell, A. Shaw, M.E. Thomas, H. Tocknell, D.R. Thomas, W. Thomas and D. Williams. Then in 1912 not only had a first-class pitch been laid at the recently completed recreation ground (the *'Rec'*) near the colliery but Archie Young was appointed as groundsman. He was a player of outstanding later talent, destined to play later for Somerset County Cricket Club, and under his expert tuition the two teams enjoyed a very successful season. Among the regular first-team players were J. Burrell, E. Dovey, A. Dinnan, R. Evans, W. Evans, A. Francis, S. Hoare, W. James, A. Johnson, T. Jones, F. Lewis, H. Powell, A. Roberts, A. Shaw, J. Stoneman, D.R. Thomas, W. Williams and Archie Young.

The *'Bluebells'* rugby team aroused great excitement in the village in its pursuit of the Lord Ninian Stuart Cup and the championship of the Second Division of the Cardiff and District League. On April 13th, 1912, hundreds of supporters journeyed to Whitchurch, very many on foot, to cheer the team against Cardiff Central in the semi-final of the Cup. The game ended in a draw but there was jubilation when the team emerged victorious at the replay a week later in Llanishen. On then to the final on April 27th against the Splott Crusaders at the Cardiff Arms Park, the supporters chartering a special train. A draw was the result and when this was repeated three days later at the same venue the destiny of the Cup was postponed until the 1912/13 season as was the outcome of the League Championship in which the team was in a very strong position.

Once again the *'Bluebells'* returned to the Arms Park in September, 1912, this time victorious, and when on October 26th they defeated Cardiff Central to be acclaimed champions of the League the joy was unconfined. The team comprised Will Pedro (Captain), Will Crook, Jim Dallimore, H. Davies, J. Davies, Will Fullalove, J. Gould, Jim Herring, Will James, J. Jones, T. Jones, E. Magee, Tom Marshall, A. Roberts, Peter Ross, Philip Skym, Jack Walters, F. Ward and Will Willacombe.

The Football Club had a full fixture list.

In May, 1912, a Sports Meeting was held at the *'Rec'*, a family affair which encompassed competitions suitable for all ages and included the tug-of-war won by a team with the unlikely name of the *'Gwernymilwr Teetotallers'*. A similar meeting was held in August in conjunction with the Flower and Vegetable Show and included a boy's race, an obstacle race and an old man's race along with more athletic events.

By the advent of 1913 the South Wales coalfield reached a peak of prosperity with the owners registering massive dividends and the work force of over 2,000 at the colliery was producing 1,800 tons of coal a day. About 50 men, affiliated to the Amalgamated Society of Railway Servants, were employed at the Sheds. The village looked forward to a trouble-free year.

Industrial calm reigned over the coalfield during the first six months and the main thrust of the Federation was devoted to the perennial question of non-Unionism. As a result *'show cards'* were organised periodically at the colliery, and one in particular was held in April in response to the Federation's declaration that it expected every miner in the coalfield to be affiliated to the Union by the general holiday on May 1st. Came that date and the Lodge held its traditional demonstration. On the following day, in common with the majority of other collieries, it declared a strike in support of the *'closed shop'* although only twenty miners were non-Unionists. Visits were made on each recalcitrant and so persuasive did they prove that all paid up and work was resumed that night with the Lodge Secretary Councillor Thomas James paying fulsome tribute to *'the housewives who have rendered valuable assistance to the Fed for they declared that lodgers who were not members would be turned out bag and baggage if they did not pay up'*. For the first time in the history of the colliery the work force had *'wiped out non-Unionism'*.

Mass meetings continued to be held at the Gwernymilwr Hotel to protest against grievances such as the excessive charge for the haulage of coal to the miners' homes. There were also a series of meetings to resolve differences within the work force as to finding an alternative method of funding the bills for medical attendance for the dependants of insured persons and others not covered by the National Insurance Act of 1911 which had been operated by a Benevolent Fund. In the event it was decided that each worker contribute 3d a week towards a Medical Fund to provide such attendance and that the deductions be made through the colliery office.

During this period from January to the end of June the village continued to be represented on Caerphilly Council by Edward Shaw, Thomas James and John Davies. The Council approved new streets in the Park Newydd Estate, the final draft conveyance of land for the Fire Brigade Station, the plan for an extension of the Workmen's Constitutional Club and the principle of establishing Workmen's Dwellings. Accepted was a tender for the supply of granite chippings and gravel, a tender of 11d an hour for street watering and the scavenging contract was awarded to Robert Alfred Bussell for which he was to be paid £270 per annum. Licences to store petrol were granted to confectioner/grocer W.T. Marshall and ironmongers Philip Richards and George Davies.

There was a negative response from the Plymouth Estate to the request for land for allotments but ongoing were the negotiations with the Directors of the Windsor Colliery via Colonel Forrest for land for a public recreation ground.

Rigorous supervision continued to be exercised over housing conditions which posed a health hazard. Yet again Stanley Street was the main source of overcrowding with closing orders served on two cellar dwellings in January, six in April and three in May. Cefn Llwyd was also served with a closing order as being unfit for human habitation. Otherwise only five Notices for the Abatement of Nuisances were issued during the six months, one of which was in respect of pigs being slaughtered in unlicensed premises at the back of Commercial Street.

There were no large-scale epidemics and there were no fatalities arising from cases of scarlet fever.

Dan Lloyd was appointed by the Council as an Overseer of the poor and funeral grants were made to four residents.

In accordance with the Closing Order: Shops Act 1912, the Council announced the closing times within the District as follows:

(A) Groceries, greengrocers, draperies, boots and shoes, furniture, iron-mongery, oil, glass, hardware, stationery, chemist, optician, plumber, pawnbroker, undertaker etc:

Monday- 7.30 p.m., Tuesday, Wednesday - 7.00 p.m., Thursday - 1.00 p.m., Friday - 7.30 p.m., Saturday - 11.00 p.m.
(B) Sale of Meat:
Monday, Tuesday, Wednesday, Thursday - 8.00 p.m., Friday - 9.00 p.m., Saturday - 11.00 p.m.
(C) Barbers and Hairdressers:
Monday, Tuesday, Wednesday - 8.00 p.m., Thursday - 1.00 p.m., Friday-9.00 p.m., Saturday - 11.30.p.m.

When the schools re-assembled in January there were 258 pupils on roll at the Infants' School, 369 at the Girls' School and 350 at the Boys' School. The Infants' School suffered staff changes as a result of the departure of Misses Greville and Wakely and the appointment by March of Miss Hoskins (C), Miss Melling (C) and Miss Gertrude Knowles (Supp.). In addition Miss John was absent ill for six weeks in February and March *'due in part to overstrain because of a very weak staff'*. At the Girls' School, Miss Evans complained about the staff being inadequate until Miss Robinson (c) and Miss Gore (C) were appointed. There were no staff changes at the Boys' School. All three schools were overcrowded.

In April came the annual visit of H.M. Inspector.

After drawing attention to the overcrowding at the Infants' School and expressing the hope that there would be no more staff changes he was able to conclude that *'The present teachers are efficient and hard working, and as they are very intelligently guided the future prospects are very encouraging'*. He again commented on the inadequate accommodation and the unsettled nature of the staff at the Girls' School before praising the teaching of cookery, the two-year course in Experimental Housewifery, English, Nature Study, drawing and painting, was not very happy with the teaching of History and Geography and very critical of the teaching of the Welsh language *'which has been practically suspended most of the new arrival teachers being unacquainted with Welsh'*, but concluding *'The condition of the school is very satisfactory'*. On the Boys' School, he reported that the accommodation was sufficient on the whole but was critical of the fact that in some classrooms there were more than 60 pupils, and that although good progress was being made in the teaching of Welsh reading this did not apply to conversation *'probably because some teachers have not the requisite knowledge'*, but he concluded *'The school continues to be maintained in a very creditable condition by the experienced Headmaster. The discipline is excellent as usual and the instruction is given with faithfulness and success'*.

The School Board members expressed their satisfaction with all three reports and the morale of the staffs was further uplifted by the prospect of overcrowding when it was announced that a Junior School was planned to be built on a nearby site.

In May and June the entries in the Log Books were sparse. Miss John welcomed the removal of Standard I to the English Congregational Chapel vestry to relieve the overcrowding and also the appointment of Miss Elsie Roberts. The unsettled nature of the staff at the Girls' School continued with the departure of Misses Bull, Irene Jones and Laura Bryant. Dan Lloyd expressed his pleasure at the use for the first time of the *'Rec'* for organised games with the kind permission of Manager Edward Shaw and also at the visit of Mr. Towyn Jones, a former pupil, *'now a student at Lampeter College where he has just passed his Responses Examination'.*

Large congregations attended the places of worship and the Sunday Schools prospered. In January Rev. Thomas Morris was inducted as minister of Noddfa Chapel in succession to Rev. James Jones. Many were the social and cultural functions. A concert at Abertridwr Workmen's Hall promoted by Salem Chapel was very successful, and even more so was a concert which featured the children of St. Peter's Church.

Cases of drunkenness and physical assaults continued to be commonplace. Typical was that of a miner, sentenced to one month's hard labour, who, in a drunken state threw a lamp at his landlady causing her bodily harm, and that of a barman at the Universal Hotel charged with assaulting a miner during a quarrel over a 6d piece. On a less serious note were the cases which indicated a *'clamp down'* on street betting. An eighteen-year-old bookmaker was fined £5 or one month imprisonment for accepting a betting slip from a lady despite his plea that he did so out of kindness, a twenty-year-old bookmaker was fined 20 shillings or 14 days imprisonment for a similar offence although he was described later by Sergeant Walters as *'a very tidy young man'* whom he had advised to *'give up the game'*, and a colliery lamp man was fined £2 and costs for passing a slip in Commercial Street.

Both the Aber Valley choirs were active as was the Aber Valley Silver Band conducted by Sam Radcliffe which came first in the Class A Competition at a Band Festival held in Pontypridd. Applauded were the successes of individual soloists at various eisteddfods - tenor Idriswyn Humphreys at Taffswell, Nantgarw and Llantrisant, soprano Mrs. J. Ellis and baritone J.D. Morgan at Caerphilly Castle, baritone Morgan John Davies at Pengam.

But pride of place in the musical field was accorded to David John Evans who was described in a *'Western Mail'* article in January as *'a remarkably clever composer and pianist'*. It continued, *'Eighteen years of age, the oldest of seven children of Mr. and Mrs. William Evans of Coronation Terrace, Senghenydd, his father an overman at the colliery and conductor of the singing at Noddfa Congregational chapel, he has displayed special musical gifts from a very early age, composing a hymn at the age of ten. Recently he has composed an operetta entitled* 'Irene', *a work of exceptional musical talent for full chorus which lasts for two and a half hours.*

When twelve he won a County Scholarship to Pontypridd Intermediate School from Senghenydd Boys' School, but he has devoted his education chiefly to music and having recently matriculated at Durham University it is his ambition to attain his degree. The residents of the village are determined to give him every opportunity of success and at a public meeting on the 14th a committee was elected to raise funds and solicit contributions on his behalf. Supported by Councillor Edward Shaw, the Chairman is Dr. Philip James, the Treasurer is Mr. Dan Lloyd and the General Secretary is Mr. B.M. Williams'. Subsequently in February the committee organised a performance of the operetta at Abertridwr Workmen's Hall. Conducted by the composer, it was widely acclaimed.

Notable also was the occasion on February 28th when the Senghenydd Cymmrodorion Society marked St. David's Day with its first celebration, a choral festival followed by a banquet. It was reported that *'The concert held at Noddfa was marked by some magnificent singing by a choir of four hundred boys and girls conducted by schoolmaster Dan Lloyd. Patriotic addresses by Rev. Price Hughes (in Welsh) and Mr. Towyn Jones were much appreciated. The proceedings at the banquet provided a meeting ground for all and a fine spirit of unity and nationalism prevailed'.*

At the Annual General Meeting of the Library and Institute, it was resolved that in order to improve the facilities, the Parc Hotel be purchased from the local group of businessmen, and appointed as Trustees were mason Rowland John Rees, collier's labourer William Thomas and clothier Dan Davies. But negotiations with the vendors were to prove very protracted and were not finalised until 1916.

The first Dramatic Society was formed by Messrs. Shell, Perkins and Griffiths in May. It gave a performance of the play *'The Porter's Knot'* at Abertridwr Workmen's Hall when the proceeds were devoted towards the Library and Institute.

Congratulated was Mr. Alfred Taylor who was awarded 1st Prize at the Caerphilly Horse Show in the category of *'Tradesmen's Turn Out'* and 2nd Prize for *'Best Hackney or Pony Mare'* with *'Queen of the Hills'*. Delighted was the Cooperative society with the award of 3rd prize in the *'Tradesmen's Turn Out'* and 3rd prize for *'Best Heavy Horse in Harness'* with *'Pride of the Valley'*.

The two rugby teams fared well in the closing months of the 1912/13 season in the Cardiff and District League, the 1st team victorious over the Grange, Machen and Rudry and performing creditably in the Hallett Cup, the United team rejoicing in a win over Penarth United. The football team was disappointed to lose to Caerphilly and dismayed in April when the Welsh League suspended W. Powell and L. Jenkins for six weeks. A games tournament was held between the Conservative and Workmen's Clubs. June saw the cricket season heralded by a victory in the *'derby match'* against Caerphilly, followed by a convincing win over St. Peter's Club, Cardiff.

The Liberals held a public demonstration at the Gelli fields which was addressed by Clement Edwards, M.P., Councillor John Davies and Rev. D.M. Jones, after which the Member of Parliament officially opened the Liberal Club.

In July, the Council, following complaints of an inadequate water supply, served Notices on the owners of 41 houses in Station Terrace, 27 in Kingsley Place, 16 in Station Road, 2 in Park Cottages, the Liberal Club and the Workmen's Constitutional Club to secure a sufficient supply from the Rhymney Water Company within seven days. Among the owners were Mrs. Clarissa Shaw of Cenydd Terrace (9 houses), Alfred Taylor (6), Fred Williams (6), butcher Frank Watts (6), Ann Lewis of Station Terrace (5) and David Griffiths of Stanley Street (5). Negotiations continued in respect of the public recreation ground and the Fire Brigade Station. Deferred was the application by W.T. Marshall on behalf of the Aber Valley Automobile Company for a licence to run a small charabanc.

Miss Evans reported the success of seven girls in the examination for entry to Caerphilly Higher Elementary School. There is no entry in the Boys' School Log Book appertaining to this examination but Dan Lloyd recorded his pleasure at a convincing victory against Caerphilly School in a baseball match and his deep displeasure by a complaint from the Colliery Sergeant that some boys had caused damage to the colliery Hospital House for Horses.

A Grand Eisteddfod, organised by Secretary Isaac Thomas, was staged in a marquee on grounds near the Park Hall with the proceeds devoted to the Library and Institute project. The music competitions were adjudicated by Professor David Jenkins of Aberystwyth University, the literary entries by Mr. Ifano Jones and Rev. D.M. Jones and the brass band competition by Mr. Sam Radcliffe. The chief competitions were: Male Voice Choir, test piece *'The Charge of the Light Brigade'*, prize £20; Class C. Brass Band, prize £15; Mixed Choir, test piece *'Yr Haf'*, prize £10; Champion Solos, prizes of 3 guineas. It attracted a large number of competitors and an enthusiastic audience although the only local winners were Nathaniel Vaughan in the Novice Solo competition and Archie Evans in the Boys' Solo competition.

The Annual Fête and Sports Meeting, the proceeds devoted this year to St. Peter's Church, followed the usual pattern of being a family affair with the musical entertainment provided by the Senghenydd Silver Band. Notable in the sports events was the success of the Gwernymilwr Teetotallers tug-of-war team, a victory which was repeated later at a Sports Meeting in Abertridwr, captained respectively by Evan Williams and Jenkin Jones.

G.S. Morgan won the 100 yards Novice Handicap race and J.L. Morgan won the 300 yards Open Handicap race at Bargoed Sports Meeting.

Exponents of the noble art of boxing such as J. Hicks engaged in contests at Abertridwr.

In August, Dr. James presided over a public meeting to mark the departure of Rev. Price Hughes, curate of St. Cenydu Welsh Church. He was presented with a gold watch and chain in recognition of his work as Secretary of the Cymmrodorion Society by Rev. D.M. Jones who extolled him as a fervent nationalist and Church defender. Rev. D. Lloyd Rees, Rector of Eglwysilan Church, made a presentation on behalf of the Welsh congregation.

The Senghenydd and Aber Valley Horticultural Society held its Annual Show, Ambulance Competition and Sports in the village under the Presidency of Edward Shaw. Colliery Sergeant James and P.C. Kirk were the main winners in the Open Classes of the vegetable section, Senghenydd came third in the ambulance competition and Stan Perry was prominent in the sports events.

Gwernymilwr Teetotallers were beaten finalists at a Sports Meeting in Llanbradach but were successful at Ystrad Mynach.

At the Annual General Meeting of the Rugby Club, Edward Shaw was re-elected as President, Peter Ross elected as Captain and the report was one of good progress with the Club being admitted again to the Hallett Cup competition.

In September the question of non-Unionism at the colliery had re-emerged and it was only under the threat of withdrawal of labour that the situation was resolved after two weeks of negotiations. There was also a meeting of railwaymen when they were urged by an organiser of their Society and by Hubert Jenkins to exercise the industrial and political powers conferred by the Trades Union Act.

The District Council, having successfully concluded negotiations for the purchase of land for a recreation ground, approved plans for a site. The Surveyor reported that there was now a plentiful supply of water to Station Terrace, Station Road and Kingsley Place. Granted free of charge for three months was a licence to W.T. Marshall for a motor charabanc. Councillor Trevor James stated that the train service to the Aber Valley was *'rotten'* and seconded a motion that the Council apply to the Board of Trade for a Provisional Order to construct and operate a system of electric tramways between Caerphilly, Abertridwr, Senghenydd, Llanbradach and Bedwas, but it was defeated as being too ambitious.

The new school year began with 276 pupils on roll at the Infants' School, 361 at the Girls' School and 348 at the Boys' School. Miss John's staff comprised Fanny Ford (C), Catherine Melling (C), Mildred Cole (C), Elsie Roberts (C), Gertrude Hoskins (C), Phyllis Austin (C), Gertrude Knowles (S), Gwen Evans (U) and Garbetta Morris (P.T.), Miss Evans's staff comprised Gertrude Roberts (T.C.), Mary Robinson (T.C.), Florence Lloyd (T.C.), Daisy Jones (T.C.), Eleanor Bractbury (C), Catherine Williams (C), C. Gore (U), Margaret Rees (U), Katie Bowen and Winifred Lewis (P.T.). Dan Lloyd's staff comprised A.J. Williams (T.C.), Miss Agnes Jones (T.C.), Thomas Morgan (T.C.), Miss Kate Clarke (T.C.), Brinley Howells (C), Benjamin Davies (U), Percival Thomas (U), John Walters (U) and Emrys Evans (P.T.). Other than the usual problem of overcrowding the month passed smoothly.

The English Congregationalists launched their annual eisteddfod. Despite pleading that he was provoked, a miner was bound over to keep the peace for six months after being found guilty of assaulting an overman in the colliery while he was walking past Eglwysilan Church.

The Rugby Club organised a fund-raising Sports Meeting in which J.L. Morgan won the 300 yards Handicap Race, S. Perry came 2nd in the 100 yards Football Race, Herbie Powell came 3rd in the 100 yards Open Novice Race and the Open Tug-of-War contest was won by a Senghenydd team captained by D. Knotts. In the Cardiff and District Union the 1st team beat Cardiff Welsh and Machen, drew with Newbridge and lost to Cardiff Central, and the United team defeated Llanbradach.

On October 3rd Dan Lloyd wrote in the Log Book, *'Another of Nature's parting days'*.

On October 4th the Rugby team played against Roath.

On October 7th the Caerphilly Council at its meeting invited tenders for the granite metalling of roads, resolved to ascertain the cost of hiring a steam roller, issued two Notices for the Abatement of Nuisances and granted licences for the sale of fireworks to W.T. Marshall and Thomas Williams.

On Saturday, October 11th, the Senghenydd junior rugby team defeated Ferndale Harriers, the football team drew with Canton, and in the evening a Senghenydd Male Voice Choir, conducted by Thomas Thomas (*'Bottanic'*), sang at the Cory Hall in Cardiff.

Sunday, October 12th, was typically sabbatarian with vast congregations and Sunday School scholars attending the places of worship.

Monday, October 13th, was of no particular local significance. The newspapers were focused on the impending marriage of the Duke of Connaught.

CHAPTER 9

On Tuesday morning, October 14th, only about half a dozen pupils were in the school yard of the Boys' School at the time of assembly, eight in the yard of the Girls' School and about thirty in the yard of the Infants' School. Dan Lloyd wrote in the Log Book, *'Appalling disaster at our local colliery. The town bereaved and frantic with grief. School closed'*. Closed also were the other schools.

On that morning, as in the normal course of events, the main force of some 945 men and boys had descended the colliery for the day shift.

By 8 o'clock, two hours into the shift, the officials had made their customary rounds of inspection in each district and reported all safe. Another routine day was in prospect.

The Explosion.

At ten minutes past eight *'all Hell'* broke loose as the roar of an awesome explosion resounded through the village and almost at the same moment a fierce blast, accompanied by a cloud of dust and smoke, swept up the Lancaster shaft, hurling upwards a two-ton cage to wreck the timber platform at the surface before crashing into the headgear. Banksman John Mogridge, standing on the platform, was killed instantly, his body decapitated, and his assistant was injured.

Down below the pit was a raging inferno, shattered with massive roof falls and enveloped in dense suffocating gas and smoke.

Said William Jenkins of High Street, *'A few minutes after 8 o'clock I was sitting down in the kitchen having a bit of breakfast when I heard a loud report. My missus said there were two reports but I cannot be sure of this. It was as if a big boiler had burst and I am sure they would have heard it miles away. I knew something had happened at the colliery and rushed for the pit'*. There he joined a mass of women, men and children *'huddled together, some weeping, inarticulate with fear of the doom of husbands, sons, fathers, brothers in the great underworld'*. Scarcely a family in the village did not number at least one member or relative working in the colliery.

At the time of the explosion Manager Edward Shaw was in the lamp room at the surface. After a quick appraisal of the situation at the mouth of the Lancaster shaft he crossed to the York pit shaft where he found both the cage and the fan in working order. Issuing instructions to replace the cage and repair the planking at the Lancaster pit head, he then, accompanied by overman D.R. Thomas, stepped into the cage and began a slow descent into the York pit to assess the conditions underground. They had descended about 15 yards when the banksman received a signal from the pit bottom and they were hauled back to the surface. Assured now that there were survivors below, the two, joined by others, began to inch their way down. Halfway down they met the up-coming cage in which was the body of a man in a tram, his legs hanging on the crossbars, it having been catapulted into the tram in the cage by the blast of the explosion. Signalling the cage to stop, they pulled in the body and continued the descent. At the Six Feet landing, 530 yards down, further progress was halted when the cage was jammed in the girders. There they got out, shouting down to the Nine Feet landing about twenty yards below to be told that the men from the East side were *'alright'* before they scrambled down to the smoke-filled bottom.

Shaw's plan was to get to the Main West Level and then via the main road to the Lancaster shaft, a route that would probably manifest the effects of the explosion. First, the party tried to go West but this was proved impassible because of the dense smoke. They then tried going East but the fires were too fierce. So they returned to try the West approach again. There, despite the burning timbers and doors blown open the fires were less intense and they were able to douse them before getting through to the Main West Level and then to the Lancaster shaft. On their way crossing the pit they found six men lying down full length, all of whom died later. A few yards from the shaft they found shackler Ernest Moses miraculously alive behind some empty trams which had sheltered him from the blast which had killed eight men working around the pit bottom.

The party then divided. The main body under Thomas made their way east to fight a fire which had re-ignited. When he reached the East York Level he found that it had not been penetrated by the explosion and the men were *'alright'* so he gave instructions that they be withdrawn from the workings and assemble at the pit bottom.

A young mother waiting alone for news.

Meanwhile, Shaw, with another man, continued west along the Main West Level. There he was met by a scene described as *'like looking into a furnace'* where all the timbers were ablaze as far as the eye could see and every working place was being swept with suffocating smoke and gas. Realising that nothing could be done there he rejoined Thomas and his party still fighting the fire. Informed that all the men on the East side were safe and of Thomas's instructions, he ordered that the men be kept back for about one hundred yards from the shaft until the debris and wrecked trams had been cleared from it. A party was detailed for the clearance and another party detailed to collect the injured and the dead. Once the shaft had been cleared, he ordered that the injured and dead be brought up, followed by the men from the York Pit.

At about 9.30, by which time work had already started to clear the shaft, Shaw returned to the surface to organise further assistance, contacting Mines Inspectors and Rescue Brigades and ordering the laying of water pipes to the nearby reservoir as work continued to repair the shattered pit pipes. He then returned underground to direct operations.

At the pithead and the surrounding area the crowds were growing into massive proportions, now joined in a constant stream of people from Abertridwr, Penyrheol, Caerphilly and other neighbouring villages. Great was the relief at the news from the York pit but enhanced was the fear for those entombed in the Lancaster pit. Equipped only with fire extinguishers and without breathing apparatus the Universal Rescue Brigade continued their gallant efforts but theirs was an impossible task.

As the magnitude of the disaster became apparent so help began to flood in from colliery managers and officials, doctors, Red Cross Nurses, St. John Ambulance Brigades, Rescue Brigades Mines Inspectors and police

Crowds waiting at the pithead for news.

and from the clergy and Salvation Army to offer words of comfort and hope. There too came the press reporters. One who journeyed by train wrote, *'I heard the tales of woe travelling up the charming Aber Valley bathed in the sunshine of a lovely October day, through the fields of verdant green and trees clustered with foliage, nothing to suggest the grim tragedy which lay just beyond the bend. What had we to do with death and disaster? Yet there it lay in the glistening heat, spreading an imperceptible haze over the whole countryside'.*

At about 10.30 came the first Rescue Brigade Car from the Rhymney Valley under the charge of Superintendent Kitto, followed at 11 o'clock by the Porth Brigade Car which had been delayed by trouble with the tyres, then shortly afterwards by Aberdare and Crumlin Cars, all the Brigades fully equipped with breathing and other apparatus.

Early on the scene had been Dr. James and other local doctors and by mid-day the roll included Drs. Burke, Donaldson and Watson (Abertridwr), T.W. Thomas, McKenzie, Richards and Tilmont (Caerphilly), Robertson and Lloyd (Llanbradach), Nolan and McManus (Bedwas) Jackson (Ystrad Mynach), Turner (Den), Leigh (Treharris), Clarke (Aberbargoed) and McGorman (Porth).

At almost a moment's notice Herbert Lewis of Cardiff, the Deputy Commissioner for South Wales and Monmouthshire St. John's Ambulance Brigade, sent a horse ambulance car followed by a motor ambulance and then despatched trained and fully-equipped squads from Caerphilly, Pontypridd, Cardiff, Newport, Rhymney, Llantwit Fardre, Aberbargoed and Cilfynydd.

Dr. James, Sgt. James and a group of miners 1913.

Under the charge of Commandant Miss Corbett of Llanbradach and Superintendent Mrs. Burke of Abertridwr came detachments of Red Cross nurses from Senghenydd, Abertridwr, Caerphilly, Llanbradach, Pontypridd, Cardiff and Barry who not only attended the injured throughout the day and night but supplied cups of coffee, Bovril and other stimulants to the rescue parties and other willing workers on the surface.

From the Glamorgan Constabulary came a strong force comprising one hundred and twenty men under the command of Chief Constable Lionel Lindsay and the Deputy Chief Constable to *'preserve order'* at the pithead where *'the scenes were harrowing in the extreme, weeping women, some with children in arms, waiting for news of husbands, sons, fathers and brothers, while strong men were dazed at the feeling of helplessness which prevailed'.*

Despite the arrival of the Rescue Brigades little could be achieved until the raging fires could be brought under some measure of control, a task which was very seriously hampered by the shortage of water Tom Purnell, one of the crew of the Crumlin Rescue Brigade, recalled, *'As we were nearing our destination we could see something very serious had happened by the thousands of people lining the streets. At last we drew near the pit and the sight is one not forgotten - the smoke belching from the pit, cartloads of coffins being hauled to the pit and the surrounding hills covered with people. But we were not able to do anything for hours because it was impossible to get past the fires. I wandered about the pit top - women crying, coffins coming in, miners making stretchers'.*

Meanwhile, at various intervals after 9.30 the first survivors were being brought up to the surface, men and boys who had been working on fringe areas of the explosion together with others recovered from the area between the York shaft and the scene of the fires. Among the gradual exodus were Sidney Gregory, fourteen-year-old Henry Wedlock who was working his first day at the pit, brothers William and Charles Wyatt, Bill Jones, Elias Morgan, Ernest Moses and Bert Williams of 2 Gelli Terrace. Said Sidney Gregory, *'I heard two heavy thuds, followed by a great deal of smoke. The air suddenly became still and this was followed by a lot of coal dust which was as thick as fog. A little boy, Henry Wedlock, was with me. I could hardly see my way out. Later on, the fireman came and told us to go out. It was an awful thing. The timber was cracking and falling about and we could hardly stand the heat and the foul air. At last we got to the bottom of the York Pit and were kept there nearly two hours. We came to the surface shortly after ten o'clock'.*

Brought up first had been the injured to be conveyed to Aberdare Hall which had been transformed into a temporary hospital under the charge of Dr. Ivor Davies of Cardiff who was assisted by Drs. Burke, Donaldson, Watson and others, St. John Ambulance teams and Red Cross nurses. Nine were critically injured. Dennis Carroll of Abertridwr and John Herring of 7 Cenydd Terrace, Senghenydd, died while undergoing treatment. The others were conveyed to King Edward VII Hospital in Cardiff by train, laid on the floor of the guard's van. William Robson of Cardiff died on the way. David Jones of 6 Cenydd Terrace, Senghenydd, died in hospital within an hour of arrival. George Smale of Abertridwr and William Charles Thomas of 21 Cenydd Terrace, Senghenydd, died the next day. William Henry Jones of 29 Cenydd Terrace, Senghenydd, died on the 17th, Gwilym Williams of 213 Caerphilly Road, Senghenydd died on the 25th, and William Barnett, age 15, of Caerphilly, died on the 27th.

Eleven bodies were laid to rest in the carpenter's a shop serving as a temporary mortuary. Here Dr. James faced the gruesome task of identification in that all were frightfully burned, some mutilated. One was described as *'nothing but a heap of blisters'*, one identified by a piece of shirt, another by the return half of a railway ticket tucked away for safety in a tin box of lozenges, another by a set of false teeth with two missing, another by his watch.

At 11 o'clock the exodus began of 489 men from the York pit in orderly batches of 20 to 28 and by 2 o'clock all had been brought up. One was my father.

At 2 o'clock the first official statement was made to the horde of pressmen. Guarded in tone, it stated, *'At 8 o'clock this morning an explosion occurred at the Lancaster Pit of Messrs. Lewis Merthyr Consolidated Collieries. There were 900 down the pit at the time. The workmen on the east side of the pit in Six Feet and Nine Feet seams have been brought out alive to the number of 489. There is a fire burning at the bottom of the downcast pit on the west side of it and it has been impossible so far to proceed beyond the fire. No workmen have been brought out from the west side of the workings. Efforts are now being made to put out the fire'.*

Sealed beyond a wall of roaring flames were some 400 men and boys, who if not already killed or suffocated were struggling to survive against the after-damp gas.

Relays of rescue and clearance parties were fighting heroically to get through to the trapped men under conditions that were described as impossible, even with the usual apparatus. So dense was the smoke that they could see only inches ahead and such was the seering temperature that work was possible only a few minutes at a time. Many were over-come by exhaustion, some were blinded temporarily. Against such overwhelming odds, coupled with an insufficient water supply and a raging fire smouldering beneath the falls, so progress was hard-fought and painfully slow.

'During the afternoon the suspense was unbearable,for there was no news from below apart from the constant repetition of the statement that the fire was being fought but little progress was being made. One could see from the sad countenances of the officials and rescuers that they held only faint hopes of recovering any entombed men beyond the fire'. When Colonel Pearson, Chief Mines inspector, arrived, he declared that there was no hope of rescue until the raging fires were put out and the *'relentless flames'* extinguished before hope could be revived *'in any shape'.*

Shortly before 3 o'clock Lord Merthyr arrived, having returned from Scotland after being informed of the disaster. He called a meeting with Shaw, Mines Inspectors, mining engineers and miners' representatives to appraise him of the conditions underground and the action being taken.

Throughout the morning and afternoon masses of people descended on the village by foot, cycle, trap, wagonette and train. As far as the eye could see were long chains of people toiling over Egwlysilan Mountain coming from Pontypridd Common and Gelligaer Common. Among a group of school boys who walked over the mountain from Bedlinog was Walter Haydn Davies, who was to leave school at the age of thirteen to work in a local colliery and destined to become Headmaster of Bargoed Grammar School. In his book entitled *'Ups and Downs'*, under the Chapter headed *'An Unforgettable Experience'* is this extract:

'As we got nearer to Senghenydd we saw suddenly the ill-fated colliery with the mangled pit gear. The tragedy was obvious for the pit head and surface works were crowded with men, women and children standing motionless, with groups scattered about the hillsides, watching and praying. There was little display of emotion - no hysterical weeping but the very grimness in the demeanour of the people added poignancy to the spectacle...

There was an air of expectancy as the great wheels above the colliery began to turn, taking the cages up and down the pit. When the wheels stopped turning there was an agony of waiting before the stretcher men came along, carrying the dead bodies of those who had just been brought up the shaft... We moved amongst the crowd, glancing at distraught faces, listening to voices thick with despair....

Towards evening, clouds began to gather and we had to begin our long trek homeward... I was just about old enough to realise that the anguish I had witnessed illustrated the degree of suffering which went hand in hand with the production of coal'.

The augmented staff at the Post Office coped with 3,000 telegraphic transcripts from an endless stream of men and women sending reassuring or hopeless messages and receiving a vast number of messages of sympathy from all parts of the kingdom. One addressed to Dr. W.N. Atkinson, Inspector of Mines for South Wales, came from King George V. It read: *'The Queen and I are appalled at the news of the terrible disaster which occurred this morning at the Universal Colliery at Senghenydd in Glamorganshire, and are all the more shocked having visited that district only last year.*

We trust that the loss of life may not be so great as were at first anticipated. We deeply sympathise with the families who have lost their dear ones, and will be grateful for any particulars regarding the condition of the injured'. George R.I.

By the evening a crowd of over 4,000 crammed the village and it was almost impossible to forge a way through the streets. On the slopes of the surrounding hills stood a vast assembly, quiet and reverend. Around the pit head, watching and waiting in a mixture of emotions of stupor, anguish, resignation and hope stood the wives, mothers, fathers, daughters, sons, brothers and sisters and other relatives of the entombed men.

At about 5.30 Mr. R.A.S. Redmayne, Chief Inspector of Mines, and Dr. Atkinson arrived and descended the pit to assess the situation. On their return they recommended an improved water supply and the removal by trams of the red-hot debriss to the surface, a process undertaken thereafter and throughout the night.

Five members of the mines' rescue team who performed the most dangerous tasks in the bid to save their colleagues. Two of these men William Hyatt and George Spreadbury died in the explosion. Also in the photograph are Sir William Thomas Lewis and Mr. Edward Shaw.

Evening merged into night, the rescue work carried out by four shifts of workers, changing every six hours, all under experienced officials belonging to the colliery and assisted by mining engineers. So great now was the danger of suffocation from the after-damp that the volunteer parties were made fully aware of the situation. Before descending, several men retired to a room in the colliery office to write letters of farewell to relatives and three made their wills. In the words of Clement Edwards, M.P., who later descended the pit with Inspector Redmayne, Colonel Pearson, Agent W.T. Rees and Miners' Agent Dai Watts Morgan, *'The heroism, energy and zeal of those I saw working is beyond praise'*.

At its weekly evening meeting the Caerphilly Urban District Council recorded its *'profound sympathy for the families who had suffered from the distressing disaster at the colliery'* and then resolved *'that the Surveyor be given plenary powers to purchase materials and engage men for preparing the necessary graves at Penyrheol Cemetery'*.

At 8.30 p.m. W.T. Rees, Managing Director of the Company issued this statement: *'The fire is now well under hand, and unless there is another fire in the workings we hope that during the night some of the rescuers may be able to make fair progress into the workings. I cannot offer you any opinion whatever as to the state of the workings inside and we shall really know nothing until the morning'*. At the pit head the huddled crowd of relatives prepared for an all-night vigil.

It was about 9 o'clock when Mines Inspectors Greenland Davies and P.T. Jenkins discovered that fresh air was entering No.1. North Heading, which communicated with the Bottanic District by means of a narrow airway 16 yards to 20 yards in length, so giving rise to the possibility that the District might not have been penetrated by the explosion fires. Joined later by Professor Redmayne and Clement Edwards, M.P., they found fresh horse droppings not covered by dust and then a live horse. Could men in the Bottanic have survived also?

When this information was reported to the committee it was decided to form a party to try to explore the Bottanic by way of the narrow airway. Led by Colliery Agent Robert Rees, it comprised Greenland Davies, Rhondda Valley Miners' Agent Dai Watts Morgan, J.A. Price the Manager of Elliott Colliery, Lewis Watkins the Manager of Bargoed Brithdir Colliery and Mechanic D.W. Price of Rhymney, accompanied by Dr. Daniel Thomas of Bargoed and seven men of the Rhymney Valley Rescue Brigade comprising Ben Rees and Charlie Williams of Aberbargoed, Tom of Bargoed Reynolds, Tom Griffiths and Frank Gregory of Bargoed and Will Williams of Pengam under the direction of Superintendent Kitto.

This initial party went down the pit at 9.45 p.m. and were joined at the bottom by Overman Ted Harris and Fireman William Thomas to guide it to the workings. Along the way they found two dead men, then a live horse fastened to a tram full of rubbish, followed by a dead horse and two bodies before arriving at the narrow airway. The air was fresh at this point and it was decided to proceed with a few men and to keep a line of communication.

Those who now went forward were Robert Rees, J.A. Price, Greenland Davies, Dai Watts Morgan, Overman Ted Harris and Superintendent Kitto. When they entered their first working place the air was a little foul, but proceeding, they found a man unconscious but alive! He was shouldered towards fresh air and Kitto rushed back to summon Dr. Thomas and the Rescue men to revive him with their oxygen cylinders. The time was 11.30 p.m. and at this juncture Greenland Davies and D.W. Price were sent to the surface to convey the news and to get more help, blankets and restoratives.

Robert Rees, J.A. Price, Lewis Watkins, Kitto and Ted Harris then began exploring the remainder of the faces. Another man was found lying on the side of the road and was shouldered back to fresh air to be attended by Dr. Thomas and the Rescue men. Robert Rees then returned to the surface.

The rest then moved to the main haulage road where over a period of time they located another sixteen survivors as well as bodies. Joined by other doctors and rescuers they then began the back-breaking task of carrying the survivors on stretchers through the narrow airway to the pit bottom, one in which the Porth and Crumlin Rescue Brigades gave valuable assistance.

Brought to the carpenter's shop between one and three o'clock on Wednesday morning were eighteen men snatched from certain death, some exhausted, some hardly able to speak, but all revived sufficiently to go home, some on foot. Home to Senghenydd went Benjamin David (159 Commercial Street), Joseph Evans (20 Stanley Street), Benjamin Hill (Parc Terrace), James Hill (15 Brynhyfryd Terrace), Ernest Jones (141 Commercial Street) brothers Evan and John Owen Jones (183 Caerphilly Road), William Jones (Coronation Terrace), William Jones (65 High Street), Charles Steel (18 Station Terrace), Wilfred Vizard (15 Alexandra Terrace) and Bert Williams (9 Grove Terrace). Home to Caerphilly went Arthur Balsom (17 Corbett Crescent), Archibald Dean (204 Nantgarw Road), Trevor Morgan (Black Cock), George Moore and his sons Evan and George (174 Bedwas Road).

Legendary is the story of how Albert Dean pressed his last drop of tea upon young George Moore shortly before he died.

One of the first to-be rescued was Bert Williams. A well-known boxer and member of the Rugby Club he said, *'I was going down on a journey of trams riding on the haulage rope when I heard a noise like a gun and was knocked of my journey as it jumped the road. Then came a dense cloud of dust and I was almost choked. I had no idea what it was. My lamp went out'*. Almost senseless and half a mile from the pit bottom he started to run blindly in the darkness, feeling his way, falling and stumbling in a desperate bid to reach safety. Then he came upon engineman Thomas Rees of Cenydd Terrace who played for the rugby team and they went forward together. But the fumes got worst and they parted company. Rees went on and died. Bert staggered back until overcome by giddiness he collapsed unconscious, remembering nothing more until he was brought round by one of the rescuers.

One of the men who helped to rescue him was his namesake Albert Victor Williams, age 18, an apprentice carpenter at the Great Western colliery,

Just eighteen men and boys were rescued from the Bottanic District and seven of them are seen here in this picture.

Hopkinstown, Pontypridd. He told a reporter, *'I belonged to the pit Ambulance Brigade so it was only natural that I should volunteer to help. A group of us tramped five miles over the mountain to Senghenydd and there were thousands at the pit head when we assembled in the carpenter's shop waiting for instructions and watching loads of fire extinguishers being lowered into the pit.*

I then joined a rescue party about to descend the pit, but first, like every other man, I made a will. Mine read, "I bequeath my property and effects to my next of kin, my father Thomas Benjamin Williams, 42 Pantygraigwen Road, Pontypridd". *I put it in a sealed envelope and dropped it into a box as I moved towards the cage.*

At the pit bottom the air, blocked in places by roof falls, was blowing so fiercely that small stones and dust were being whipped into our faces as we edged forward... There seemed to be dead everywhere... At Bottanic airway the team of rescuers who had gone down before us were on their knees dragging survivors through the tunnel on brattice sheets... Then we helped to carry them on stretchers to the surface, and after I went to the carpenter's shop where I was given a drink of rum and hot coffee'.

Five years later, their war service over, the two Berts met by chance in a military camp at Boulogne when they chatted about *'the man who came back from the dead'.*

Rescued Ernest Jones told how he and other colliers heard a loud report from the direction of the Lancaster Pit. They got together and moved gradually forward, but with great difficulty. One by one the party became separated until he and another man he did not know were left, but as they moved forward his companion had to give up after a few yards, the air being thick with smoke. At about noon he felt too weak to proceed any further laid down by the side of the road and gave up hope. There he was found unconscious.

John Owen Jones said, *'I heard a report like thunder. I came back from the surface where I was working and tried to dress. I stumbled trying to get out and then became unconscious. The first thing I remember after that is being in Aberdare Hall. My brother, cousin and uncle were rescued with me.'*

Archibald Dean recounted, *'I heard the blast shortly after 8 o'clock.* "What was that?" *asked 16-year-old Thomas Cook who was working with me. I said that something had happened somewhere, perhaps a fall in the main.*

Within about two or three minutes a number of other colliers came rushing up and wanted to know what was the matter. We all went towards the airway but were driven back by the smoke and fumes. Then we made for the York West return, the boy a little ahead of me, but the smoke was so stifling that we had to go back again. I looked round for Cook but I could not see him anywhere. Where he had got to I don't know. After that I began to get unconscious. That was about 10 o'clock on Tuesday morning and it was about 1 o'clock on Wednesday morning when I came to myself again.

The first thing I saw when I came round was a light about twelve yards away. I crawled up to the light and found it belonged to a man who was dead. I took the light and then I saw a boy named George Moore and another man who was able to speak but couldn't get up. Then I went towards the intake as the air seemed clearer and saw some men up there huddled in a heap apparently dead. I was feeling done up and after about half an hour the rescue party came along and I was brought out'.

Described Wilf Vizard, *'I was working by myself that morning when I heard a bang and felt the shock. The place was filling with dust and my lamp dimmed. I put my coat on. My lamp went out and I had to feel my way out along the tram rail. I went into the next heading and called out. There was no sound or light there so I came out and made for the straight. When I got there I could hear a boy shouting* "Where's my father? I want my father!" *Making my way, I felt the legs of a man and then his face which was covered by a scarf. He recognised me and said,* "Wilf, I've had enough. I'm going off. My legs have no feeling". *I was getting groggy myself by this time so I pulled myself to one side of the tunnel, put my cap over my face and poured water over it from my bottle. Just after that I was gone. The first thing I remember is having a tube in my mouth and a voice saying* "That's good, that's good". *It was the voice of a doctor'.*

Haulier George Moore senior, who was driving a horse at the time of the explosion, said, *'I heard a loud report and was stifled for some time. I fell down once but I managed to get up again and went back to the parting where there was a big fog of dust. I had my lamp in my hand and hid it under my coat to save it. Then I rushed to the face and shouted to the men working there to get out.*

Then I went towards the main entrance but failed to get out.When I returned I captured my youngest son George, he being a weak and delicate boy. His partner on the coal was called Dean. The air was greatly affected and we took off our mufflers and saturated them with tea from our jacks and tied them round our mouths. This undoubtedly saved our our lives. My horse was killed'.

His son Evan told how he had been working on the same side as his father and brother. He joined the rush of men trying to get to the pit bottom but had to turn back because the smoke was so thick and they could see fire ahead. As they went back to the workings he saw men stagger, then, one by one, fall unconscious. He became dizzy and remembered falling, striking his forehead as he went down, and landing with his face partly in a pool of horse's urine. He maintained that the proximity of his nose and mouth to this urine was his salvation.

The last to be brought out was Arthur Balsam. He said, *'About 8 o'clock I heard a terrific explosion followed by a cloud of dust and smoke. Haulier George Moore shouted something had happened and told us to get out. We picked up our lamps and ran about 20 yards. Then I suddenly remembered about my tea jack and ran back to get it from my work place. I then tried to get to the pit bottom by the nearest way but I was driven back by the fire. I then tried to escape by another way but was driven back again. Soon I felt dizzy and lay down with my handkerchief soaked with tea over my mouth to keep it moist. I then became unconscious and I do not remember any more until Colonel Pearson and his party found me. Almost immediately I was attended by Dr. Leigh of Treharris. As I was being carried out by a couple of men two big stones fell and the three of us were knocked over. I can feel the effects on my head now. It was a miracle how I came out. I cannot realise it'.*

To the waiting crowds at the pit head came renewed hope, an air of expectancy that this would be the prelude to the rescue of more men and boys. With it came rumours of voices, of singing, of knockings being heard from trapped men *'who would soon be brought up'*. But as each hour passed with only the recovery of twenty bodies from the District so the hopes of a major rescue receded.

The *'Western Mail'* of Wednesday the 15th reported, *'Senghenydd presents a touching scene. There are darkened homes into which the light will never come again'*. The *'South Wales Daily News'* commented, *'The annals of disasters in the coalfields of South Wales provide no parallel in the circumstances of horror and doom to the overwhelming calamity which has overtaken the mining village of Senghenydd'*. The Archbishop of York, opening a session of the Church of England Men's Society in Cardiff called for special prayers with these words, *'I bid you commend our brothers who have lost their lives to God's mercy and care those who are still in danger to His protecting Providence; those who are attempting to rescue them to His guidance and protection; those who are mourning the loss of those dear to them to the comfort and strength of His Holy Spirit'*.

At the colliery a committee of mining engineers was appointed to oversee the operations and issued a statement of intent to fight the fire with all the force of water possible, to bring out in trams all moveable burning material, and after the fire had been extinguished to send in rescue men to examine the ventilation systems. But with its optimistic anticipation that the fire would be successfully controlled *'within a short time'* was the ominous statement that no purpose would be served as yet in sending rescue men into the workings. Relays of men laid a pipe line from the reservoir into the pit but the fire raged all day and in the words of Page Arnot, *'Beneath was still an inferno of flames and stench of noxious vapours. Those who went down found themselves fire-fighting and exploring chaos'.*

In a scene described as like Dante's Inferno the heroism again displayed, enriched the history of valour. Wrote one reporter, *'I have jostled all day with the exploration parties and colliers who worked like Trojans, heroes who count not their lives dear unto them if they can do something, be it only wielding a pick axe from an unstable mass of debris in the bowels of the earth, to rescue their fellows from death. It is always thus when one of these great calamities overwhelm a Welsh colliery. The miner stands out as a man of high courage and unstinted labour'.* One man *'who did not count his life dear'* was William John of Abertridwr, killed that day by a rock fall while engaged in clearance work. Despite all the superhuman efforts only corpses were brought to bank that day bringing the total number to fifty six.

Another team of rescue workers pictured at the colliery following the explosion.

Messages of sympathy poured in from all parts of Britain, from France, Belgium, Spain, Portugal, Italy, Austria, Hungary, Russia, Canada, the United States of America, Australia, New Zealand and South Africa.

At about 7 o'clock that night the Home Secretary Reginald McKenna arrived, stating that the King would have made a personal visit were it not for the Royal marriage that day. After being informed of the situation he inspected the pit and then, accompanied by Clement Edwards, he made an extensive tour of the village to visit homes and offer sympathy to the widows and families of men already known to be dead or entombed. One of the homes he visited was that of Mrs. Anne Thomas of Brynhyfryd Terrace whose husband Evan was among the dead, leaving her to care for seven children, the oldest age 14. When McKenna asked her how she would manage she replied, *'I will try to bear up and will lean on Him who is the Father of the fatherless'*, and thanked him for coming. Later, he stated, *'The patience, amounting to heroism, displayed by the bereaved people is beyond all praise'.* Clement Edwards also added words of admiration for *'those whose beloved ones and breadwinners are entombed'.*

Thursday, October 16th, was a day of despair. *'No Hope for Men Below'* was the stark headline of the *'Western Mail'* which commented, *'There now seems no hope for preventing the Senghenydd calamity from ranking as the biggest mining disaster which has occurred in South Wales. There is no justification now for, encouraging hope that any of the victims will be found alive'.*

The Committee's optimistic report of the previous day had proved ill-founded. The fires were still out of control, burning underfoot. Men were coming up for fresh air from the intolerable heat with their clothes singed and the soles of their boots scorched. Not only that, but as the fires were being driven back so a fresh hazard emerged, the increased danger of explosions from the ignition of concealed pockets of gas. A new strategy had to be devised, but in the meantime all work of exploration and rescue had to be suspended, a tacit admission that all who remained in the pit had perished. Early in the morning all ambulance men from outlying districts left for home to await further instructions. *'The hills around were dotted with groups, and in the roadways along the valley there was movement, but near the colliery the crowd was tense, voiceless, almost motionless. The numerous ladies of the Red Cross Brigade, Salvation Army officers and clergy busied themselves trying to console those to whom the certainty of bereavement had come'.*

In the afternoon, Mr. David Rees, Coroner for East Glamorgan, formally opened the Inquiry at the Gwernymilwr Hotel into the cause of death of the victims. The foreman of the jury was grocer J.J. Thomas. The Coroner stated that he opened the Inquiry so that the bodies might be identified and so facilitate their burial. They then proceeded to the temporary mortuary to view the bodies, and after taking evidence of identification the Inquest was adjourned sine die. In Cardiff the Coroner W.L.Yorath took similar action in respect of three men who had died in King Edward VII Hospital.

Following the Inquest at Senghenydd the Executive Council of the South Wales Miners Federation met at the Gwernymilwr Hotel and called upon the Home Secretary to institute a full and independent Inquiry into the circumstances of the disaster. It also decided to impose on members of all Lodges a levy to relieve the great distress of the bereaved and also to launch a public appeal as well as to seek an interview with the Lord Mayor of Cardiff and the Lord Mayor of London with a view to opening official Appeal Funds.

These were two distressing photographs that made the national newspapers in 1913 with recovered bodies being moved in their coffins to a final resting place.

Keir Hardie, the veteran Labour Member of Parliament for Merthyr, toured the village of drawn blinds and later at Merthyr made a speech in which he alleged the disaster would never have occurred if the safety regulations of the Coal Mines Act had been fully observed. The Bishop of Llandaff also toured the village accompanied by the Rector and curate to offer sympathy to some of the bereaved in their homes. There came too a party of Salvation Army field officers from the London Training College *'to do all we can in assisting the injured and do what is in our power to alleviate the distress and suffering'*.

A telegram was received from Queen Alexandra, the Queen Mother. It read, *'I am distressed beyond words at the news of the terrible disaster which has occurred at the Universal Collieries, Senghenydd, Cardiff.*

The loss of life is truly appalling and my heart is very full of grief for those who have sustained such a crushing sorrow.

Will you please convey to the bereaved families of the poor miners my very sincere and heartfelt sympathy'.

It was addressed to Dr. Atkinson.

'As the third night commenced the moon shone gloriously over the tragic scene and the gaunt grim colliery shone out against a clear sky. A horrible prospect faced the weary watchers, for whereas there was hope last night now there was little but despair. Many of the women who for so long had hoped against hope now sought refuge for their grief in their homes. Only a few remained at the pit head. Some hovered about the ambulance room and the mortuary with its ranks of coffined dead'.

On Friday, October 17th, a new strategy was put into operation, that of damming off the fires by a *'bashing'* of sandbags and turf, hundreds of men working feverishly to the point of exhaustion. Gangs of men cut the turf from the mountain sides around the colliery then rushed it to the pit in trams on a roughly constructed tramroad. On the surface other gangs filled sandbags. Both turf and sandbags were taken below to be tightly packed up to the roof of the road leading into the Lancaster Level.

'The crowds in the village and around the colliery are much less numerous. One girl held vigil still, said to have spent most of her time there since the explosion, watching, watching, hoping, hoping for the return of the sweetheart who is below and to whom she was to be married tomorrow'.

On Saturday, October 18th, a vast multitude converged on the village to pay a last tribute at the funerals of eleven victims. It lined the streets in awesome silence as the mile-long cortege, headed by Salvation Army massed bands, moved off at 3 o'clock. So immeasurable was the pervading depth of grief and despair that no hymns were sung at the *'rising'* as was the immemorial custom. Although all available carriages had been engaged yet they were insufficient and *'it was all the more pitiful to watch the weeping women and children walk slowly and silently behind the hearses. In one instance, a widow walked with her eight children behind her husband's coffin, all attired in mourning, seemingly dazed in their woe'.* At Abertridwr the cortege divided, eight hearses destined for Penyrheol Cemetery, three for Eglwysilan Churchyard. At the gravesides the officiating clergy included Revs. David Roberts (Welsh

Baptist), Thomas Morris (Welsh Congregationalist), Evan Thomas (Welsh Calvinistic Methodist), D.M. Jones (English Baptist), Rector D. Lloyd Rees, Curate Campbell Davies and Brigadier Greenway (Salvation Army). Only at the interment of the Salvationists did the service include a hymn.

Conveyed *'back home'* by rail and road were the coffins of other victims.

Extraordinary scenes were witnessed on Sunday, October 19th. By 8 o'clock hundreds of sightseers had come from the surrounding villages, *'the mountains literally black with processions of men and women'*. As the day wore on so trains, motor cars, motor cycles and other conveyances brought thousands to swell the crowds of those who had come on foot. It was estimated that 100,000 - 150,000 people descended upon the village. From Penyrheol onwards the road was a solid mass of humanity, the vehicles reduced to a walking pace. While the press correspondents wrote of *'knots of men and women whose pallid anxious faces betokened something more than sympathetic curiosity'*. Fred Parrish said, *'some came out of curiosity. I remember feeling disgusted. The road from the Universal Hotel to the pit was filled with sightseers and the* "Holy Joes" *playing musical instruments. It was like a fair'*.

By the common consent of the clergy the normal morning service was suspended to be replaced by a brief prayer meeting. Very few attended. The Roman Catholics met at Cwmaber School where a Mass for the dead was officiated by Father Knight.

At 1.30 p.m. a mass cortege began to assemble on the square for the funerals of another eight victims and notwithstanding the crush of the crowds the sense of decorum prevailed. So late did the last hearse arrive at Penyrheol Cemetery that the rites were not completed until 6.00 p.m. and conducted by lantern light.

Throughout the United Kingdom special services were held in churches, chapels and the 1,200 Salvation Army Halls, the collections being donated to the Appeal Funds.

So ended a week of tragedy unparalleled in the annals of British coal-mining. Of the 945 men and boys who had descended, 489 were brought up from the York Pit. From the Lancaster Pit, 18 were rescued from the Bottanic District, 9 critically injured who were brought out on Tuesday were to die later. Recovered were 55 bodies. Entombed were 374 bodies. Left to mourn were widows, fatherless children and dependant parents estimated at about 800.

At home and abroad public reaction had been swift and overwhelming in response to the Appeal Funds launched by the South Wales Miners' Federation, the Lord Mayor of Cardiff, the Lord Mayor of London, the Chairman of Caerphilly Council and other cities and towns. Among the early donations had been £500 from King George V, £200 from Queen Mary and £100 from the Queen Mother. On the Saturday afternoon spontaneous collections were made at football and rugby matches throughout the United Kingdom, the Salvation Army and organisations invaded the streets to raise money.

Throughout the week-end the construction of the bashing continued and on the Saturday night shift three men were so badly gassed that they had to be carried out to receive medical treatment before they recovered.

By Sunday night the situation had improved greatly with the level of smoke and temperature much reduced.

On Monday, October 20th, with the fire subdued and entry secured into the Lancaster Level so the exploratory parties made a cautious entry into the workings with the object of trying to reach the Mafeking District. But they were halted by massive falls.

The schools re-opened. The attendance at the Infants' School was only about 30% and that of the Girls' School about 28% and remained open, but so few were present at the Boys' School that it closed.

On Tuesday, October 21st, the exploratory parties renewed their efforts towards the Mafeking and Kimberley Districts, and in the process they retrieved nine bodies before reaching their objective by nightfall. But convinced that no one was alive in either District and encountering massive falls so penetration was deferred. One of the parties was composed of mining engineers, Assistant Mines Inspectors, Miners' Agents and a number of men. They found the roadways difficult to negotiate because of heavy falls but they pressed forward only to be overcome by gas about 80 yards from the workings of the Kimberley District and had to be rescued by the Crumlin and Aberaman Rescue Brigades. Carried on stretchers or supported by the rescuers until they reached the surface, the nineteen men were given medical treatment, seventeen recovering within the hour, the other two recovering later at Aberdare Hall.

The schools were opened and remained so although the attendance at the Infants' School was 58%, that of the Girls' School was 33% and that of the Boys' School stated as very few.

In the evening a special meeting of the Caerphilly Council resolved to open a Fund to deal with immediate cases of distress. The Health Committee resolved as a matter of urgency that the Sanitary Inspector be authorised to store a supply of disinfectant at Senghenydd and that he attended there to give whatever assistance was necessary to abate nuisances.

Also on that day a meeting of the Monmouthshire Congregational Union at Abersychan passed a resolution of sympathy with the families of the bereaved. It then passed another resolution which protested strongly against the showing of pictures of the disaster at cinemas and condemning the commercial spirit which would exploit its tragedy and horrors in order to make money. There were many such protests voiced at places of worship and District Councils.

On Wednesday, October 22nd, it was announced that all work of exploration would be deferred because the heavy rock falls and the accumulation of gas made it imperative to concentrate on strengthening the bashing at the Lancaster Level to improve the ventilation.

The pit top was deserted on Thursday, October 23rd, the first of five days to be devoted to the bashing. Two members of the Salvation Army were buried at Penyrheol Cemetery, the bands playing hymns all the way to the graveyard with *'all the beautiful emotion and feeling that music can express given forth by the working men and boys. In the triumphant phrases of the changes of melody the music seemed to defy the monster of industrialisation which had robbed the mourners of their bread winners'*. Some victims were laid to rest at Eglwysilan churchyard, the services extending into the late evening with the mourners holding lanterns.

By Saturday, October 25th, such was the response to the Appeal Funds launched by the Miners' Federation, the Lords Mayors of Cardiff and London, the Salvation Army, Newport, Swansea, Merthyr, Aberdare, Llanelly, Barry, Ebbw Vale, Margam, Aberavon, Pontypool, Cardiganshire, Wrexham, Abertillery, Aberystwyth, Abergavenny, Monmouth, Mold and other towns and cities that the combined total stood at £54,170. Among the donations was £1,000 derived from the entry charge to the exhibition of the Royal Wedding presents at St. James's Palace. From two hundred children of a Band of Hope in Leicester came a letter of sympathy accompanied by a donation. Unwashed, dressed in working clothes, carrying lighted lamps, a group of Western Valley colliers went straight from work to make street collections in Newport. The Federation recommended a levy of 1/- per man and 6d per boy on all its members.

But a very considerable time would elapse before the distribution from a Central Fund could be formulated and meanwhile the bereaved were suffering great financial distress. Consequently the Committee of the Lord Mayor of Cardiff's Fund administered temporary relief at a weekly rate of 7/6d for a widow or adult dependant and 3/6d for a child, then increased it to 10/- and 5/- respectively, the arrangement made with Evan Owen, Secretary of the Miners' Permanent Provident Society, Councillor James and other members of the Senghenydd Relief Committee to make the payments at Bethel Chapel. Further assistance for necessitous cases came from the special Fund provided by Caerphilly Council

The Executive Council of the S.W.M. Federation met at the Gwernymilwr Hotel to consider claims that there was insufficient assistance given in respect of the organisation of funerals, bearers and carriages. As a result several Lodges offered to assist.

On Monday, October 27th, a deputation from the Miners' Federation of Great Britain met the Home Secretary to press for a full-scale Inquiry into the circumstances of the explosion.

The Executive Council of the S.W.M. Federation met again, this time to consider how best to help those out of work as a result of the explosion. Hundreds were seeking work at Cardiff Docks and elsewhere as a temporary measure but alternative employment was scarce, and it was estimated that 541 were out of work with 721 dependant wives, children and parents facing increasing financial hardship.

On Tuesday, October 28th, an Inquest was opened at the Gwernymilwr Hotel when only evidence of identification of bodies was taken, most of whom were identified by clothing or a possession but three were buried as *'Unknown'*.

Exploration was renewed on Wednesday, October 29th, with an attempt to penetrate Ladysmith but progress was painfully slow, excruciating and hazardous and eventually it came to a halt when faced by massive rock falls and an accumulation of gas.

The S.W.M. Federation Executive Council met Mr. Shaw with a request that house coal be provided for both the bereaved and the unemployed but it received only a non-commital reply.

On Thursday, October 30th, the falls encountered the previous day in Ladysmith District were cleared, vast tons of debris were removed and four bodies were recovered.

At the colliery office a deputation comprising Miners' Agent Hubert Jenkins, William Thomas the Treasurer of the East Glamorgan Miners and Councillors Trevor James and John Davies met Lord Merthyr to discuss the plight of the unemployed. He offered to cooperate with the Unemployed and Distress Committee and donated £100 but his only practical suggestion was to indicate that 200 colliers were required in the Rhondda, one which met with little sympathy from the deputation.

At the close of the month the combined total of the Appeal Funds stood at £67,500. A donation of 10/- was enclosed with a letter from Sunday School scholars at a Lincolnshire church *'as a token of sympathy for the bereaved children'*. A cheque for £1 *'for a woman most in need'* was sent by a family in Lydstep, Penally. Among the mass of donations were cheques from Taunton Fire Brigade, Eastbourne boatmen, employees of a Bristol Tobacco Company, employees of a Glasgow Tube Company, the operatives of a Manchester Card and Blowing Room, church/chapel congregations at Briton Ferry, Fishguard, Pembroke Dock, Cross Hands, East Kirby, Ealing, Exeter, Farnborough, Liverpool, Shrivenham and Hoylake.

'A parcel of clothing to distribute among the most needy' was sent by a lady in Cornwall to Police Sergeant Walters.

General Booth offered to take fifty orphan children into Salvation Army Homes. A Shropshire family with two children, the husband a miner, offered to adopt an orphan girl about 8-9 years of age. Many families in different parts of the country offered to provide holidays for widows and children.

In the village the Cardiff Fund Committee distributed the weekly allowances of 10/- and 5/- to a quoted number of 207 widows, 436 children and 50 parents. The Secretary of the Miners' Provident Society distributed sums of money and sums from the Caerphilly Fund were given to the most distressed by Rev. Douglas Evans, Secretary of the Senghenydd Relief Committee, at Salem Chapel.

On Saturday, November 1st, further falls were encountered in Ladysmith. A delegate meeting of the S.W.M.F. held at the Cory Hall in Cardiff voted to assist wageless workers by a weekly levy of 6d to provide 10/- for a man and 1/- for a child each week until work would be resumed.

By Thursday, November 6th, more bodies had been discovered in Ladysmith but because of obstructive falls the last was not recovered until Saturday, the 8th, bringing the total to 144. Officials of the S.W.M.F. doled out the weekly relief money to the unemployed numbering 540 of which 446 were married with 721 children. Sums of money were allocated to the most distressed by the Senghenydd Relief Committee.

The combined total of the Appeal Funds now stood at £85,535. Donations included another £1,000 from the Royal Marriage Presents Exhibition, the proceeds from a concert held at the Central Hall, Westminster, organised by the Glamorgan and Denbighshire Societies, attended by Mrs. Lloyd George and daughter Olwen, a cheque from the Halifax Homing Society. Locally, donations came from the proceeds of a concert held at Caerphilly Castle Cinema, of a concert promoted by the Nelson Choral Society and one promoted by the Aber Valley Silver Band at Abertridwr Workmen's Hall.

With Ladysmith having been explored the attention was focused on Kimberley, Mafeking and Pretoria, but no exploration was carried out on Sunday, November 9th, in order to erect another bashing. It was completed the next day and on Tuesday, November 11th, thirty bodies were found in Pretoria and a further twenty five bodies in Kimberley on Thursday, November 13th, despite encountering massive falls.

Mafeking had been breached also and the way was open, as it was for further exploration of Pretoria. From Friday, the 14th, to Monday, the 17th, almost two hundred bodies were raised to the surface, discovered in groups, grossly decomposed, many badly mutilated. At the Aberdare Hall mortuary there began the prolonged, gruesome and sickening task of allocating names instead of numbers to the bodies. In the very many cases where facial identification was impossible the bodies were wrapped in winding sheets and on top were placed any item of clothing or possession which would help recognition. Once identified the body was coffined immediately. The coffin was never reopened.

On Thursday, November 20th, a statement was issued to the press that a total of 406 bodies had been recovered of which 6 had been buried as *'unknown'*, 352 identified, 48 unidentified and 33 still in the pit.

On Friday, November 21st, the miners met to appoint representatives to serve on an inspection party of the Lancaster pit to consider the prospects of it reopening.

On Saturday, November 22nd, *'A sadly depleted rugby team, the players wearing black arm bands, journeyed to Ferndale in aid of the Disaster Fund, winning by 7 points to 6, a try by Herbie Powell and a drop goal by Will Willacombe'*.

The combined total of the Appeal Funds stood at £95,000.

On Sunday, November 23rd, Gunner Gomer Green and Private William Evans of Senghenydd, both members of the National Reserve, were buried with full military honours at Eglwysilan churchyard. Headed by the Aber Valley Silver Band, the Union-Jack-draped coffins borne on gun carriages, the cortege was escorted by 700 reservists under the command of Colonel Pearson. The service, conducted before a massive concourse, concluded with the firing of three volleys and a trumpeter sounding the *'Last Post'* over each grave.

The inspection of the Lancaster pit took place that day.

Two harrowing scenes from that fateful day Tuesday October 14th 1913.

On Monday, November 24th, a mass meeting of miners was held to consider the report of Miners' Agent Hubert Jenkins and his team of ten miners on the situation at the Lancaster pit. This being favourable, the meeting voted in favour of a partial return to work.

On Wednesday, November 26th, partial work was resumed, some coal was raised and the 410th body was recovered, that of Evan Jones, Senghenydd.

On the afternoon of Saturday, November 29th, the rugby team journeyed to Treorchy where *'the team, which was terribly affected by the mining disaster, gave a spirited plucky display with Bert Williams, Pedro, Dallimore and the Goulds always dangerous, losing only by 3 points to nil'*. In the night, a Boxing Tournament in aid of the Appeal Fund was held at Caerphilly Virginia Park and featured an exhibition bout by Jimmy Wilde, the Welsh 7-stone Champion.

On December 9th an Inquest held at the Gwernymilwr Hotel was confined to evidence of the identification of forty bodies.

By December 12th eight more bodies had been recovered, including those of Ellis Davies of Abertridwr, Francis Hollister, John Davies and Thomas Tucker of Senghenydd, bringing the total to 418.

On December 15th there were still 15 bodies unrecovered.

The various Appeal Funds were officially closed with a combined total of over £120,000. It was agreed that until such time as the Trust Deed would be formulated the Committee of the Lord Mayor of Cardiff's Fund would continue to allocate the weekly grants. For those still out of work the S.W.M.F. continued to give financial support and the Caerphilly Council voted an extra allowance for Christmas to those who were in greatest need.

On December 17th the body of Archie Williams of Senghenydd was recovered.

On December 31st two bodies were buried as *'Unknown'*. Twelve bodies were unrecovered.

In the most devastating catastrophe in the annals of the British coalfield 440 men and boys had perished, including one killed by a rock fall while engaged in clearance work. At the Inquest on the death of 422 victims the causes of death were listed as: Burns and suffocation 251; Suffocation 74; Burns, injuries and suffocation 68; Burns, injuries and shock 13; Burns and shock 15; Wounds and suffocation 1. An explanatory note stated that *'suffocation'* meant poisoning by carbon monoxide (*'after damp'*) and not suffocation in the meaning of asphyxiation.

To some, death came mercifully swift. An aged haulier was found grasping the sprag of a tram, another man was found on his knees chalking his number on a full tram of coal, another *'with his hands held out as if to push back, the terrible fate which was upon him'*, another with his hands covering his face before being overcome by the after damp. Equally swift was the fate of four men discovered *'sitting down in their place of work apparently having a chat when death overtook them'*, and that of a group of eight men *'who did not have time to dress, their lamps found still hanging on nails or spikes on the coal face'*.

Others suffered a more protracted fate. When a group of thirty men and boys were located *'it was evident that the unfortunate victims had got together after being aware of what had happened and had made an attempt to get away. They had put on their clothes and had their food tins with them when they succumbed in groups to the deadly fumes'*. Of another group of eleven *'the indications were that the foreman had realised what had happened and had called the men to make a dash for safety, but they did not proceed very far before they succumbed to the deadly fire damp'*. Another report was of a group of nine, then a group of eight, followed by another group of five *'who had evidently got together after the explosion and had attempted to escape through the intake airway. They had got to the point where they were found when they were met by the deadly, after damp. They were lying in various positions, some on their backs, some on their faces, some on their knees in a crouching position. Most of them had their coats on and had brought their teajacks and food tins with them. It is evident that they had lived some time after the explosion but it is impossible to say how long'*.

Agonising was the fate that awaited others. Four men *'lay as if they had been running together for escape, arm in arm, when they were struck down in a heap by the after damp. There they lay, breast to breast, arms interlocked'*. Two men *'appeared to have gone about 100 yards from their working places'*, a repairer and his assistant *'had travelled a considerable distance from their working places when they were overcome by the fire damp'*. Found was *'a group of six men, five lying down as if asleep, the other on his knees as if in an attitude of prayers. It is quite evident that they lived some time after the explosion, having left their places of work, but probably not more than half an hour before meeting their death through after damp'*. Four men *'having fought a gallant fight through 900 yards of dense fumes and after damp and having reached the main return, dropped dead literally within 30 yards of an abundance of fresh air'*.

A father died clasping the hand of his dying fourteen-year-old son only yards away from the body of another son aged sixteen, a father and his two sons were found locked arm-in-arm in a group of eleven bodies, a father and son were found locked in each other's arms.

Some died in the noblest tradition. *'We came to the bottom of the Pretoria incline and found two bodies lying in the road. One was evidently the engine boy, the other a roadman. From the position where they lay the man was carrying the boy when he was overcome and fell - the boy still had his arms around the man's neck'*.

Eight bodies were buried as *'Unknown'*. A vast number were so badly mutilated, burnt or decomposed that facial identification was impossible. One body was identified by having one arm shorter than the other, one by a set of false teeth in which some were missing. One was identified by a black patch on his singlet, one by a pair of boots with notches, one by a leather belt repaired with copper wire, one by a Boys' Brigade belt. Some were identified by inscribed tobacco boxes, some by a watch, one by a a railway ticket in a box of lozenges, one by an inscribed food box containing cake.

Wales never knew such grief.

Two hundred and twelve married men, eight widowers, two hundred and twenty single men and boys had perished in the most appalling circumstances. Eight were age 14, four age 15, eleven age 16, forty two between the ages of 17 and 19, one hundred and seventy three in their 20s, one hundred and four in their 30s, sixty nine in their 40s, twenty four in their 50s, four in their 60s and one age 72. Forty-six families had suffered more than one bereavement.

Left to mourn were 212 widows, 20 orphans, 489 fatherless children of which 39 were born subsequent to the day of the explosion and 35 dependant parents.

The figurative *'Angel of Death'* claimed the souls of one victim from Newbridge, one from Tongwynlais, one from Cilfynydd, one from Groeswen, four from Rhydyfelin, six from the Rhymney Valley and ten from Cardiff. Mrs. Elizabeth Dew of Tongwynlais *'lost'* her husband on his first day at the colliery and only a week or so since he rescued a woman from drowning in the Glamorgan Canal, leaving her with two children. Mrs. Mary Gwynne of Rhydyfelin *'lost'* her husband and a stepson on his second day at the colliery, leaving her with four young children, and Mr. & Mrs. Hallett from the same village *'lost'* their fourteen-year old son. In Cardiff, Mrs. Jenkins *'lost'* two sons, Mrs. Dorothy Peters *'lost'* two sons, one married, and Mr. & Mrs. Mansfield *'lost'* a sixteen-year-old son.

Claimed from Penyrheol were 16 souls. Mrs. Mary Jones of St. Cenydd Terrace *'lost'* her husband and a son and was left with eight children, the oldest being 14. Mr. & Mrs. Jones of Brynhyfryd Terrace, Energlyn, *'lost'* a sixteen-year-old son.

Claimed from Caerphilly were 32 souls. Mrs. Mary Morgan of Ty Melyn, Black Cock, *'lost'* her husband and two sons and was left with five children, the oldest being 13. Mr. & Mrs. Henry Morgan of Nantgarw Road *'lost'* a sixteen-year-old son and a married son. Mrs. Rachel Davies of Bradford Street *'lost'* her husband and a brother-in-law. Pregnant Mrs. Mary Rowlands of Donyfelin Street who *'lost'* her husband was left with six children, the oldest being 12. Fifteen-year-old William Barnett of Bartlett Street died on his way to hospital, Mr. & Mrs. Attewell of Pontygwindy Road *'lost'* their fifteen-year-old son, Mr. & Mrs. Cook of Nantgarw Road their sixteen-year-old son.

Claimed from Abertridwr were 63 souls. Mrs. Ethel Priest of Ilan Road mourned the deaths of her husband and two sons aged fourteen and sixteen. He was found clasping the hand of the former and only yards away from the latter. Mrs. Edwards of Tridwr Road *'lost'* her husband and a son Mr. & Mrs. Button of Ilan Road, Mr. & Mrs. Morgan of Ilan Road, Mr. & Mrs. Morris of High Street, Mr. & Mrs. Davies of Cwmceffyl Road, Mr. & Mr. B. Fern of Lower Francis Street each *'lost'* two sons. Mrs. Ethel Carroll of Lower Francis Street *'lost'* her husband and a brother-in-law who lived with her. *'Lost'* were brothers David Williams of High Street and Llewellyn Williams of Bryngelli Terrace, both married. Margaret Jane John of Thomas Street mourned the death of her husband killed by a rock fall when he was engaged in excavation work on the day after the explosion and was left with two children. Widowed were Polly Jones of 40 King Street and Anne Jones of Ilan Road each left with seven children of which the oldest was 12. Orphaned were Bromley (12), William (10) and Ruby (5) Ferris of High Street, as were Elizabeth (13) and Emlyn (2) Hughes of Bridgefield Street.

Claimed from Senghenydd were 305 souls - 145 Married men, 6 widowers, 154 single men and boys. In age, six were 14, two were 15, six were 16, twenty nine were between the ages of 17 and 19, one hundred and fifteen were in their 20s, seventy in their 30s, fifty two in their 40s, twenty two in their 50s, two in their 60s and one age 72. A young generation had been decimated.

Two hundred and twenty households were touched - 45 victims from Commercial Street, 39 each from Caerphilly Road and High Street, 22 from Cenydd Terrace, 20 from Stanley Street, 19 from Grove Terrace, 15 from Parc Terrace, 14 from Graig Terrace, 12 each from Station Terrace and Woodland Terrace, 11 from Coronation Terrace, 9 each from Alexandra Terrace and Phillips Terrace, 8 each from Station Road and Brynhyfryd Terrace, 6 from The Huts, 4 from Kingsley Place, 3 from Clive Street, 2 each from Cross Street, Windsor Place and School Street, 1 each from Gelli Terrace, Gelli Villas, Parc Cottages and Wesleyan Cottage. Including both family and lodgers 3 households suffered four bereavements, 8 suffered three and 48 suffered two.

Left to mourn were 145 widows, 14 orphans, 339 fatherless children of whom 30 were born subsequent to the day of the explosion and 23 dependant parents.

Widow Mrs. Elizabeth Twining who kept a shop in Commercial Street *'lost'* three sons, one age 14, another age 16. Mrs. Elizabeth Ross of Coronation Terrace *'lost'* her husband, two sons of whom one was married, a brother and a lodger. Mrs. Margaret Downes of Caerphilly Road *'lost'* her husband and two sons, as did Mrs. Catherine Lewis of High Street.

Buried in Penyrheol were three single brothers living in Stanley Street who hailed from Blaenau Ffestiniog where lived their dependant mother Mrs. Hughes. Buried there too were Edmund Small and his son living in Cenydd Terrace who hailed from the village of Orcop in Herefordshire where fifteen-year-old Mary was left to care for five younger sisters.

Mrs. Margaret Ann Baker of Alexandra Terrace, who *'lost'* her husband and 14-year old son was left to care for nine children, the oldest age 13, the youngest age 2 days. Mrs. Hannah Hyatt of Caerphilly Road, who *'lost'* her husband and son was left to care for six children, the oldest age 13. Pregnant Mrs. Esther Kenvin of Graig Terrace, her fourth child born in February 1914, *'lost'* her husband and a son. Others who each *'lost'* a husband and single son were Mrs. Catherine Edwards of Commercial Street, Mrs. Mary Evans of Parc Terrace, Mrs. Louise Harrison of Cenydd Terrace, Mrs. Esther Kestell of High Street and Mrs. Mary Williams of Caerphilly Road. Pregnant Mrs. Mary Humphries of High Street, her sixth child born in May 1914 and the oldest age 14, *'lost'* her husband and a married son.

Widows Mrs. Davies of Station Terrace, Mrs. Jones of Woodland Terrace, Mrs. Lower of Coronation Terrace and Mrs.Vranch of Cenydd Terrace each *'lost'* two sons, as did Mr. & Mrs. Davies of Commercial Street, Mr. & Mrs.

Pritchard of Caerphilly Road, Mr. & Mrs.Richards of Caerphilly Road, Mr. & Mrs. Rowland of Grove Terrace, Mr. & Mrs. Cotterell of Commercial Street (one married) and Mr. & Mrs. Jones of Caerphilly Road (one married).

Orphaned by the deaths of their widower fathers were: Minnie Maddocks (9) of Woodland Terrace, who also *'lost'* her 16-year-old brother; Hugh (14), Laura (12) and William (10) Williams of Coronation Terrace; Joseph (11) and Alice (8) Hopkins of High Street; Robert John Morris (1) of Brynhyfryd Terrace ; Alice Maud Davies (8) of Station Road.

In the home of pregnant Mrs. Edith Edwards of Caerphilly Road, her fourth child to be born in February 1914, lay the coffins of her husband and two brothers-in-law who lived with her. Among others who suffered the loss of their husbands were Mrs. Boswell of High Street left to care for seven children, the oldest age 10, Mrs. Thomas of Brynhyfryd Terrace left to care for seven children, the oldest age 11, and Mrs. Evans of Coronation Terrace to care for seven children, six under the age of 11, 18-year-old David John the oldest.

Mourned were the deaths of Alfred Tudor by his mother at Alexandra Terrace, William Eldridge of High Street, Reuben Jones of Phillips Terrace at the age of fourteen, Alfred Milton of Parc Terrace and William Uphill of Station Road at the age of fifteen, David Hill of Parc Terrace and Ernest Petherick of Grove Terrace at the age of sixteen

On the third day after the explosion Mrs. Sarah Twining of Station Terrace gave birth to her second child, on the fourth day Mrs. Mabel Parrish of Cross Street gave birth to her first child, on the seventh day Mrs. Emma Evans of Stanley Street gave birth to her fourth child and on the ninth day Mrs. Blodwen Herring of Phillips Terrace gave birth to her second child. In November, Mrs. Margaret James of Grove Terrace gave birth to her seventh child, the oldest being 14, Mrs. Margaret Anderson of Woodland Terrace gave birth to her sixth child, the oldest being 12, and Mrs. Mary Jones of Parc Cottages gave birth to her second child. In December, Mrs.Louisa Jones of The Huts gave birth to her sixth child, the oldest one being 8, and Mrs. Edith Griffiths of Commercial Street gave birth to her third child.

In January 1914 Mrs. Mary Pegler of Phillips Terrace gave birth to her fifth child, Mrs. Kesiah Rees of Commercial Street to her first child. In February, Mrs. Susannah Lewis of High Street gave birth to her sixth child, the oldest age 8, Mrs. Edith Edwards of Caerphilly Road to her first child. In March, Mrs. Jemima Lewis of Caerphilly Road gave birth to her eighth child, the oldest being 13, and Mrs. Mabel Kelly of Graig Terrace, Mrs. Catherine Seager of Grove Terrace and Mrs. Alberta White of Caerphilly Road gave birth to the first child, Mrs. Mary Dillon of Alexandra Terrace, Mrs. Anne Jones of Caerphilly Read and Mrs. Annie Prosser of High Street gave birth to the second child and Mrs. Elizabeth Rees of High Street gave birth to her fourth child. In May Mrs. Eva Pritchard of Commercial Street gave birth to her sixth child, the oldest age 11, Mrs. Lucy Scott of Graig Terrace to her first child, Mrs. Gertrude Green of Grove Terrace to her second child, and Mrs. Eliza King of Cenydd Terrace to her third child. In June, Mrs. Janet Jones of

Cenydd Terrace gave birth to her second child. In July, Mrs. Mary Jones of Phillips Terrace gave birth to her fourth child, and Mrs. Margaret Moran of High Street to her second child.

So the tragic tale continued.

An uncertain future faced every bereaved family which had lost the bread-winner. Under the terms of the Workmen's Compensation Acts of 1897 and 1906 the maximum sum that could be awarded to an applicant was £300 assessed on the basis of the deceased wages and family circumstances, the amount determined by the Judge at the Pontypridd County Court. After the deduction of £10 for funeral expenses the Registrar was instructed to *'pay a sum in respect of the past maintenance of the dependants'* and the balance then invested by him in the Post Office Savings Bank *'for the benefit of the dependants'* out of which a sum would be paid each month *'for her own maintenance and for the maintenance, education and benefit of the dependant children'*. A proviso stated that *'The said widow and children, or any or either of them, shall be at liberty to apply to the Judge from time to time for any further order as to the application of any of the sums so ordered to be invested'*. For a single man or boy without any dependants then the maximum sum sum of £10 was awarded for funeral expenses.

As each claim would be heard individually and open to challenge from the Lewis Merthyr Consolidated Collieries Limited and would take very many months to finalise so in the meantime the dependants would have to rely on the financial support provided by the Appeal Fund and the local Distress Funds.

Not only had the lives of the bereaved families been shattered but the fabric of the community had been grievously affected. The membership of the places of worship had been depleted - the St. Peter's Church by forty nine members, including a lay preacher, the Treasurer, a Churchwarden and an organist, the Roman Catholic Church by thirty two from the valley including half the choir, Noddfa Chapel by twenty including two deacons and the Arweinydd y Gan, Salem Chapel by a similar number, Ebenezer Chapel by eighteen, Tabernacl Chapel by sixteen, St. Cenydl Church by seven, all officers, the Salvation Army by five, all band players. The Rugby Club was left without its Captain, six other players, the Treasurer, the Assistant Secretary and three committee members. Five players, all under sixteen, were missing from the Junior Football team. Fifty were members of the Conservative Club and twenty were members of the Liberal Club. Depleted were the choirs and the Silver Band as were the Friendly Societies now exhausted of funds. Bankrupt was the Colliery Sick Fund faced with claims for over £2,000.

No visit came either from Prime Minister Asquith or from a member of the Royal Family and the media had quickly lost interest. By the end of November some miners had left the stricken village never to return but there was no difficulty in the gradual replacement of the lost work force which in the main came from the depressed agricultural areas of mid Wales and south west England. Partial work had been resumed at the Lancaster pit and the schools were functioning normally. With the overwhelming number of dead now *'brought home'* and buried so the pall of grief and the agony of suspense began to ease a little. For the bereaved there began the slow, bitterly painful process of rebuilding their lives, drawing upon all their inner resources of stoicism and dignified self-reliance forged over a life-time's endurance of the dangers and hardships associated with the miner's calling, sustained also by a deep religious conviction and the embracing communal care. This spirit of resolve not to submit in the face of *'the slings and arrows of outrageous fortune'* was typified by the regrouped rugby team renewing matches and the football team playing friendly games against Abertridwr.

But also growing in intensity was the sense of anger and outrage not only in the village and the surrounding area but in mining communities throughout the land. What caused the explosion? Why was the effect so devastating? Was there criminal neglect of the 1911 Coal Mines Act by the management and the Company? Was the devastation caused by the failure to implement the lessons learned after the 1901 explosion? Could more lives have been saved? These were some of the questions which demanded an answer.

The bitter feelings were exacerbated by the tardiness of the Home Office in setting up an Inquiry despite repeated demands from the Miners' Federation of Great Britain. It was not until December 18th that it appointed a Commission of Inquiry into the cause and circumstances attending the explosion under Mr. R.A.S. Redmayne, H.M. Chief Inspector of Mines, with Mr. Evan Williams, Chairman of the South Wales and Monmouthshire Coalowners Association, and Mr. Robert Smillie, President of the Miners' Federation of Great Britain, as Assessors. At Christmas time the Royal and Ancient Order of Buffaloes organised a tea and a cinema performance for 250 children, and on Christmas Day the Picture Palace Company was granted a licence for a cinema performance provided the pictures were of a suitable nature.

On December 31st two bodies were buried as *'Unknown'*. Some bodies were still unrecovered.

CHAPTER 10

On January 2nd, 1914, the Court of Inquiry opened at the Cardiff Law Courts but was adjourned the next day because of the impending Coroner's Inquest and these two proceedings were to overshadow the village for the next seven months.

The Coroner's Inquest opened on January 5th at the Gwernymilwr Hotel. In his opening remarks the Coroner stated, *'Gentlemen, this Court has criminal jurisdiction... We are inquiring into the deaths of four hundred and thirty nine persons. I think it is due to them and those who mourn them that we should sift every fact which would enable us to apportion blame - if blame there be - and to place it on the proper shoulders'*. The hearing lasted eight days over a period until the 14th, during which Mr. Shaw, under cross-examination, agreed that *'it was safe to assume that the pits were dangerous'*. At the conclusion of the hearing the jury recorded some criticisms of the operation of the colliery such as the accumulation of dry coal dust and offered some recommendations. But in answer to the critical question *'Did the neglect of any person or persons cause or contribute to the death of the deceased persons?'* the answer was *'No'*. By doing so the jury absolved both the management and the Company from any responsibility for the holocaust and returned the verdict of *'Accidental Death'*.

The Court of Inquiry was resumed at the Law Courts on January 27th and completed on February 21st. The Lewis Merthyr Consolidated Collieries Limited and Mr. Shaw the Agent and Manager were represented by Mr. John Sankey, Q.C., and the Hon.Trevor Lewis with him. The Miners' Federation of Great Britain and the South Wales and Monmouthshire Colliery Enginemen were represented by Mr. W.P. Nicholas with Mr. W.E. Harvey, M.P., and Mr. Edward Hughes, the South Wales Miners' Federation and the Senghenydd workmen by Mr. William Brace M.P., with Mr. Thomas Richards, M.P., Messrs. Alfred Onions, James Winstone, Hubert Jenkins and D. Watts Morgan, the General Association of Firemen and Deputies by Mr. E. Williams, a number of bereaved families by Mr. Clement Edwards, M.P.

In the course of the hearing 21,837 questions were put to the witnesses. Among them were Edward Shaw, David John Morris (Under Manager), D.R. Thomas (Overman), William Williams (Overman), Richard Davies (Deputy), Griffith Morgan (Surveyor), William Henry Chidsey, James Opie, Richard Davies, Morris Roberts, John Skym, Ben Thomas and Richard Howell (Firemen), Charles Waddon (Electrician), William Morse (Lampman), Benjamin Price (Panman), William Thornton, Benjamin Thomas Davies, Archibald Dean, Ben Hill, Thomas Jones, Edward Gill, John Powell and James Williams (Colliers), Ernest Moss (Shackler), Edward Edwards

(Timberman), William Henry Lasbury (Assistant Timberman), Griffith Humphreys (Ripper), William James (Repairer), James Hill (Collier Boy), Hubert Jenkins (Miners' Agent) and Dr. Philip James (Medical Practitioner).

A significant omission from the array of experts who gave evidence was that no Company Director was called. When this was questioned by Clement Edwards M.P., the Company's legal representative stated that *'they had no practical knowledge of the working of the mine and to have called Lord Merthyr or any other Director would have been wasting the time of the Court'.* Yet Sir William Thomas Lewis, Bart., G.C.Y.O., Baron Merthyr of Senghenydd, had extensive technical knowledge and mining experience and as president of the Mining Association of Great Britain and President of the Institute of Mining Engineers he *'had served on more Royal Commissions that any man alive'*. From 1879 to 1886 he had served on a Royal Commission to inquire into *'Accidents in Mines'*, the causes and the possibility of preventing their recurrences or limiting their consequences. In November 1881 the press reported, *'Another subject of Inquiry by the Commissioners, and a very important one, has had reference to the influence of suspended dust in causing or aggravating explosions, experiments having shown that percentage of fire-damp which would be perfectly harmless in air alone is rendered highly dangerous by the presence of dust and that such a mixture is immediately kindled with a rapidity not distinguishable from an explosion by the contact of an open flame'*. When the Chairman of the Royal Commission presented his Report in 1886 to parliament he bore testimony to the valuable assistance of Mr. W.T. Lewis to whose ability and practical knowledge of the working of coal that the success of the Inquiry had been mainly due. As a mark of appreciation for his services to the Commission he was knighted in 1885.

The Report following the Inquiry was submitted to the Home Office on March 31st but it was not issued until April 23rd despite complaints by the Miners' Federation over the delay.

In the opening paragraphs of the Report, Mr. Redmayne referred to the explosion as *'constituting in point of life the greatest disaster in the annals British Mining'* and also to the Report which followed the 1901 explosion *'in which all three gentlemen emphasised the danger of coal dust and made definite suggestions in respect thereof'* with Mr. S.T. Evans, Q.C., M.P., stressing the importance of making provisions to prevent the accumulation of coal dust in dry and dusty mines on the roads, roofs and sides in the main haulage and travelling ways by regular and efficient watering. He also stated that the mine generated large quantities of gas typical of the more fiery mines in the South Wales coalfield and that no blasting or shot-firing had taken place on the day of the explosion.

As to the place of origin and the cause of the explosion there was a divergence of views. He believed there was a strong possibility that it originated in the Mafeking incline where rock falls liberated gas which was ignited either by sparks from the electric signalling system or from the rock falls. This opinion was supported by Mines Inspectors Dr. Atkinson, Dyer Lewis and Greenland Davies and Assessor Mr. Smillie. The alternative theory was that it originated at the Lancaster Level where heavy rock falls liberated gas which was carried to the lamp-locking station and there ignited by a flame from an open lamp. This was the view supported by Mr. Shaw, representatives of the men, mining engineers representing the management and Assessor Mr. Williams. Discarded as the cause was ignition by matches.

Redmayne was highly critical of many aspects of management. He criticised the methods used by firemen for testing the presence of gas, their manner of reporting its presence, the absence in their reports on the condition of the roof and sides of the road in respect of coal dust so breaching the Coal Mines Act and was of the opinion that the time allocated for a thorough inspection of the districts was inadequate.

He criticised the practice of opening safety lamps in a mine which was notoriously gassy and also the use of an electric signalling system in a part of the mine where there was likely to be a dangerous quantity of inflammable gas.

He criticised the fact that the arrangements for reversing the air current had not been completed by the ascribed date of September 30th so breaching the requirements of the Coal Mines Act. Whether lives would have been saved if it had been possible to effect this reversal immediately after the occurrence of the disaster he was of the opinion that it would not.

Dealing with the crucial question of the extent of dry coal dust in the mine, the factor responsible for the devastation of the 1901 explosion, he reported that the open character of many of the trams and the fact that the coal was piled high above the top of all trams were *'fruitful'* sources for the accumulation of coal dust. As to the methods of dealing with it, they were quite inadequate, the roof and sides of the roads never cleaned or watered. He concluded, *'From my inspection of the mine I have no doubt whatever that coal dust existed on the roof, sides and timber of the roadways in dangerous quantities, that in this respect the mine was not in a satisfactory position, a breach of the Coal Mines Act seems clearly to have been committed and I am of the opinion that the considerable violence of the blast was due to the large quantities of coal dust'.*

Although acknowledging that Manager Shaw and others *'had done all that was humanly possible with the means at their disposal'* to combat the fire, Redmayne was critical of certain aspects of the rescue operations. In view of the experience of the 1901 explosion he criticised the fact that the Universal Rescue Brigade was ill-equipped and expressed the opinion that *'if within an hour of the explosion breathing apparatus had been available and rescue men had gone into the return of West York District some persons might have been saved in that part'*. Also, he condemned the management's failure to provide an adequate water supply to meet an emergency and observed that *'had an adequate water supply been available within an hour of the explosion, and had the brigades of rescuers attacked the three fires simultaneously, I am convinced the fires might have been extinguished in a comparatively short time. I should have thought, in view of the fact that the colliery was such a gassy one, and as already it had been devastated by an explosion in 1901, that the management would have made arrangements for a supply of water adequate to meet an emergency of the kind that actually occurred'*. Nor was he entirely satisfied with the Bottanic rescue, commenting, *'I am of the opinion that these men might have been rescued earlier but whether more lives might have been saved is problematical'*. He was also sceptical about what he thought was the delay in the decision to dam off the fires by bashing.

Chief Inspector Redmayne's conclusion was that *'some of the breaches of the Coal Mines Act may appear trivial but taken in the aggregate they point to a disquieting laxity in the management of the mine'*.

Mr. Smillie, the Assessor appointed by the Miners' Federation of Great Britain, was in general agreement with Mr. Redmayne's Report, but he condemned the extension of time allowed to provide the means for the reversal of the air current and that it had not been completed even by the close of the Inquiry. Differing from Redmayne, he was firmly of the opinion that had the air been reversed then it would have saved the lives of all men in the West York District and possibly in the Pretoria and Bottanic Districts.

Far different was the response of Mr. Williams, the Assessor appointed by the Coalowners' Association to the Report by Mr. Redmayne. Regretting that he was unable to subscribe to it *'owing to my differing from him to a greater or lesser degree upon several material points'* he submitted a separate report. As to the cause of the explosion he believed it resulted from a big rock fall in or near the Lancaster Level releasing a gas stream which was ignited by an open light in the lamp cabin. He then proceeded to stoutly defend the management. He refuted all criticisms of the firemen's procedures and the suggestion that the districts were too large for them to make an efficient examination, stated that the electric signalling system was not capable of sparking and that the failure to reverse the air current would not have been beneficial under the circumstances. Dealing with the question of coal dust on the sides and roof of the roadways he asserted that *'no system had been proved efficacious in preventing the accumulation of coal dust in heavily timbered roads of large areas as those at Senghenydd'* and that all was done within the limit of practicality.

He considered the colliery was *'well and efficiently staffed, and neither in the number of officials nor in the provision of labour, materials or any arrangements necessary for the safe working of the mine was there any evidence having been spared, but quite the contrary.'* Furthermore, he defiantly declared, *'I am of the opinion that the explosion was not consequent upon any breach of the Act or Regulations, nor due to any lack of provision of a kind not required. by law other other than that which may be attached to the positions of the relighting station. While there were some contraventions of the statute, they were all, with the exception of the failure to complete the means of immediately reversing the ventilation, of the nature of neglect to comply with the formalities of no importance in themselves'*. Four hundred and thirty nine men and boys had been killed as a result of contraventions of the Act which he termed were of no importance in themselves!

The Report aroused a furore of anger. Mr. Redmayne's testimony together with the bland rejection by Mr. Williams of managerial and

Company responsibility only served to increase the bitterness, re-awakening the anguish of the bereaved and causing dismay in every mining community in Britain. Was it not the tragic truth that if the management and company had implemented the lessons learned from the 1901 explosion and conformed to the Coal Mines Act then this catastrophe would have and should have been averted? In the event, how many more lives would have been saved if the Universal Brigade had been properly equipped and if there had been an adequate water supply? Were the management and Company not to be made accountable?

So great was the public outcry and the pressure from the Miners Federation of Great Britain that a reluctant Home Office was compelled to institute proceedings against the Manager and the company for breaches of the Coal Mines Act. The case was first heard at Caerphilly Magistrates Court on May 5th when Mr. Shaw was charged with seventeen offences and the Company with four. Neither party appeared nor were they represented and the magistrates decided to adjourn the hearing *'sine die'*. The hearing was resumed on June 17th before a Bench comprising Mr. W. Ware (Chairman), Mr. C.E. Forester-Walker and Mr. David Prosser, adjourned until July 4th, then again adjourned until July 17th when its wisdom the same Bench dismissed nine charges against the Manager including that related to the accumulation of coal dust in that *'he had done all that was reasonably practicable under the circumstances'*, found him guilty on eight accounts and fined him a total of £24. The four charges against the company were dismissed on the grounds that *'the offences were committed without the knowledge, consent or connivance of the Company'*, and the prosecution claim for costs was rejected. The press headline of *'Miners Lives at 1/1¼d each'* reflected the widespread disgust and anger felt by mining communities at this travesty of justice.

All this while the task continued of clearing the falls and making the Lancaster pit secure for full operation, and as more areas were cleared so more miners were engaged and production improved. Of the eleven bodies still unrecovered by the end of March, that of Drychan Jones of Abertridwr was brought to the surface in April, that of William George King of Senghenydd in May, followed later by those of George Chant, William O. Williams and Simeon Worman of Senghenydd.

All this while, too, the claims for compensation for the dependants were being heard at the Pontypridd County Court. The Trust Fund was not yet formulated but they continued to be supported from the unified Appeals Fund and in the early months of the year by Caerphilly Council which made grants from its Distress Fund of £250 to the Senghenydd Distress Fund and £300 to the Miners' Sick and Accident Fund provided that it be distributed irrespective whether or not the victim had been a member.

Edward Shaw was re-elected unopposed to the Council so re-joining Councillors Thomas James who was appointed as a Manager of the Caerphilly Group of Schools and John Davies. Representations were made to the Rhymney Valley Water company when the residents of Station Road were without a supply for many days in May and when there was an inadequate supply to the Park Newydd Estate in June. Mr. R.A. Bussell of Caermoel farm was again awarded the contract, valued at £280, for scavenging and cleaning the cesspools. Tenders were approved for the erection of a public urinal at the top end of Commercial Street, the supply of limestone for the roads and watering of the roads. The Police Sergeant reported the street lighting as satisfactory. Fourteen Notices for the Abatement of Nuisances were served in respect of blocked drains, two in respect of dilapidated shop floors and in June the inspector was asked to report on the Stanley Street cellars.

A virulent epidemic of scarlet fever extended from late April to June.

The Allotments and Recreation Ground Committee reported no progress in the quest for land for allotments. But there was more encouraging news concerning negotiations for land for a public recreation ground after a meeting with Colonel Forest in July when he stated that Lord Windsor would be agreeable to the sale of the land on condition that the price be fixed and the Council communicating with the landowners in the district to ascertain whether they would be prepared to contribute towards the gift of the land to the Council, he being prepared to pay his quarter. The Council resolved to despatch a letter to the Colonel requesting his price and to arrange a further meeting.

Fred Williams was appointed an Overseer of the Poor and in May the ratepayers held an election to appoint members to the Board of Guardians. Thomas Williams was granted permission to build a motor shed. Five businessmen were prosecuted and fined for contravening the Shops Act in relation to exceeding the permitted opening hours and employing lads beyond the permitted hours at night, often up to 11 o'clock.

At the schools there were 320 Infants, 350 Girls and 340 Boys. After years of complaining about the inadequacy of the coal fires, the installation of a coal-fired central heating system in the two buildings came as a boon in January. Attendance was of a high order, St. David's Day was celebrated in the customary manner, medical inspections were carried out including *'special cases'* followed up by Nurse James. Periodical visits were made by School Managers Councillor Trevor James, Rev. Tawelfryn Thomas and Rev. David Roberts. In March had come the annual Ministry Inspection but no Reports were recorded in the Log Books.

The Infants' School continued to suffer from a changing and inadequate staff. The year began with Misses Hoskins and Roberts having departed to take up posts as Head Teachers and with the appointment of Miss Mary Jones (U) the staff was short of Certificated Teachers. There was no relief until April when Miss Alice Burke (C) was appointed. Then in May when Miss Knowles (Supp) left and was replaced by Misses Annie James and Gwendraeth Enid Davies, both supplementary Teachers without any experience, so at the end of the month Miss John was constrained to write in the Log Book. *'The strain upon both the Head Teacher and teachers has been very great because of the shortage of staff'*. In July Miss Mary Jones left and

Miss Margaret Thomas (T.C.) was appointed but the staff remained inadequate.

At the Girls' School the staff changes were limited to the departure of Miss Catherine Williams and the appointment of Misses Phyllis Evans (C) and Gertrude Rees (T.C.) so that Miss Evans had no problems in this respect. A Laundry Course was introduced into the curriculum and there was great jubilation in July when seventeen pupils were successful in the examination for entry to Caerphilly Higher Elementary School.

Staff changes at the Boys' School were also minimal, confined to the departure of Miss Agnes Jones and the appointment of Mr. Stanley Chivers (C). Also recorded by Mr. Lloyd in the Log Book was the departure in January of David John Evans (Provisional Unqualified Teacher appointed in December) for Cardiff University College of Music, the fact that all the Irish boys were absent on St. Patrick's Day and his pleasure at a victory over the Caerphilly School in a baseball match. Absent is any reference to the Caerphilly Higher Elementary School examination.

Very heartening was the progress of the Rugby Club which had been reorganised under Edward Shaw as President and Herbie Powell as Secretary. In January the team registered a narrow victory over Barry in its first official fixture, losing later in the month at Penarth by 33 points to nil but thereafter it went *'from strength to strength'*. Then on April 2nd came the eagerly awaited official opening of the new ground (the *'Rec'*) which had been constructed near the colliery by the Company, the occasion marked by a game against a representative team drawn from the Cardiff and District union. Additional cause for joy was the provision of *'dressing rooms'* by Crosswell's Brewery at the Universal Hotel. The necessity for the team players to change at home, the visitors to change in the cellar of Alf Littlemore's barber shop or at Aberdare Hall was now a thing of the past as was the trek up the mountain to the Gelli field.

Enthusiasm reached its peak as the team reached the final of the Mallett Cup competition against Grange Barbarians at the Cardiff Arms Park on April 30th when it was represented by Will Willacombe (Captain), Jim Dallimore, Geo Gould, J. Gould, P.C. Hayes, Bryn Howells, Will James, Geo Jones, J. Jones, Tom Jones, Llew Jenkins, W. Ormonde, Will Pedro, H. Skym, B. Williams and W. Woolbridge only to suffer the disappointment of defeat. However, this was forgotten when the cherished membership of the Welsh Rugby Union was bestowed upon the Club and admitted into the Glamorgan League.

At midnight on August 4th Great Britain declared war on Germany. Still striving to rebuild the family units and the community fabric and with compensation claims still to the fore the village greeted the announcement with little patriotic fervour. As to the miners, their ambivalent attitude was one shared throughout the coalfield. Not that they were unpatriotic or unwilling to fight but they were sceptical that the *'sacrifices'* that the war would entail would be equally matched by the profit-making coal-owners. Bitterly ironic, too, was the fact that with the outbreak of hostilities and the supreme necessity of supplying coal for the navy so the miners now assumed such a vital national role that the government made every effort to keep them in the collieries.

Of more immediate import was not the war against the Hun but the battle being waged by the Miners' Federation of Great Britain to reverse the scandalous verdict of the Magistrates in relation to the culpability of the Manager and company for the explosion. So greeted with satisfaction was the news that the Home Office had given its approval for the Inspector of Mines for the South Wales Division to file appeals at the Court of Appeal in respect of two specific charges which had been dismissed, one against the Manager for failure to prevent the accumulation of coal dust, the other against the Company for failure to provide for the immediate reversal of the air current.

Poignant was the occasion this month when a tablet to the memory of forty-nine communicant victims was unveiled at St. Peter's Church by Mrs. Griffiths of Craigyrhufan farm, the tablet fashioned by communicant Mr. J. Franklin.

The announcement of the death of Lord Merthyr of Senghenydd on the 29th with the accompanying press obituary notices lavish in their praise of his character, career, achievements and philanthropy brought only bitter memories to the village. One newspaper observed, *'The terrible disaster last year in Senghenydd, one of the mines with which he was associated, and the suffering and loss of life which was thereby entailed were a heavy grief to him'*, but in vain would one search the press to learn the reaction of the widows or the Federation.

As the year progressed so the thoughts of the miners and villagers turned increasingly towards the war effort but they were still exercised by the aftermath of the explosion with many fundamental aspects still unresolved.

Happily, on September 14th the administration of the Appeal Funds was incorporated into a Deed of Trust with an Executive Committee of thirty-nine members including eleven trustees comprising the Lord Mayor and ex-Lord Mayor of Cardiff, the Lord Mayor and ex-Lord Mayor of London, the Earl of Plymouth, Baron Merthyr of Senghenydd (Rt. Hon. Herbert Clarke), Baron Tredegar, Sir William James Thomas, Colliery Proprietor David Alfred Thomas, Miners' Agent William Brace, M.P., and Miners' Agent Alfred Onions. Included in the other twenty-eight members were Miners' Agent Alderman Hubert Jenkins, William Thomas the Treasurer of the East Glamorgan Branch of the South Wales Miners' Federation and Rev. David Myrddin Jones.

Its terms of reference were *'to make weekly payments not exceeding 15/- to widows and other dependants, 6/- for boys under the age of 14 and for girls under the age of 16'*, and that *'payment to widows shall in every case continue as long she shall lead a chaste life and shall conduct herself with becoming propriety to the satisfaction of the Executive Committee.'* The actuarial figures quoted as the number of dependants were 211 widows, 516 children, 33 mothers and 2 fathers.In addition the terms of reference included the dependants of eight men killed in an explosion at the Merthyr Vale Colliery on October 22, 1913.

The amalgamated sum subscribed amounted to £126,615 and with accrued interest stood at £127,324. Of this, £12,416 had been expended. In temporary grants to leave £114,907 for investment to provide a weekly pension of 10/- for an adult and 5/- for a child. By wise investment £195,353 had been distributed by 1951. When the Fund closed in 1952 only forty remained to receive the last payment.

Claims under the Workmen's Competition Act continued into the next year the last of the 439 not finalised until April 1915. On September 1st, 1915, Mr. R.H. March, Chartered Accountant, Mount Stuart Square, Cardiff forwarded to the Lewis Merthyr Consolidated Collieries Limited an itemised list of the sums paid into Court in respect of each case between March 17th, 1914, and April 28th, 1915. The total, calculated to the last penny, amounted to £75,855. But as this included the sum of £4,158 for funeral expenses which were deducted from the sums awarded then the cost to the company was £71,696.

Compensation was awarded in 396 cases only, and in all but six, £10 was deducted for funeral expenses. The levels of compensation awarded were as follows:

Sum.	Number of Cases.
£300	6
£290	130
£250 - £289	50
£200 - £249	32
£150 - £199	6
£100 - £149	21
£50 - £99	94
£1 - £49	57

Thus only 13% (34%) received the maximum sum of £300 and 151 (39%) received less than £100, the lowest being £8 6s 8d.

No compensation was awarded in respect of 43 cases, the reasons cited as *'No claim received', 'Proceedings withdrawn', 'Liablity not admitted', 'Liability rejected'* and *'Verdict in favour of Company'*. In 37 cases £10 was awarded for funeral expenses, in 3 cases only partial expenses were awarded and in 3 cases no funeral expenses were awarded on the submission of *'Body not recovered. No claim received. Liability not admitted'*.

In a covering letter Mr. March concluded, *'The average cost per case amounts to £172 15s 9d and having regard to all the circumstances I think the settlement can be regarded as extremely favourable from our mutual point of view'*, a sentiment, no doubt, shared by the Company.

At the colliery an extra hour a day was being worked in accordance with an agreement made by the Federation to aid the war effort. Viewed with mixed feelings was the news in October that the Court of Appeal had dismissed the charge against the Manager but that against the Company had been referred back to the Magistrates for further information. No further progress was made this year and it was not until February 26th, 1916, that the Caerphilly Magistrates, on the instructions of the King's Bench, found the charge proved against the Company and imposed a fine of £25 with five guineas cost. It was a derisory sum but finally the partial culpability of the Company for the obscene tragedy had been legally established.

Municipal affairs were conducted in the normal way. Representations were made to the Water Company following complaints in October that the supply to the Park Newydd Estate was *'dirty'* and again in November when the inhabitants of Station Road, Station Terrace and Kingsley Road complained of its impurity and inadequacy. Much anxiety was caused by the report that the sewer underneath the Ash Depot was in danger of being crushed by the weight of refuse and the problem was not solved until November when Mr. S.P. Evans who took over the tenancy of the Caermoel farm and the scavenging contract agreed to tip more refuse on its land. Preliminary Closing Orders were served on the Colliery Company in respect of Maesdiofal farm and on the owner of 24 Stanley Street unless the properties were put in a fit state for human habitation. Notices for the Abatement of Nuisances were served on the owners of five houses in Stanley Street.

There was no further progress in the negotiations with Colonel Forrest in relation to the public recreation ground but he was also considering the availability of land for allotments. The street lighting was reported as satisfactory by the police and two more fire hydrants were installed. The grant in September of licences to three shopkeepers to sell fireworks was followed by a request to the police to investigate complaints of boys setting them off in the streets.

Cause for great delight were the major changes in educational provision after the Summer Vacation consequent upon the opening of a Mixed Junior School. Opened on the morning of August 31st the formal ceremony was performed in the afternoon by Councillor Thomas James assisted by the Manager and Clerk of the Caerphilly Group of Managers in the presence of several members of local public bodies. Mr. Albert John Williams, formerly on the staff of the Boys' School, was appointed as Head Master with a staff comprising Misses Alice Burke (C), Margaret Thomas (C) and Phyllis Austin (Prov. C) transferred from the Infants' School, Miss Daisy Jones (C) transferred from the Girls' School, together with Evan Roberts (C) and Miss Lizzie Swaithes (C).

By the end of September the number on roll had increased from 239 to 292 and in October a Manual Instruction Centre was opened in the basement of the building with Mr. Way as Instructor.

During the course of the term visits were made by the Manager, Rev. David Roberts, District School Nurse Miss David, the Primary Schools' Inspector and by H.M.I. who conducted an inspection in November. Apart from a Log Book entry that *'The majority of staff members being monoglot English-speaking the Council's syllabus of Instruction in Welsh is not at present being thoroughly carried out'*, one which must have pained Mr. Williams, a fervent Welshman, bard and essayist, the first term passed smoothly and efficiently with no staff changes and the high order of attendance earning half-holidays on three occasions. Absent from the Log Book is any reference to the War.

The opening of this school not only eliminated overcrowding in the other three schools but the restructuring of the age groups made them more educationally effective.

At the Infants' School some classes which were previously accommodated there were transferred to the Junior School so that the number on roll was reduced to 242. Miss. John's staff now comprised Misses Fanny Ford (C) ,Mildred Cole (C), Gwen Evans (U), Annie James (Supp.), Gwendraeth Davies (Supp.), Sarah Thomas (P.T.), joined later by Misses Carbetta Morris (C) and Mary Collins (Supp.). Notable was the appointment of the first married woman Mrs. Hetty Lewis (U), the engagement to terminate when her husband returned from military service, but she resigned after two days because the trains were not convenient. Entries in the Log Book were scant with no reference to the War.

At the Girls' School, with the former Standards I and II now transferred, so the number on roll was reduced to 245. Here too there were major staff changes. Miss Daisy Jones was transferred, Miss Phylliss Evans left, Misses Margaret Rees and Katie Bowen departed for Barry Training College so that the staff under Miss Dinah Evans comprised Misses Mary Robinson (T.C.), Gertrude Roberts (T.C.), Florence Lloyd (T.C.), E.J. Bradbury, Mary Jones (C), Catherine Gore (U) and Winifred Lewis (P.T.) to which Miss M. Morris (P.T.) and Cookery Teacher Miss Broad were added later.

Particular attention was paid to health care. In addition to the normal medical inspection and the follow-up of special cases by Nurse Coverley the pupils were examined for personal cleanliness by County Council Nurse David and the senior pupils given a talk on *'Tuberculosis and the Laws of Health'*.

Due regard was paid to the war effort. The Log Book records on November 5th, *'The scholars have been given lessons on the war such as the causes and have been busily employed in their spare time in knitting helmets, mufflers, socks and body belts for our soldiers and sailors. Materials have been provided by the local Sewing Guild. An appeal was made also for bandages, so the scholars have brought old garments from their homes to be cut and joined into bandages. A large parcel weighing 42lbs has been despatched to the front today.'*

The number on roll at the Boys' School had also been reduced by the withdrawal of the previous Standards I & II. Mr. Lloyd's staff included Thomas Morgan (C), John Walters (C), Brinley Howells (C), Moelwyn Samuel (C), Benjamin Davies (U), Percival Thomas (U) and Emrys Evans (P.T.), four of whom were to enlist in 1915. As in the Girls' School particular attention was paid to health and personal cleanliness. Noted in the Log Book were a visit from the Inspector of Drawing and the boys no longer having to attend Cwmaber School for Manual Instruction. Apart from recording the visit of an ex-pupil who had joined the 17th Lancers there was no reference to the War.

Epilogue

In many respects the tale which has been unfolded is typical of the pioneering days in other south Wales mining villages. In the space of twenty-five years Senghenydd was transformed from a quiet secluded rural sylvan hamlet into a booming boisterous community.

What differentiates it, is that no other coal-mining village in Great Britain was subjected to so many slings and arrows of outrageous fortune. It is a remarkable story of indomitable courage and great endeavour in the face of fearful adversity.

The year 1914 marked the end of an era.

CHAPTER 11 - More Pictures of Senghenydd

The Square Senghenydd in about 1912-13.

A quiet-looking Lower Commercial Street some 90 years ago.

The colliery building remnants with the shafts and winding gear still in place.

Welsh mining communities drew strength from their close camaraderie encountered through years of strife and tribulation in the coal industry and this picture portrays the local workmen's committee in 1915.

The town band, St. John Ambulance members and local choir are seen assembled around the cenotaph in Senghenydd Square.

A view overlooking Senghenydd as it appeared in about 1903.

From 1905 comes this photograph of the young lady participants in a concert held at Salem Welsh Baptist Chapel. Such a gathering today in such circumstances, would not be easy to find, but 1905 was period of fervent religious revival throughout Wales.

The town's Square as it would have looked a century ago.

Difficult to imagine these days in Senghenydd is this picture of such an industrious scene in the district, the laden wagons of coal waiting to be transported onwards. These were days when 'Coal was King'.

These gentlemen are described as the 'Town Guard' with instructor Sergeant James on the far left. Photograph taken in 1914.

A final picture of the colliery from the days when it meant so much to the economy and welfare of the town of Senghenydd.

H. Walters of Gelli and Parc Dairies.

Once sinking of the colliery began and with the numbers of men required for the task, a short-term housing shortage became apparent. The quick solution was the construction of some temporary huts in 1891 to house the workers and their families. The houses above were built some time later.

The Railway Station post 1915.

A Rhymney `railway 'motor car' at Senghenydd, c. 1908.

BIBLIOGRAPHY

Caerphilly Journal
Merthyr Express
South Wales Daily News
Pontypridd Chronicle, Pontypridd Herald
Western Mail
Glamorgan Free Press
The Cambrian
Aberdare Leader
South Wales Echo
Glamorgan Gazette
Glamorgan County Times
Cardiff Times
Western Daily Press
Llais Llafur (The Labour Voice)

Ness Edwards *'The History of the South Wales Mines'.*

P.N. Jones *'Colliery Settlements in the South Wales Coalfields'.*

Eric Wyn Evans *'The Miners of South Wales'.*

Morgannwg IX *'The Great Miners Strike of 1898 in South Wales'.*